A Gift for

_____

From

LIVING WATER FOR THE THIRSTY SOUL
365 STORIES OF HOPE HEALTH & HEALING

LIVING WATER FOR THE THIRSTY SOUL: 365 STORIES OF HOPE
HEALTH & HEALING
Copyright 2019 Juanita Fletcher Cone
Cover Image: Tywebbin Creations
Author Photo: Takia Lamb, TK Consulting & Design

LIVING WATER FOR THE THIRSTY SOUL

365 STORIES OF HOPE HEALTH & HEALING

Juanita Fletcher Cone MD MPH

Acknowledgments

God's human family is amazing. I've been blessed to meet some of these extraordinary people. It was their miraculous faith stories that contributed to this book of reflections. They are the true witnesses of the power of the living Almighty Sovereign God. I thank and praise God for each and every one of them.

One of my dear friends encouraged me to consider writing a book of reflections. I'm not sure if Joyce remembers making this suggestion. I thought and prayed about it and decided to give it a try. It made sense since I've always wanted to share lessons learned over my lifetime. Now, I had an opportunity. God kept filling my heart and soul with memories, stories, and insights on a variety of topics. Thank you, Mrs. Joyce Watson, for sweet words of inspiration.

I was fortunate to spend two years in seminary. My late husband encouraged me to go at the age of fifty-three. This book would not have been possible without the wisdom, ethical, and biblical learnings gained in seminary. I'd also like to acknowledge my classmates and professors who helped make this an unforgettable experience. Thank you, Rhonda McKnight and your editorial team, interior, and cover designer. You guided me through the development and production process. You added a level of excellence that was supportive, creative, and instructive.

Introduction

How often have you thought, "If I can get this job, get married or divorced, retire, build my financial portfolio, raise the children, or purchase my dream home, then I'll be satisfied?" Even if you achieved your specific goals, before long, you'd probably start to feel like something is still missing. So you start searching for another quest. Human contentment is elusive. Every time you think you've found it, it slips away. When Jesus met the Samaritan woman at the well, he knew she was not satisfied. That's why he said to her, "Whoever drinks the water I give will never thirst. Indeed, the water I give him will become in him a spring of water welling up to eternal life." (John 4:14 NIV) A glass of life-giving water goes a long way.

Living Water for the Thirsty Soul: 365 Stories of Hope Health & Healing is for the divine well in your soul. It has its own unique flavor, and there is a variety. I share my own faith journey through a collection of personal and family stories. These stories are blended in with miracle stories of everyday people and Bible wisdom. Also included are present and past historical figures whose faith in God changed the course of history. There are reflections on love, fear, choice, courage, grief, death, giving, and forgiving. Lastly, I'm a physician who believes in caring for the body, mind, and soul so I share reflections that focus on my holistic approach to health.

Everyone deserves daily quiet time. I invite you to spend some of your time with me. Let each reflection be a sacred experience. As you reflect and meditate, you'll gain personal insights and wisdom. God's well never stops flowing. Each person has their own personal experience with the Divine. Embrace the experience and allow it to penetrate your mind, body, and soul! May a small daily dose of wisdom help to fill you divine well.

January 1
Go Forward, I Prepare the Way for You

Forty years ago, while earnestly praying, I received a word from God that was crystal clear and brought me much peace. The message was, "Go forward, I prepare the way for you." I heard no voice. It was as if the message was imprinted on my mind. This is the best way to explain the experience. I'll also say, it has been the only personal divine message given to me this way.

Often, during my walk with the Lord, I hesitate in some action, and then remember the message, "Go forward, I prepare the way for you." I relax and move forward.

When my relationship with God was not personal, I moved forward without thinking about decisions, guidance, or consequences. As a young college student, life just happened. For example, while it was my intention to go to medical school, my grades in college were not medical school quality. As a result, my medical school dream died.

A year of poorly compensated work at the Smithsonian Institution prompted me to try graduate school. My admission to Howard University (HU) graduate school was provisionary. I had to take graduate school courses for no credit. The embarrassment was almost more than I could bear. However, I persevered and accepted the challenge. By the middle of the first semester, my endocrinology professor encouraged me to apply to medical school. I forged ahead and applied to HU medical school and was accepted. The only requirement was to continue to maintain a high level of scholarship.

The Almighty Sovereign God was preparing the way for me every step of the way even when I didn't realize it. When God says to move forward, go, for the way has been prepared. We need to trust God and walk by faith.

"For I know the plans I have for you, declares the Lord, "plans to prosper you and not to harm you, plans to give you hope and a future" (Jeremiah 29:11, NIV).

January 2
God's Temple

"... Offer your bodies as a living sacrifice, holy and pleasing to God—this is your true and proper worship" (Romans 12:1, NIV).

A temple is a building devoted to the worship of a deity. According to the Bible, our body is God's temple. Its primary purpose is to bring glory and honor to God. "Do you not know that your bodies are temples of the Holy Spirit, who is in you, whom you have received from God? You are not your own; you were bought at a price. Therefore, honor God with your bodies" (*1 Corinthians 6:19-20, NIV*). How is this done?

We honor God's temple when we become instruments for God to use in everyday life, a life filled with godliness in giving, forgiving, kindness, and patience. These are not easy tasks, but with the help of the Holy Spirit, you begin to walk the talk.

To glorify God in our temple is to spend time in prayer and meditation. Prayer strengthens your relationship with God. Prayer has its greatest effect on 'me' and changes my response to life's circumstances. Sometimes you may not even know what to pray. That's when you get quiet. When you do, "the Holy Spirit prays for us with groanings that cannot be expressed in words. And the Father who knows all hearts knows what the Spirit is saying, for the Spirit pleads for us believers in harmony with God's own will" (*Romans 8:26-27, NLT*).

Meditation is another way to honor God. You may decide to practice being still with God, sitting quietly for a period of time. Or, you may choose to select a passage of scripture to reflect, study, or ponder over. The more you allow your temple to bring glory and honor to God, the more your mind, body, and spirit will align with God's will, purpose, and plan for your life here on earth.

"May God equip you with everything good for doing his will, and may he work in us what is pleasing to him, through Jesus Christ, to whom be glory for ever and ever. Amen" (Hebrews: 13:21, NIV).

January 3
The Daniel Fast

"Who satisfies thy mouth with good things so that thy youth is renewed like an eagle" (Psalm 103:5, KJV).

Are you familiar with the Daniel Fast? In the first chapter of Daniel, the story begins after Daniel and his companions are imprisoned in another country. The king observes their high intellect and wisdom and uses both to benefit his kingdom. They were given the privilege of eating the king's food (meats) and drinking the king's elegant wine. "But Daniel purposed in his heart that he would not defile himself with the portion of the king's meat, nor with the wine which he drank" (*Daniel 1:8, KJV*).

Daniel appealed to the chief steward to permit a ten-day test for him and his companions to eat only vegetables and water. Then he asked him to observe and compare their physical appearance with the king's youth. If no differences were observed, Daniel would willingly eat the king's food. The test was approved. To their amazement, ten days later, Daniel and his companions were fairer and more robust in appearance than all the other youths.

With faith in God, Daniel practiced courageous discipline. It couldn't have been easy to stick to a healthy diet when rich foods were in abundance to tempt his taste buds. Passionately, he held to his beliefs. As a result, the king recognized Daniel and his companions to be far above all the other youth in matters of wisdom and understanding.

This story is as relevant today as it was two millenniums ago. It's worth a ten or even twenty-one day trial. Should you decide, please check with your physician to see if it is appropriate for you. (On the Daniel Fast, generally fruits, vegetables, beans, quinoa, plenty of water are allowed. No caffeine or decaf, soft drinks, sweets, or meats are consumed.)

"The good man eats to live, while the evil man lives to eat" (Proverbs 3:25, TLB)

January 4
Never Give Up!

In the Gospel of Luke 18:1-8, Jesus tells a story about a widow who was being harassed for her property. During the time of Jesus, widows were not allowed to inherit their husband's estate. It was either passed to a man's sons or his brothers. She went to the judge whose job it was to hear complaints with fairness but was met with a man who was heartless and unjust. Jesus described the judge this way: "He neither feared God nor cared about people" (*Luke 18:2, NLT*). The judge regarded the widow as an invisible nuisance. She was poor and as young people say, she had no sway.

Although the widow's socioeconomic status was low, she had the courage and determination to be patient and persistent in her plea for justice. She refused to become weary in doing the right thing. As a result, the judge became exasperated and gave in to her steadfastness. She never gave up!

Jesus told this story to encourage us to have faith. I suspect her prayer life mirrored her outward character of courage, patience, and persistence. Our faith in a just God grows as our prayer life becomes more steadfast. Our faith in a just God empowers us with courage to be all that God intended us to be. God answered her prayer and moved through an unjust judge.

"So, let's not get tired of doing what is good. At just the right time we will reap a harvest of blessing if we don't give up" (Galatians 6:9, NLT).

January 5
Transforming Fear into Triumphant Faith

"Do not be anxious about anything, but in every situation, by prayer and petition, with thanksgiving, present your requests to God. And the peace of God, which transcends all understanding, will guard your hearts and your minds in Christ Jesus" (Philippians 4:6-7, NIV).

It is a challenge to be "calmly happy" in today's topsy-turvy world. Feeling anxious, afraid, and worried about personal issues and societal concerns can be exhaustive and make one feel helpless. I am one who does a lot of worrying. My late husband used to tell me that I suffer from the "what if syndrome" and worry about ships that never sail. He would say that I did enough worrying for both of us.

In this passage of scripture, Paul is encouraging the church not to worry. Mind you, Paul is innocent but in jail, facing the threat of being killed. There is no greater humiliation than to be labeled a criminal, particularly when you are innocent.

While the letter that Paul writes from jail is replete with love and strength, he confesses his fear and anxiety. This is a normal response, but Paul never lost hope.

Are you feeling anxious? Share your fears with God. Then, like Paul, expect to be delivered. He writes, "For I fully expect and hope that I will never be ashamed, but that I will continue to be bold for Christ, as I have been in the past." (*Philippians 1:20, NLT*). Paul turned his fear into power. During an anxious time in my own life, God gave me victory with this acronym for FEAR:

1. Faith in God
2. Expect God to make a way
3. Always remain prayerful
4. Rest in the Lord and wait patiently for God to act

"Do the thing you fear, and the death of fear is certain."
~Ralph Waldo Emerson

January 6
Prosperity in Health

"Dear friend, I pray that you may enjoy good health and that all may go well with you, even as your soul is getting along well" (3 John 2, NIV).

This is a new year. What's in store for you? Expect great things. Spread your wings. Soar like an eagle. Visit new places. Meet new people. Dance, sing, smile and have some fun. Dare to be different. You have a lot to do.

I am a physician and passionate about preventive health. Please pardon me while I ask a few questions centered around prevention.

When was your last wellness check-up? If you can't remember, call, and schedule an appointment. What about your dental hygiene? Besides flossing every day, follow up with your dentist or dental hygienist for regular teeth cleaning. Take care of your oral health because it is linked to your physical health.

Ladies, are you in the age group to have a periodic mammogram? Just, get it done. Ladies and men, if you are forty-five years or older, have you been screened for colon cancer? Screening is all about saving your most valuable life.

And don't forget about your precious eyes. Be sure to check with an eye specialist to make sure that eye pressure is normal. High pressure in the eyes could indicate signs of glaucoma. It is the leading cause of blindness in the United States. But the good news is that it is easy to treat.

Taking time to care for our bodies is just as important as carrying for our souls.

"There is a time for everything, and a season for every activity under the heaven" (Ecclesiastes 3:1, NIV).

January 7
The Daniel Fast—Part 2

Our church is in the midst of the Daniel Fast. In the January 3rd reflection, I shared the Bible story behind this fast. Like many churches, at the start of each year, our pastor leads us in a twenty-one-day Daniel Fast. It is a period of consecration and preparation for the year to come individually and collectively. A lot of planning takes place leading up to the fast.

A month before the fast starts, the pastor invites willing participants to the altar for prayer. Each member is given a Daniel Fast devotional booklet prepared by the ministerial staff, which describes the fast and what foods to include and those to exclude. It also has a daily devotional message, names and addresses of vegetarian restaurants in and around metro Atlanta, as well as a number of vegetarian recipes. Our church does not leave this activity up to chance.

Each year, I look forward to my annual Daniel Fast. Eating lots of fresh fruits and vegetables derived from mother earth is a challenging task in the twenty-first century, but that's what's needed to improve our overall health. Daniel demonstrated this healthy way of eating 600 years BCE and science confirms its value in helping to manage weight, reduce joint inflammation, and improve diabetes.

Our temple (body) needs our care. Do you struggle to eat healthy? Has your physician recommended making changes in your diet? The Daniel Fast is an excellent way because it is based on biblical precepts and has been scientifically tested.

"And God said, 'Look I have given you the seed-bearing plants throughout the earth and all the fruit trees for your food'" (Genesis 1:19, NLT).

January 8
Kindness

People with different worldviews have been at odds as far back as biblical days. In the fourth chapter of the Gospel of John, Jesus starts a conversation with a Samaritan woman, crossing two boundaries. First, Jewish people considered Samaritans to be outcasts and adversaries and did not form relationships with them. Secondly, there were boundaries between men and women which he broke by talking to a woman.

Jesus challenges the social norm. He is not governed by fears and biases but by respect for all human beings. As a result, Jesus opens the eyes of the Samaritan woman to his power and love. Not only is her life turned around, but many others in her community as well.

A new decade is here. It is time to move to a higher level of understanding and thinking about those who appear different from you. You never know whose life you will change when you bless them with a smile, or when you open up a conversation, or take the time to encourage them with a random act of kindness.

If you can, the next time you are in a coffee or fast food drive-through, give the attendant money for the person in line behind you. Consider keeping some lunch or dinner money, or a gift card in a sealed envelope in your pocket or handbag, and hand it to the next person you see holding a sign asking for help. I believe this is called paying it forward. You decide how much you want to give. Cross the *imaginary* boundary between us. When you do, not only will you touch their heart, your heart will be touched as well.

"What have you done today to make you feel proud?"
~ Heather Small

January 9
The Effect of Gratitude on One's Attitude

After missing a flight, I shared an elevator ride with a young African American man who worked at the airport. I was feeling a bit annoyed and frustrated, but his attitude changed my perspective. As we rode the elevator, I asked how his day was going. He spoke softly, humbly expressing his love for life and how grateful he was just to have woken up that morning.

I thought about the stress young African American men live under daily, facing violence of every kind, including police violence. In a recent scientific study reported in the *Journal of Epidemiology and Community Health*, police violence disproportionately impacts young people of color, greatest among those between ages twenty-five to thirty-four.

This young man had a beautiful outlook on life. His response to my question suggests that he appreciates the gift of life and that we do not know when our earthly time will be up, but he will love the time he has. I wonder what would happen if more of us expressed love for life simplistically rather than complaining about what we have or don't have, or like me, complaining about my missed flight.

"You are my God, and I will give thanks to you; you are my God; I will exalt you. This is the day that the Lord has made; let us rejoice and be glad in it" (Psalm 118:28, NIV).

January 10
Giving

"It is possible to give freely and become more wealthy, but those who are stingy will lose everything" (Proverbs 11:24, NLT).

There is a story in the Book of Acts, Chapter 5 about a married couple named Ananias and Sapphira. They were a part of the early Christian church. In the early church, everyone freely and cheerfully shared their material possessions with the church. In this way, poverty did not exist.

Ananias and Sapphira chose to sell a piece of their property for the church. Instead of placing all the money at the altar, they held back a portion. I guess they felt it was their money and could give what they chose. Perhaps they felt the people who were to benefit from the money didn't need that much or didn't deserve it. Still, they wanted to give the impression they were giving all the money. It was their little secret. Ananias and Sapphira didn't know that God has unlimited knowledge (omniscient) and is present everywhere at the same time (omnipresent). And that God searches our hearts and examines our deepest motives.

As a result, the Bible says when confronted about their actions, they fell down and died. They ended up paying a huge price.

Like Ananias and Sapphira, when we hold back untruthfully, it affects us spiritually. When we pretend to do what we are not doing, we stunt our own spiritual growth. We may not die physically, but we die spiritually. Our gain is in giving not in holding back. A person's security is not their savings but in their giving.

"The generous prosper and are satisfied; those who refresh others will themselves be refreshed" (Proverbs 11:25, NLT).

January 11
Keep an Eye on the Birds

When I was about five years of age, I recall my great aunt saying to me that "a bird told her what I had done." I wasn't convinced, but it made me more mindful of birds. Since that time, birds have been special, bringing messages of hope to me.

Years ago, when Cecil and I lived on Amelia Island, a bird (probably a pigeon) perched on our balcony rail for at least three or four days. We lived in a condominium on the fifth floor, and every day when I opened the front door, the bird was there. He sat perfectly still, even when approached. It was amazing to watch. Then one day, he was gone. I surmised the bird must have been sick and upon recovery mounted his wings and flew away.

Similar to birds, we need time for our body and our soul to be still. Rest is an excellent way to get reinvigorated. A fatigued body is less focused, less likely to exercise, sing, dance, pray, or study the Bible. Rest and sleep are like renewable energy. Adults need eight hours of sleep, and children less than twelve years old need ten to eleven hours of sleep each night.

Quiet time with God nourishes our soul and our relationship with God. When we are still spiritually, we are better able to hear God speak. If we wait until our being is befuddled or bewildered, God's message is harder to hear. Also, being still could mean to wait. Sometimes God says, now is not the time to move. The prophet Elijah lost his confidence until he sat long enough in a quiet place to hear God's direction. We all need to "Be still in the presence of the Lord and wait patiently for Him to act" (*Psalm 37:7, NLT*).

"They that wait on the Lord shall renew their strength. They shall mount up with wings of eagles; they shall run, and not be weary; they shall walk, and not faint" (Isaiah 40:31, KJV).

January 12
The Helper

We all know people who are always ready to help—24/7. Or, are you that person? Taking days off from work is just not possible for the helper. The work won't get done. Missing a day from church for the helper is out of the question. She is responsible for counting the offering. Vacations are infrequent and if taken, most of their time is spent checking emails and making phone calls.

My brother is a dedicated taxi driver and has what he refers to as regular customers. Oftentimes, I've heard him say, "My customers depend on me to get them to work." Family time and vacations are ignored or not taken because nothing interferes with his taxi duties.

It is hard for helpers to relax or sleep well. Their bodies and minds stay in overdrive. In Martha Hickman's book, *Healing after Loss*, she tells the story about a typical helper named Charles Carter. He was exhausted from all of his responsibilities. Charles became ill, but for him being sick was out of the question. There was no way he could fit an illness into his busy schedule. Charles cried, "Too many people are depending on me!" One day he fell into a deep sleep and had a dream. In the dream, God was pacing the floors of heaven wondering, "What shall I do? Charles is going to be sick."

Thank God, that was just Charles' dream. But there are many like Charles who think they are the only ones who can handle a situation. No human being is invincible. We live and we die. The world is in the hands of God.

"I will lie down in peace and sleep, for you alone, O Lord, will keep me safe" *(Psalm 4:8, NLT).*

January 13
Healing and Hope for the Future

It's an honor to see God's healing hands in the lives of others, especially in one who is like a sister. Joyce went to see her gynecologist for a yearly check-up. She was not feeling ill. The doctor's visit was supposed to be routine. However, her doctor did a biopsy because she saw a spot that didn't look right. The results showed cancer. This was a startling discovery, and in the course of a few minutes, Joyce's life story changed. She remained hopeful, and there was good news throughout her journey.

Joyce was blessed to only need eight weeks of radiation treatment and was able to continue working. Chemotherapy and surgery were not necessary. The doctors gave her a list of symptoms to expect from radiation, but she experienced none until the very end of her treatment.

She is now cancer free and continues to work. Most importantly, Joyce says that she owes her recovery to God. She is grateful for the physicians and nurses God used in her magnificent healing. She is a living testimony at work, home, and in her church.

If you know someone who has been diagnosed with cancer or experienced it yourself, you probably would agree that it can be a lonely journey with uncertainty at every corner. Remain hopeful and you'll see God's hand ordering your steps. Each individual's situation is unique, but God always provides a way of escape that we might be able to bear our burdens.

"Even to your old age and gray hairs I am he, I am he who will sustain you. I have made you and I will carry you and I will rescue you" (Isaiah 46:4, NIV).

January 14
Family

Family is important to Jesus. In the Gospel of John 12:1-7, Jesus visits Lazarus and his two sisters, Martha and Mary. During his visit, each sibling had a unique way of relating to Jesus: Martha served. Lazarus sat at the table with Jesus, and Mary knelt at Jesus' feet.

For Martha, service is important. Martha does what most women do when they're expecting a special guest. She ensures the house is fresh, the bathroom tidy, the table set, and the aroma from the kitchen inviting. This takes a lot of work and Martha expects Mary to assist. She becomes frustrated when Mary doesn't. In fact, Martha is so outdone that she asks Jesus to nudge Mary to help. For Lazarus, talking with Jesus is important. The hymn, "Just a little talk with Jesus" written by Cleavant Derricks expresses it well. A conversation with Jesus changes my outlook, my situation, and most of all, it changes me.

For Mary, worship is important. In the presence of Jesus, Mary forgot about service and preparation. At this point, nothing else matters. She is in the presence of the Lord. All she wants to do is kneel at his feet and pour out her love, thanksgiving, and praise. As a result, a holy fragrance fills the entire room.

What would the worship experience be like without the due diligence of the pastor, choir, ushers, stewardesses, trustees, stewards, deacons, and deaconess? Indeed, service, prayer, and worship are important, but as one matures in their Christian walk, they soon discover that which brings the most meaning to their innermost being.

"Martha, Martha," the Lord answered, "you are worried and upset about many things, but only one thing is needed. Mary has chosen what is better, and it will not be taken away from her" (Luke 10:41, NIV).

January 15
Happy Birthday Dr. King!

Ninety years ago, Dr. Martin Luther King, Jr. was born. He was a twentieth century prophet and Civil Rights leader. In my opinion, Edgar Guest's poem, "I'd rather see a sermon than hear one any day" describes Dr. King. His life was a living sermon. He lived and taught nonviolence as a strategy against injustice. Dr. King preached an inclusive 'gospel of freedom' throughout the United States and globally.

Dr. King was a preacher, scholar, and philosopher. He demonstrated courage, compassion, dignity, humility, justice, and service to humanity. His life was always at risk for harm. Dr. King endured beatings and provocation and was jailed twenty-nine times for taking direct action against oppression and unjust laws.

One month before the Poor People's Campaign was to begin in Washington, DC, King was assassinated. The purpose of the campaign was to lobby for an "economic bill of rights" for jobs, unemployment insurance, a fair minimum wage, and more low-income housing.

In 1983, a national holiday was established to commemorate the life work of Dr. King. This holiday is a day of service where followers of Dr. King give their time and talents in homeless shelters, prisons, hospitals, and in tutoring and mentoring programs; wherever people need assistance. A Dr. King comes only once in three or four lifetimes.

Dr. King's answer to discord, turmoil, misunderstanding, and disharmony was and still is LOVE.

"Without love, there is no reason to know anyone, for love will in the end connect us to our neighbors, our children and our hearts."
~ *Dr. Martin Luther King, Jr.*

January 16
Fear

"But the boat was now in the midst of the sea, tossed with waves; for the wind was contrary" (Matthew 14:24, KJV).

In the above passage of scripture, the disciples are at sea [without Jesus] and are facing strong winds and heavy waves. The situation is terrifying. To add to their fear, Jesus appears and walks towards them. At this point, Peter puts the Lord to a test. He said, "Lord, if it's you, tell me to come to you on the water" (*Matthew 14:29, NIV*). Peter starts to take the risk and walk toward Jesus. When he notices the strong winds, he is filled with fear, takes his eyes off Jesus and starts to sink. Jesus reaches out his hand and catches him.

Not unlike Peter, storms rage in our lives. Oftentimes caused by our own choices. Regardless, God is always there to catch us. And like Peter, we put God to the test: *I know you can get me out of this trouble... Show me your power...Heal me.*

The answer may be just what we are looking for and we rejoice. But sometimes when the hand of God reaches out to save us, God's response is not what we expected.

We have two choices. Either we look to God whose hand is always there to catch us. Or, we look away and do it our way. I know someone who was in trouble and reached out to God. When things didn't work out to his liking, he became angry and turned away from God. To this day, he says, "I got up off my knees and did it myself." Little did he know that God had answered his prayer. God gave him the strength to move in a different direction and become highly successful.

Regardless of the mountain of difficulties, God is always close by. It may not feel like it when the storms of life are raging. But, stay anchored in the Lord. God knows what is best for you and will not test you beyond what you are able to bear.

"My soul has been anchored in the Lord."
~ *Douglas Miller*

January 17
Grace Versus a Squeak

Michelle Obama was born on this day in 1964. All I could think when I read her book, *Becoming* is the word heartwarming. Her memoir made me laugh and sometimes made me cry tears of joy. The relationship she had with her parents was not only one of love but one of humility and reverence.

There were several instances that illustrate her humble nature. She refused to let her parents know about the trip to Paris being planned by her French class. Mrs. Obama's first thoughts were the extra financial burden it would cause. Her parents found out anyway and without hesitation made sure she was on the plane to Paris.

Another time occurred while she was away in college. By this time, multiple sclerosis was overpowering her father. She found simple ways to connect with him without burdening him with worry. Mrs. Obama writes about finding comfort in hearing his soft, joyful voice with "no trace of pain or self-pity." At the end of their conversations, he always wanted to know if there was anything she needed. "But I never said yes." She had a way of placing her parents' needs first. Some people might refer to her as an "old soul."

Lastly, Mrs. Obama shares the joy of being accepted to Harvard Law School. She admits that she 'squeaked in' off the waitlist. It might appear that way from human thinking. Christians call it grace rather than a 'squeak'. Grace is a special favor from God. It's hard to figure out why God pours out grace.

Was it the result of her hard work starting as far back as first grade? Or the reverence she gave to her parents? No one knows the mind of God or why grace is given, but it sure feels good when you receive it!

"Honor your father and your mother, that you may live long in the land which the LORD your God is giving you" (Exodus 20:12, NIV).

January 18
An Athlete in Training

"Like an athlete I punish by body, treating it roughly, training it to do what it should, not what it wants to" (1 Corinthians 9:27, TLB).

At the beginning of every year, many people commit to a healthier lifestyle. This is great since the leading chronic diseases in the United States that account for 75% of the $3.2 trillion spent annually on healthcare are preventable.

Unfortunately, if it's not the lack of motivation, it's the other life factors that interfere with healthier lifestyle commitments made at the beginning of the year. I recommend trying a different strategy.

Listen to your body. When do you feel most energized? What exercises are more apt to get you moving?

Work your plan. What time of the day is easiest to achieve self-care? Perhaps ten to fifteen-minute intervals work best. Or, consider a thirty-minute walk once a day. There are many exercise programs on television and online. Though, going to the gym or line-dancing may be the right experience for you.

Before beginning your exercise program, it's a good idea to check with your physician to make sure your blood pressure and heart are healthy.

Rest and sleep are critical to good health. Lack of sleep affects your ability to exercise safely.

Finally, make sure you are eating plenty of energy foods and keeping the sugary and fast foods to a minimum.

What is the best exercise? The best exercise is the one that will get you up and moving.

January 19
A Higher Level of Understanding About Self and Others

While childhood is filled with fun, discovery, and excitement, there are some experiences that lead to fear, self-doubt, self-hate, and selfishness in adulthood. The ego sets up a strategy to compensate for these insecurities. As a result, our true authentic identity is in bondage. Compassion, love, patience, and empathy are suppressed. When this happens, human beings exhibit more insensitive attitudes, intolerance, self-righteousness, and even hate. If you are to be, the soul must escape from bondage. Being true to self is a major pathway to freeing the soul. When the soul is free, fear, self-doubt, self-hate, and selfishness wane, and we move to a higher level of understanding about ourselves and people.

Psalm 51:6 (*KJV*) says, "Thou desires truth in the inward parts; and in the hidden part, thou shall make me to know wisdom." Through wisdom, we learn to be honest with ourselves. Then, we can love ourselves just as we are, every aspect of our being. The more self-love is demonstrated, the more we love others.

A higher level of understanding moves away from an attitude of disconnection and pretense toward wholeness. We begin to feel connected with human beings we meet. We are more open to other people's truth. We acknowledge their viewpoint with attentiveness and respect. We are willing to understand people's behavior and to understand the impact of culture on individual and community behavior. It is time to make the decision to move to a higher level of understanding about people who don't look or think like me.

"Wisdom is the principal thing; therefore, get wisdom. and in all your getting, get understanding" (Proverbs 4:7, KJV).

January 20

Grace

"Then Jesus stood up again and said to the woman, 'Where are your accusers? Didn't even one of them condemn you?' 'No, Lord,' she said. And Jesus said, 'Neither do I. Go and sin no more" (John 8:10-11, NLT).

It is a blessing to have Jesus around when we're in trouble. Like the biblical story about the woman caught in adultery where the self-righteous religious leaders demand Jesus respond to Mosaic law and stone her to death. Even though the Mosaic law stated both the man and the woman were to be stoned, the attention of the religious leaders was solely on the woman. Jesus did not respond to their accusation. He remained quiet. I believe he was thinking about the humanity of the woman.

I suspect she is embarrassed and ashamed as she stands accused and alone in front of a heartless crowd. Jesus understands human nature. Human beings react differently when their actions are hidden. Once exposed publicly, we lose support, friendships, and other things most valuable to a person, including your job. In our society, the media has a way of making you appear at fault whether you're guilty or not.

People need love most when they are in trouble. Jesus did not react to their accusation or what the Mosaic law said. Rather, he dealt with the sin. He knew that none of us are sinless. That's why he said, "He that is without sin cast the first stone." One by one, her accusers walked away.

Jesus responded to the woman with grace, the unmerited favor and love of God. This response makes a difference. I imagine she must have felt loved. She was finally able to speak and then hear Jesus say she was not condemned. She had peace to go on and live a life that pleased the Lord.

"Do not judge, or you too will be judged. For in the same way you judge others, you will be judged, and with the measure you use, it will be measured to you" (Matthew 7:1-2, NIV).

January 21
"I Feel Great at Ninety-Eight"

The above words were expressed by one of my patients after hip replacement surgery. This patient (I'll call her Ms. AC) was a vibrant 98-year-old lady who walked on a treadmill two to three times a week until she began having severe pain in her right hip. She was referred to an orthopedic specialist who recommended hip replacement surgery.

This recommendation did not seem like a good idea for someone her age. I explained that surgery was more likely to result in complications, including death. None of this mattered to her. The pain was unbearable. She made the decision to proceed with hip surgery. To my astonishment, Ms. AC had a complete recovery that exceeded my expectations.

When is too old—*too old* for surgery? I'm not sure, but when there is a willing patient with faith in God, a skillful surgeon, optimal physical therapy, and advanced medical technology, age doesn't seem to matter, because age was not the determining factor for Ms. AC.

On her last visit, I thanked her for the privilege of caring for her. She was one of my last patients before I retired. I felt extra privileged to hear her say, "I feel great at 98!"

Regardless of our age, when we trust in God, we can see the hand of God moving in us and in others.

"Trust in the Lord with all your heart and lean not on your own understanding" *(Proverbs 3:5, NIV).*

January 22
Is Food Medicine?

"Let food be thy medicine and medicine be thy food."
~Hippocrates

Our church has just completed a twenty-one-day Daniel Fast. I am thankful and excited about the results and want to continue this way of eating. (See January 3 devotion for the story behind the Daniel Fast.)

The Daniel Fast consists primarily of fruits, vegetables, complex carbohydrates (beans, lentil, quinoa, potatoes) nuts, olive oil and water—foods known to fight excess inflammation in the body. Foods to be avoided include soft drinks and other sugar-sweetened beverages, meat, margarine, fried foods, and refined carbohydrates (white bread, pasta, pastries, white flour, white rice, and most breakfast cereals). These foods cause inflammation in the body.

God has given us an immune system that protects from harmful substances in the environment. Overindulgence of these foods produces an overabundance of inflammation. Chronic inflammation can cause conditions like arthritis, diabetes, depression, and even Alzheimer's is linked to chronic inflammation.

In Genesis 1:29 (NIV), God says: "I give you every seed-bearing plant on the face of the whole earth and every tree that has fruit with seed in it. They will be yours for food." These are the foods recommended in the Daniel Fast and the same foods that reduce inflammation in the body. In 400 BCE, Hippocrates, known as the father of medicine, associated food with medicine. I believe he was saying that fruits and vegetables are like medicine.

Our Lord wants us to prosper physically and spiritually. When we make healthier food selections, not only do we feel better, but our overall physical health improves.

Almighty Sovereign God, thank you for providing what we need to live the best possible life. Satisfy my desire for foods with the nutrients that come directly from Mother Earth. AMEN

January 23
Life is in the Breath

"And the LORD God formed man of the dust of the ground and breathed into his nostrils the breath of life: and man became a living soul" (Genesis 2:7, KJV).

The above scripture does not say that water invaded our nostrils and we became a living soul. Nor does it say that food nutrients went into our nostrils and we became a living soul. Nor does it say that blood cells entered our nostrils and we became a living soul. No, the substance that distinguishes the living from the dead is the breath of God. In other words, you can live for days without water, food, or a low blood cell count. But it's near impossible to live without breath for more than one minute.

Breath is critical to life. Unless we develop a condition that impairs our ability to breathe normally, we don't have to think about it.

Consider taking time during your meditation and prayer time each day to practice deep breathing. Deep breathing helps you to relax. When we are angry or upset, our breathing becomes shallow, increasing anxious feelings more. The practice of taking deep breaths relaxes the muscles, including the heart and lowers the blood pressure.

Are you getting the most from the gift of breath? It's a new year, a great time to start increasing your energy by taking time to take deep breaths at meditation time and periodically throughout the day. Life is in the breath!

"The Spirit of God has made me, and the breath of the Almighty gives me life" (Job 33:4, NIV).

January 24
A Shero (A female hero)

"Buy the truth, and do not sell it—wisdom, and instruction, and understanding as well" (Proverbs 23:23, NIV).

A few years ago, she was unknown to most people until a movie told her life story. Mrs. Katherine Johnson was a genius. At age ten, she was a freshman in high school and graduated from college at age eighteen. After college and graduate school, she taught mathematics in junior and high schools. I can only imagine how her students must have felt to learn of their teacher's vast accomplishments after she left them.

The National Aeronautics and Space Administration (NASA) was fortunate to discover the brilliance of Katherine Johnson, an African American mathematician whose calculations of orbital mechanics at NASA was critical to the success of U.S. manned spaceflights. At NASA, because of her brilliance, she stood head and shoulders above her colleagues. She wanted to know the 'how' and the 'why' and then the 'why not.' Her gifts and talents did make room for her in the field of science and mathematics. She earned a reputation for mastering complex manual calculations and helped the space agency pioneer the use of computers to perform such tasks.

Mrs. Johnson's talents and contributions were hidden for many years, but now the world knows and are proud of her tremendous contributions to the United States space program. In 2015, President Barack Obama presented her with a Presidential Medal of Freedom.

"No one lights a lamp and puts it in a place where it will be hidden, or under a bowl. Instead, they put it on its stand, so that those who come in may see the light" (Luke 11:33, NIV).

January 25
A Poem of Love by Cherita

"Did I learn to love, not with a fair-weather love but with a love that accepts unconditionally; love not with a quick and passing love but with a love that is a quiet peace within your heart."

The above poem was written by a twelve-year-old girl. I still have the poem thirty-eight years later. Back then, it surprised me that a pre-teen could write with such wisdom and insight. I like to think it was written through her ageless and eternal soul.

We met her when my husband pastored a small church on the outskirts of Jacksonville, Florida. I recall helping coach Cherita for an upcoming church program. She was to recite 1Corinthians 13, a chapter in the Bible about love.

When she read the sentence, "When I was a child, I spoke as a child, I reasoned as a child, but when I became a [man], I put away childish things," I asked her to change the last portion of the sentence to, when I became a [woman], I put away childish things.

When Cherita recited the scripture with this small change, I noticed the difference in her being. She stood taller and appeared more confident. Her words were distinct, and the sound of her voice was stronger. I could tell she liked making the change to emphasize her value as a female creature with unique gifts to give to the universe. Nothing like being yourself.

"When you try to be somebody else, you can only be second best."
~ Cecil Wayne Cone

January 26
Identity

".....Who do people say the Son of Man is" (Matthew 16:13, NLT)

In Philippians, we get an accurate description of Jesus: "Who, being in the form of God, thought it not robbery to be equal with God; but made himself of no reputation, and took upon him the form of a servant, and was made in the likeness of man; he humbled himself, and became obedient unto death, even the death of the cross" (*Philippians 2:5, NIV*). To put it simply, Jesus says, I am a servant. I am humble. I am obedient to the Almighty Sovereign God. And no experience, no matter how horrible it might appear, will cause me to question who I am.

Jesus wanted his disciples to be clear about his identity. Accordingly, he asks them, "But who do you say that I am?" Peter spoke, "You are the Messiah" (*Matthew 16:15-16, NLT*). Peter's answer suggests he knows Jesus. However, when Jesus says that he will be rejected, and killed, Peter thinks Jesus is insane. In Peter's mind, it is impossible for the Messiah to suffer. After all, Jesus was all powerful. Moreover, Jesus had come to rescue them from their enemies. How could anything bad happen to him?

Jesus rebukes Peter in the harshest way, "Get away from me, Satan! You are a dangerous trap to me" (*Matthew 16:23, NLT*). Peter forgot the true mission of Jesus. Peter wanted Jesus to be the King and not the suffering servant. Peter was ready to receive the glory of following the Messiah but not the persecution. Jesus made it clear that nothing or no one would stop his reason for being.

Who do people say that you are? Are you a believer, a follower of Jesus Christ? What does it mean for a Christian to suffer, be obedient, be humble? How do you respond to people who think differently, talk different, or look different from you?

"Then he called the crowd to him along with his disciples and said: 'Whoever wants to be my disciple must deny themselves and take up their cross and follow me'" (Mark 8:34, NIV).

January 27
Your Gift Will Make Room For You

"A man's gift maketh room for him, and bringeth him before great men" (Proverbs 18:16, KJV).

On this day in 1961, Leontyne Price's gift made room for her as she debuted at the Metropolitan Opera. Out of Laurel, Mississippi, a woman was born with unparalleled operatic talent. In the 1990s, an article in the *Washington Post* characterized her as the most important prima donna America produced since Rosa Ponselle in the 1930s.

Ms. Price showed an interest in music at the young age of five. At age nine, she attended a recital by contralto Marian Anderson that helped her visualize her own dream of singing. She was awarded a scholarship to study at the Juilliard School of Music. From there, her career blossomed.

She received empowering messages from her mother and father. "My parents told my brother and me that there is nothing that you cannot achieve if you aim high enough," she recalls. "I don't remember them ever asserting that being me, being black, being Afro-American, was anything but positive. It was always approached as aiming high ~ climbing a mountain with your head held high, because you can't climb a mountain looking down; you're bound to fall."

Although she was a gifted artist, it was her family support, parental wisdom, and faith in God that were the catalyst for her successful career.

"I have a very pristine belief in God—untampered with—as fresh as it was when I was in Sunday school in Laurel, Mississippi. I don't intellectualize about it; I know it's there—I am part of a plan, and I go with it."
~ Leontyne Price

January 28
A Broken Chain Experience

God helps us even when we have broken the laws of the state. A young married woman with four children is involved in a car accident. She is the driver of the car. It was a rainy day. She had just picked up her children from school. There were no serious injuries or fatalities. The police arrive and discover that not only does she not have a driver's license, but she is an undocumented immigrant and does not speak English.

She is arrested and separated from her children (ages 5, 9, 12, and 17). Her husband arrives and picks up the children while his wife is handcuffed and taken away in a police car. The extended family is close-knit and supportive. Although a bit worried, they make sure the children have warm meals, continue in school, and complete their homework. The husband and nephew hire an immigration attorney.

Three days later, after paying a substantial bond, she is released. By this time, she had been transferred to a facility four hours away. She arrives home around midnight and although a bit shaken and showing signs of fatigue, the joy of seeing her children again make up for the last seventy-two hours.

The final outcome for this young woman is uncertain. Still, her release did not have to happen. She could have been required to remain in jail and eventually transported back to her home country, but the Almighty Sovereign God performed a miracle and brought joy to a family when hope had become hollow.

"I believe if you keep your faith, you keep your trust, you keep the right attitude, if you're grateful, you'll see God open up new doors."
~Joel Osteen

January 29
My Personal Plea

"Rejoice in the Lord always and again I say rejoice" (Philippians 4:4, KJV)!

Years ago, the Lord gave me my own song. I sing it to the melody of the spiritual, "I'll be alright." It is taken from Psalm 139:

Search me O God and know my heart. Try me and know my thoughts. And see if there be any wicked ways in me and lead me in the everlasting way.

I wanna be led in the way. I wanna be led in the way. I wanna be led in the everlasting way. So, see if there be any wicked ways in me and lead me in the everlasting way.

The everlasting way, the everlasting way, I wanna be led in the everlasting way. So, see if there be any wicked ways in me and lead me in the everlasting way.

This song describes the depth of my relationship with God. It's a relationship that began before I was born. God understands my thoughts, my words, and all my ways. And wherever I go, God is there, even if I make my bed in hell. What is even more astonishing is that God's thoughts about me are innumerable, more in number than the sand.

To ask God to search me is surprising since God knows me from top to bottom. So, I guess the request is a reality check to remind me of who I am, what I am capable of, and who I really want to follow. Thank you, Almighty Sovereign God.

"Search me, O God, and know my heart: try me, and know my thoughts: and see if there be any wicked way in me and lead me in the way everlasting" (Psalm 139: 23-24, KJV).

January 30
Eternal Life

In the Gospel of Luke 18:18-27, a rich young ruler asked Jesus what is required to inherit eternal life. He had kept all God's commandments since childhood, but Jesus told him he still lacked one thing. "Sell everything you have and give to the poor, and you will have treasure in heaven. Then, come follow me" (*Luke 18: 22, NIV*). That's when the rich young man walked away sad and empty-handed. What did he lack?

He needed humility. He thought his entry into the kingdom ought to be inevitable since he had been in the church all of his life. To add to this, the young man's wealth was a stumbling block. Money was so important, he walked away sad when it appeared he would lose his money.

The rich young ruler lacked faith in God. He didn't have to leave empty handed. The gift of eternal life is free. It is impossible for anyone to buy their way into heaven. In fact, you don't have enough in your bank account or portfolio to pay for eternal life. Neither is eternal life dependent totally upon your church work. Further, with faith in God, Jesus would not have to chide him about his wealth. He would want to cheerfully share God's blessings with the poor.

Are there stumbling blocks that hinder your faith walk? It's easy for you to admire your Christian service when you've been in the church for years and you are doing a lot of good work. But frequently remind yourself that your walk with the Lord is not based on what you do right. It will always be based on what Jesus did. In the words of songwriter, Elvina Hall, "Jesus paid it all. All to Him I owe; Sin had left a crimson stain. He washed it white as snow."

"And without faith it is impossible to please God, because anyone who comes to Him must believe that He exists and that He rewards those who earnestly seek Him" (Hebrews 11:6, NIV).

January 31
Jesus' Answers About Death

Have you ever listened to conversations people have when someone they know dies? Comments like, my cousin just died from a heart attack. I'd better get checked out...He drank all the time. I'm glad I stopped drinking...Recently, I read about a fifty-year-old physician who died in the midst of taking care of her patient...so young to die. In my opinion, loss of life stirs up angst about death, when one no longer exist.

In the Gospel of Luke 13:1-5 (KJV), Jesus has a conversation about death with his disciples. A band of people died, one group was murdered, and the other group died as a result of an accident. Jesus asks his disciples a series of rhetorical questions. Why was their death so harsh? Was it because they were worse sinners? What is Jesus saying? The cause or the timing of death is not yours to control. Life is fragile and can change in the twinkling of an eye. What happens after we perish is more important.

Oftentimes, we look at the miracles Jesus performed. He healed the sick, raised the dead, opened blind eyes, and even turned water into wine. However, Jesus was more concerned about eternal life. "Whosoever believes in him will not perish, but have eternal life" (John 3:16, KJV).

In answer to their questions about death, Jesus is saying that death is not the end of the story. Those who believe in him have eternal life. This is where the Christian's primary hope lies. If you have not given your life to Jesus, now is an excellent time: "That if you confess with your mouth, "Jesus is Lord," and believe in your heart that God raised him from the dead, you will be saved." (Romans 10:10, NIV).

"The Lord is not slow in keeping his promise, as some understand slowness. He is patient with you, not wanting anyone to perish, but everyone to come to repentance. But the day of the Lord will come like a thief" (2 Peter 3:9, NIV).

February 1
The Heart of the Matter:
Reducing the Burden on the Heart

February is American Heart Month. Its purpose is to raise aware-ness about heart disease and how to prevent it. The heart is the most important part of the body. The less the heart is burdened, the better. It is burdened by unhealthy blood pressure, blood sugar, and choles-terol. Regular safe exercise strengthens the heart. Fruits and vegetables protect the heart. Rest and joy energize the heart. Emotions affect the heart. A merry heart does good like a medicine, but a broken spirit dries the bones (*Proverbs 17:22, NKJV*). A healthy heart matters for the body and the soul.

In Psalm 51, David's heart was burdened from sin. There were known as well as hidden factors that weighed heavy on his heart: deceit, dishonesty, sexual exploitation, and murder. The result was a shattered relationship with God, and it was more than he could bear. For David was considered to be a man after God's own heart. Now, his spiritual heart was clogged up. He cried out to God. David asked God for for-giveness, to create in him a clean heart, and restore their relationship.

Our lives are similar to David's life predicaments. Whether there is a physical or spiritual burden on our heart, healing starts when we take the necessary steps to allow God to heal our hearts.

"Create in me a clean heart, O God, and renew a right spirit within me" (Psalm 51:10, KJV).

A Voice Crying in the Wilderness...

"My drive comes from just wanting to see myself and my family be in a better situation and I do think drive is important for everybody, but what's more important is that once you find what it is that you want, you have to keep working for it. People may think that they've done enough, but it's never enough."
~ Richard Jenkins

Richard Jenkins spent the early years of his life living in homeless shelters and motel rooms. In addition to housing issues, he had medical problems and was hospitalized for long periods of time.

Mr. Jenkins' passion to achieve academically started when he was in the eighth grade. As a result of his hard work, he received a full-scholarship to a boarding high school for students from single-parent families and limited resources. This young man graduated as the class valedictorian and was accepted to Harvard University undergraduate class of 2021. He was waitlisted at the University of Pennsylvania and rejected by Yale.

In addition to being a high-achiever, Mr. Jenkins didn't want to accumulate debt while getting his education. Since Harvard pays 100 percent of tuition for students from households earning $65,000 a year or less, his college debts would be less.

There is wisdom to gain from Mr. Jenkins' life story: 1) Never give up. He refused to let serious health challenges and being homeless hold him back. 2) Dream big for God. He had hope for the future. He was able to visualize himself and his family doing better. 3) Keep working and growing. You can always learn more.

Mr. Jenkins was a voice crying in the wilderness. Thank God, his cry was heard and answered.

"For I know the plans I have for you," declares the Lord, "plans to prosper you and not to harm you, plans to give you hope and a future" (Jeremiah 29:11, NIV).

February 3
A Living Will

"I don't want nobody pounding on my chest."

These were words I heard my ninety-two-year-old mother say to the staff attending her at a rehabilitation center. She was sent there to recuperate from pneumonia. During her hospital stay, an aneurysm was discovered on the large artery (aorta) in her abdomen. An aneurysm causes an artery to swell like a balloon. It has the potential to rupture at any time and cause massive bleeding and/or death. Understanding the implications of her decision, she declined surgery to repair the aneurysm and opted to go to a rehab center for physical therapy. Although she had not completed a written living will, she verbalized her wishes.

A living will describes one's wishes should they become terminally ill. It takes the burden off the family when situations appear futile. My mother's first twenty days at the rehab center were smooth. Each day her strength increased, and it looked like she would be able to return home. Then one day, she cried out in pain, blacked out, and stopped breathing. The rehab staff started resuscitation efforts including chest compressions. I am told that my mother opened her eyes and looked annoyed as if to say, *I told y'all, I don't want nobody pounding on my chest.* She was transferred back to the hospital where she died one hour later.

Regardless of what caused the sudden worsening of her condition, her decision had been made. She lived out her faith in God in everything she did. She was courageous and decisive. When her mind was made up, her mind was made up.

Have you completed a living will? Do you think this is only for the elderly or people with terminal illnesses? While we do not have control over death, we have control over how we prepare for death.

"For to me, to live is Christ, and to die is gain" (Philippians 1:21, NIV).

February 4

Rosa Parks

"People always say that I didn't give up my seat because I was tired, but that isn't true. I was not tired physically, or no more tired than I usually was at the end of a working day. I was not old, although some people have an image of me as being old then. I was forty-two. No, the only tired I was, was tired of giving in."
~ *Rosa Parks*

On February 4, 1913, a quiet but courageous woman was born in Tuskegee, Alabama. Parks was an established organizer and leader in the Civil Rights movement by the time she boarded the bus in 1955. She was destined to set in motion one of the largest social movements in history, the Montgomery Bus Boycott.

At the time of the incident, Mrs. Parks was seated in the front of the black section. When the bus started to fill up with white passengers, the bus driver asked Parks to move. She refused to give up her seat and was arrested. Her action heralded the onset of the Montgomery Bus Boycott that lasted 381 days. The boycott led to the integration of public transportation in Montgomery.

Parks' strong faith in God was at the core of everything she did, providing her strength and courage. Her courageous act resulted in the loss of her job, but it changed the course of history.

"For whoever wants to save their life will lose it, but whoever loses their life for me will find it" (Matthew 16:25, NIV).

February 5
Rejoicing in the Lord

"This is the day that the LORD has made; we will rejoice and be glad in it"
(Psalm 118:24, KJV).

My daily meditation time includes writing in my journal. Some-times I choose a spirited word and try to think of other words that align with each letter in the word. You will see this exercise intermit-tently throughout this book. Today, the word is Rejoice: I rejoice in the Lord because:

- Redeemed – My life has been redeemed from destruction.
- Enheartened – I am enheartened to serve humanity.
- Joy – The joy of the Lord is my strength.
- Omnipresent – There is nowhere I can go where God is not present.
- Identity – God *identifies* with me.
- Comforter – The Holy Spirit is the Comforter and lives inside me.
- Everlasting–From everlasting to everlasting is God's mercy to-ward them that fear God.

This is a positive exercise that clears my mind and gets me ready for a great day. To serve God is to serve humankind. To serve humanity is to serve God.

"Rejoice in the Lord always: and again I say, Rejoice" (Philippians 4:4, KJV).

What is More Important?
When You Were Born or Why You Were Born?

There was a time in the United States when the date of birth was unknown for most of the enslaved population. One such person is Harriet Tubman born a slave somewhere around 1820.

Tubman was described as fearless and strong. Her biography, *Harriet Tubman*, written by Earl Conrad, tells the story of how she blocked a doorway to prevent the overseer from seizing a fugitive slave. He picks up a heavyweight to hit the fugitive but misses and hit Harriet instead. This left her unconscious for a long period of time. Eventually, she awakens from the coma and develops into a strong, intuitive, and more courageous woman. Not only did she think a lot about escaping to a free country, she visualized it as well. After learning that she was about to be sold into slavery into the deep south, she makes her decision to move forward.

Harriet knew about safe houses (Underground Railroad) where she could stop for rest and food. Conrad says she traveled by night using the north star as her guide. Eventually, she arrives on free soil in Pennsylvania. However, she did not rest on her own laurels of success. She became a champion for others to find freedom as well. It is reported that she made nineteen trips back through the Underground Railroad to rescue enslaved relatives and anyone else she could lead out of the oppressive system.

Harriett Tubman continues to be a source of inspiration for many. In 2016, it was announced that Harriet Tubman would be the new face on the twenty-dollar bill. I hope to hold that bill in my hand one day.

"There's two things I've got a right to and these are death or liberty. One or the other I mean to have. No one will take me back alive; for I shall fight for my liberty, and when the time has come for me to go, the Lord will let them kill me."
~ *Harriett Tubman*

February 7
A Higher Level of Thinking

"And now, dear brothers and sisters, one final thing. Fix your thoughts on what is true, and honorable, and right, and pure, and lovely, and admirable. Think about things that are excellent and worthy of praise" (Philippians 4:8, NLT).

If you can fix your thoughts on truth, honor, wholesome living, and excellence, you have moved to a higher level of thinking. However, this is not easy to do. Our minds are like an electronic message board. Like cell phone app ads, all kinds of messaging pops up in our thoughts. Some imaginable, unimaginable, some positive and some negative thoughts. Most thoughts pass through unnoticed by us. But many thoughts occur based on past and present experiences.

Because of thoughts, even before a conversation starts, we make inferences about another person's behavior based on personal and sometimes paranoid ideas floating in our own mind. Sometimes, our impressions are far from reality.

There are many life experiences, fearful events, and anxious times that paralyze our thinking and keep us from thinking the beautiful thoughts described in Philippians 4:8. Our minds are quick to move to what happened in the past or what might happen in the future rather than the present situation.

What is the answer to a cluttered mind? How does one reduce over-analyzing situations? Both meditation and prayer help. Unfortunately, as one attempts to engage in quiet time, every thought imaginable starts wandering across the mind. Still, try and keep at it. Here are suggestions for beginning a quiet time routine:

- Turn off the computer, phones, iPad, TV and radio. Set a stopwatch for how long you want to meditate.
- Before beginning the meditation process, start with prayer.
- Sit upright in a comfortable chair. Place your hands on your lap with palms facing upward. Relax and breathe naturally.
- Relax your legs and feet to your liking.
- Let go of your will, your agenda, your desire.

- Start slow. Sit still for two minutes. As you continue to practice this exercise, increase the time spent in meditation.
- When thoughts pop up in your head, take a few deep breaths in and out. Keep at it until your timer goes off.

"Truly, sacred rest is soul care. We honor quiet time alone with God. We intentionally step away from the chaos of life. We unplug from noise and distractions. We relish moments of tranquility."
~*Dana Arcuri*

February 8
Relationships Matter

"Healing starts in the relationship."
˜Cecil Wayne Cone

My late husband was a pastor. In many of his sermons, he would say, "Healing starts in the relationship." Relationships in families, marriages, churches, communities, nation, and in the world are dependent on mutual trust and respect. With so much division in our country, it's time to become more mindful of the importance of building relationships. Listening to others is paramount, and we must listen with our heart. To listen with your heart means to be present. Thinking about what you're going to say when it's your turn to speak is not active listening. Before saying what's on your mind, paraphrase what you heard. This is a sure way for the other person to know they have been heard.

Diana Ross sang a song titled, *Reach Out and Touch (somebody's hand).* In the song, she implored us to make the world a better place. Simple words that are sometimes hard to put into action but make a world of difference when practiced.

My husband used to say, "Your journey to your destiny goes through those persons you most despise. Therefore, you must come to terms with your perceived enemies." Jesus said it this way, "But I tell you, love your enemies and pray for those who persecute you" (Matthew 5:44, NIV). It is the connection between and among human beings that heals and moves us to a higher level of living.

"All human beings have an emotional bank account where love, forgiveness, respect, patience, and warmth are stored. Be outrageous in the amount you withdraw to build and strengthen a relationship. The more you take out, the more you gain back"
˜Juanita Fletcher Cone

February 9
Wholeness—Mind, Body, and Spirit Connection

The connections between the body, mind, and spirit are incredible. It's what makes us human. We're at our best when all three are functioning in a synchronized way. The Bible wrote about these relationships thousands of years ago. Science has confirmed what was already written. Let's look at a few examples found in the Bible.

Proverbs 17:22 (NIV) says, "A cheerful heart is good medicine, but a crushed spirit dries up the bones." In other words, our mood affects our mental and physical health. Science has discovered a chemical imbalance in the brain in some forms of depression. Anti-depressant medication corrects this imbalance.

1 Corinthians 6:19 (NIV) says, "Do you not know that your body is the temple of the Holy Spirit, who is in you, whom you have received from God? You are not your own." The Holy Spirit lives inside the physical body. A weak physical body affects the spiritual body. Cigarettes, cigars, high fat and high sugar foods, alcohol, marijuana, and other illegal drugs steal energy from the body. Fatigue and weakness make it less likely you'll feel like reading or meditating on God's Word. Fasting, prayer, and meditation strengthens the spiritual body and in turn gives energy to the physical body as well.

The physical body is only one quality of a human being. The physical body works together with our emotions, intellect, and spirit to create health and wholeness with God, ourselves, our fellow human beings as well as every other part of this magnificent universe.

"Beloved, I wish above all things that thou mayest prosper and be in health, even as thy soul prospers" (3 John 1:2, KJV).

February 10
Grace and Mercy

My upbringing was in the church. Our mother made sure we attended Sunday School and participated regularly in all youth activities. But things changed after I left for college. I didn't attend chapel or say my prayers regularly. Before long, I began to feel like I was on my own, making unsafe choices in college and medical school.

In spite of me, the Almighty Sovereign God was still watching and protecting me. I don't want to know where I would be or what could have happened if it had not been for the Lord showering me with unmerited grace and mercy. I owe my life to God.

Where are you on your spiritual journey? Wherever you are, God is as close as each breath you take. We can never be out of the boundary of God's love. God sees and hears you at all times. "Does He who fashioned the ear not hear? Does He who formed the eye not see" (*Psalm 94:9, NIV*).

"If I ascend up into heaven, thou art there: if I make my bed in hell, behold, thou art there. If I take the wings of the morning, and dwell in the uttermost parts of the sea; Even there shall thy hand lead me, and thy right hand shall hold me" (Psalm 139:8-10, KJV).

February 11
Happy Birthday to Jarena Lee—
Born February 11, 1783
The Passion of Her Calling to Ministry

"For as unseemly as it may appear nowadays for a woman to preach, it should be remembered that nothing is impossible, heterodox, or improper for a woman to preach, seeing the Savior died for the woman as well as the man." ~Jarena Lee

These are the words found in the *Religious Experiences and Journal of Mrs. Jarena Lee: "A Preach 'in Woman,"* a biography of her life by A. Lee Henderson. Mrs. Lee was the first woman preacher in the AME Church (African Methodist Episcopal Church).

This quote speaks to her insight and courage to address sexism in the eighteenth century. The denomination to which she belonged had encountered racism causing black people to separate from the Methodist church and form the AME church. Although they challenged racism, the church leadership was blind to their sexism.

The response of Richard Allen, bishop of the AME church to her request to preach was typical: "The doctrines and discipline of the AME church knew nothing at all about women who are called."

Lee was not deterred. She continued to pray and make preparation for the day when she would preach. After waiting eight years, recognition as a preacher came in an unusual way. Indeed, God's ways are not our ways.

A minister scheduled to preach suddenly was loss for words. Without effort or premeditation, Lee leapt to her feet and preached a powerful message. The bishop of the church witnessed the spectacle. After the impromptu sermon, Lee assumed that not only would she never preach again, she expected to be expelled from the church.

Instead, Bishop Allen rose up in the assembly and confirmed that she had approached him eight years earlier about preaching. "After this sermon," he stated, "I now as much believe that she is called to the work."

This event shows her passion and readiness to preach, the Bishop's humble and level temperament and most of all, the power of God. "When a woman's ways please the Lord, God makes her enemies to be at peace with her" (*paraphrased Proverbs 16:7, KJV*).

"Opportunity does not waste time with those who are unprepared."
~Idowu Koyenikan

February 12
God Provides

"Be not dismayed, God will take care of you."
~ Civilla Martin

In my opinion, this old hymn is a pure love song. When I hear it's heartening words, my faith is strengthened. The third verse says, "All you may need, God will provide." I am a living testament to this truth.

Before my husband passed, he was in an intensive care unit for six and a half weeks. My heart's desire was to be with him day and night. As a result, I missed many days from my work as a physician.

The majority of my work compensation was based on productivity (number of patients seen each day). During this time, my productivity dropped significantly. Salaries were adjusted twice a year. I expected a substantial drop given the number of days I missed working while he was in the hospital.

However, things turned out differently. The leadership team advised me, as I expected, that my salary was to take a big drop. However, the decision was made to not reduce my salary. They decided to keep it at the same level and re-evaluate in six months. I was so grateful. Indeed, God will take care of us.

"No matter what may be the test, God will take care of you. Lean weary one upon God's breast, God will take care of you."
~ Cevilla Martin

February 13
Responsibility

Responsibility means not blaming anyone or anything for your present situation. When you are able to do this, you can engender a creative response to the situation you find yourself in. Making excuses and blaming others only brings temporary satisfaction.

"If you had done your part, things would have worked out."

"My blood sugar is out of control because I have no one to help

me cook."

"Vegetables are too expensive."

"I am late to work because of the traffic."

We can always see how someone, or something, has handicapped us. When we blame others, we block the seeds of opportunity. When we own it, we can do something about it.

I make the decision to eat healthy foods, exercise regularly, and get enough sleep every night. I am responsible for getting to work on time. I am responsible for the impact alcohol, cigarettes, and illegal drug use have on my body. Care of my body and my health begins with me.

"Each of you must take responsibility for doing the creative best you can with your own life" (Galatians 6:5, MSG).

February 14
Celebrating Love: Valentine's Day

Today, we celebrate love. We honor that which never fails, that which continues after death, which heals the wounded heart, satisfies the starving soul, conceives life, and saves lives for eternity.

Love is calming, courageous, creative, curious, forgiving, generous, kindhearted, magical, patient, powerful, tender, and redemptive.

Love makes you laugh. Love makes you cry. Love awakens. Love admits when its wrong. Love believes the best. Love feeds the hungry and houses the homeless. Love gives and forgives. Love heals. Love sedates. Love soothes.

Love is agape (unconditional). Love is eros (passionate). Love is phileo (brotherly and sisterly). Love is born of God. God is the source of all love.

"And may you have the power to understand, as all God's people should, how wide, how long, how high, and how deep God's love is. May you experience the love of Christ, though it is so great you will never fully understand it. Then you will be made complete with all the fullness of life and power that comes from God" *(paraphrased Ephesians 3:18-19, NLT).*

February 15
The Lazarus Syndrome

"Now a man named Lazarus was sick. He was from Bethany, the village of Mary and her sister Martha. (This Mary, whose brother Lazarus now lay sick, was the same one who poured perfume on the Lord and wiped his feet with her hair.) So the sisters sent word to Jesus, 'Lord, the one you love is sick'" (John 11:1-3, NIV).

As a physician, it's worth noting the word 'sick' is mentioned three separate times in the above scriptures. In the African American community, there are many Marthas and Marys with sick husbands, fathers, and brothers who do not live out their full life expectancy. The life expectancy for African American men averages out at a low of seventy-one years.

Too many men don't like making doctor visits. Some keep working while sick. Others mask their symptoms or deny warning signs until it's too late. While the decision to seek medical care belongs to the individual, it brings worry to the Marys and Marthas of the world. And then there's the economic cost. Full social security benefits start at age sixty-seven. If one dies between age sixty-seven and seventy-one, only four years of social security benefits are collected. Additionally, those who die in their fifties and early sixties end up receiving no benefits (after working all those years).

In the referenced scripture, Lazarus is sick and dies. Jesus performs a miracle and brings him back to life. There are several things that happen before his resurrection: Jesus orders Martha to roll the stone away. Because of its weight, Martha needs help. Unhealthy communities are a heavy burden on society. The entire community of families must start making healthy decisions and leverage resources to build social programs around health. It takes a village to build strong healthy communities.

Lastly, Jesus calls Lazarus to come out of the cave. "Unwrap him and let him go" (John 11:3, NLT). No one can make Lazarus change his lifestyle. Lazarus must take ownership of his spiritual, physical, and mental health. Now, Lazarus wants to speak:

Thank you, Jesus for giving me a second chance at life. My desire is to live like it is my second time around. The past is behind me. Each day will count. I will not waste one minute of this God given time. This is the day that the Lord has made. I will rejoice and be glad in it. Health is a way of life, a habit that enables me to meet and adjust to life's challenges. I invite all of you to join me in my new health journey. Let's make this an opportunity for the entire family and community to take the best care of our bodies, minds, and spirits.

"... I am come that they might have life, and that they might have it more abundantly" (John 10:10, KJV).

February 16
The Soul Within

"I will bless the Lord at all times: God's praise shall continually be in my mouth. My soul shall make her boast in the Lord. The humble shall hear thereof and be glad" (paraphrased Psalm 34: 1-2).

One of the first truths I learned after being born again was that Christians were to bless the Lord regardless of their life situations. My mentor used the scripture, "No matter what happens, always be thankful for this is God's will for you who belong to Christ Jesus" (*1 Thessalonians 5:18, TLB*). When life is mellow, it's easy to give praise to God. But when things are not going well or we feel rejected or discouraged, the mind and heart may not feel up to it.

When we bless the Lord, it demonstrates our faith in God. When we bless the Lord, we are in communion with God. When we bless the Lord, it enriches our soul to the true source of what brings value to life. Power, wealth, strength, or position in society are fleeting. While it is true that every blessing comes from God, all are not connected to God and therefore do not add value to the soul.

"My soul shall make her boast in the Lord." The soul is our eternal connection with God. That's what Douglas Miller means when he sings, "My soul is anchored in the Lord"," or as Kenneth Morris wrote, "Yes God is real, real in my soul."

When my soul magnifies the Lord, it is boasting in the Almighty Sovereign God's omnipotence, omnipresence, and omniscience. Boasting about God in our alone time is sacred, but when the humble saints commune together, there is a ground swell of unspeakable joy and bliss that binds believers together as one.

"My soul glorifies the Lord and my spirit rejoices in God my Savior" (Luke 1:46-47, NIV).

February 17
Brotherly and Sisterly Love

In Maya Angelou's autobiography, *I Know Why the Caged Bird Sings*, she writes about the many stressors she faced during childhood including being raped at the age of eight.

Her brother (one year older) became more like a Godbrother to her. His life validated her to the point that, "she wanted to live a Christian life just to show God how grateful she was for his comforting presence in her life." They memorized poetry together, and then recited it to each other. Her brother was the first person she told about the rape. His response was not only to show empathy, but also to encourage her to name the rapist, which she did. In fact, after the rape, she rarely talked to anyone else.

Often, we hear about sibling rivalry and less about the deep connection between brothers and sisters. In my own family, there were two girls and one boy. We did have occasional conflicts, but we spent much more time enjoying each other as we learned to swim, play instruments in the school band together, participate in a youth dance troupe, and other activities. We spent more time showing love than being contentious.

"A friend loves at all times, And a brother is born for a time of adversity" (Proverbs 17:17, KJV).

February 18
I Sent You a Rowboat
(Source Unknown)

A very religious man was once caught in rising floodwaters. He climbed onto the roof of his house and trusted God to rescue him. A neighbor came by in a canoe and said, "The waters will soon be above your house. Hop in and we'll paddle to safety."

"No thanks," replied the religious man. "I've prayed and I'm sure that God will save me."

A short time later, the police came by in a boat. "The waters will soon be above your house. Hop in and we'll take you to safety."

"No thanks," replied the religious man. "I've prayed and I'm sure God will save me."

A little time later a rescue service helicopter hovered overhead, let down a rope ladder and said, "The waters will soon be above your house. Climb the ladder and we'll fly you to safety."

"No thanks," replied the religious man. "I've prayed to God and I'm sure God will save me."

All this time, the floodwaters continued to rise until soon they reached above the roof and the religious man drowned. When he arrived at heaven, he demanded an audience with God. Ushered into God's throne room, he said, "Lord, why am I here in heaven? I prayed for you to save me. I trusted you to save me from that flood."

"Yes, you did, my child," replied the Lord. "And I sent you a canoe, a boat, and a helicopter. But you never got in."

Too often, we imagine God to look or act a certain way. We miss opportunities, blessings and even divine interventions because of narrow minded thinking. The scripture says that God provides a way of escape. It does not give specific descriptions of what to be on the lookout for.

"For we live by faith, not by sight" (2 Corinthians 5:7, NIV).

February 19
Give Up on Despair

Sometimes the heart overflows with tears of despondency. Newsflash—it is okay to cry. "When they walk through the valley of weeping, it will become a place of refreshing springs where pools of blessings collect after the rains" (Psalm 84:6, NLT).

The earth needs rain for the flowers to blossom, the plants to grow and turn green, and for vegetables and fruits to grow and nourish our bodies. If there was no rain, the earth would shrivel up for lack of moisture. In a similar manner, we need rain (challenges) in our lives. Rain helps us grow in wisdom and patience.

There is a reservoir of godly love and compassion in the human community. Don't be afraid to open your heart and reach into this bottomless reserve. Go to the reservoir of godly love. In other words, spend time at church and bible study. If you don't belong to a church or know where to go, seek guidance from family or friends. Volunteer activities are most useful and rewarding.

"We often can't see what God is doing in our lives, but God sees the whole picture and His plan for us clearly."
~ *Tony Dungy*

February 20
The Power of Prayer

Years ago, I heard a story about a woman whose husband was ill and needed the care of a doctor. The couple lived during a time when physicians made house calls and racism was at its peak. The doctor was white, and the patient was black. Refusing to go to their home, the physician goes home and tries to sleep, and the sick man's wife goes to God in fervent prayer.

The physician tried to fall asleep three times. Each time, he would be awakened from a dream where he saw the sick man in need. He was so troubled by the dream, he got up and went to the ailing man's house and provided the medical care he needed. Prayer makes a difference.

I have a long list of people I pray for every day. Some are family members, friends, former co-workers, acquaintances, and people I have or had business dealings with. Most of them don't know that I pray for them. It is an honor and a privilege to pray for their health, safety, and prosperity.

Oftentimes, one will tell me something good that has happened in their life, and I let them know that I take a little credit because of my regular prayers on their behalf. Some laugh and make jokes, but they never ask me to stop praying for them.

Pray for healing, peace, forgiveness, generosity, understanding, and for unconditional love to abound.

"The effectual fervent prayer of a righteous man [or woman] availeth much" (James 5:16, KJV).

How Does the Picture Look?
Maybe It's Time for Some Reframing

A few years ago, I decided it was time to declutter our garage. During the process, I found some family pictures that I had completely forgotten existed. They had been packed away for years and were grubby and covered with spiderwebs. Even in their dirty condition, they were too precious to dispose of.

I had the pictures reframed, and what a difference it made. I hung them along the staircase and not only were they revitalized but the walk up the stairs was no longer boring.

How does the picture of your life look? Is it grubby, uneasy, dark, or light, joyful, or fulfilling? Consider stepping outside of the picture. Look at it from different angles. Before you go back inside the picture, modify what you see, what you desire. There are so many ways of looking at your life picture. You may not be able to change the particulars, but you can change how you interpret them. In other words, reframe the picture. When you do, you become refreshed, revived, and recharged.

"It is difficult to see the picture when you are inside of the frame."
~*Author Unknown*

February 22
Justice

What is just? What is fair? For me, it is treating everyone equally. As I write this reflection, there is a lot of tension and divisiveness in our country. This causes fear, mistrust, and stress filled lives even among those with similar beliefs.

There is limited patience. This is sometimes manifested by reckless driving, road rage, impatient shoppers, disparaging comments to innocent workers just doing their job, and many other acts of pettiness and meanness. By the time you read this, I am hopeful that our citizens will have moved to a higher level of thinking, understanding, and being about each other.

I believe that the Almighty Sovereign God created different races, genders, ideologies, religions, traditions, and cultures to demonstrate that we can live together in harmony. It cost nothing to be fair or to be respectful. Treat everyone the way you want to be treated.

We are connected to every human being, and this connection makes us ONE. Herman Melville expressed it this way, "We cannot live only for ourselves. A thousand fibers connect us with our fellow men [and women]; and among those fibers, as sympathetic threads, our actions run as causes, and they come back to us as effects."

Connect with the soul of people. The soul is where love, patience, empathy, and compassion live in every human being.

"If we have no peace, it is because we have forgotten that we belong to each other."
~Mother Teresa

February 23
Take Another Look!

"...Jesus asked, 'Do you see anything?' He looked up and said, 'I see people; they look like trees walking around.' Once more Jesus put his hands on the man's eyes. Then his eyes were opened, his sight was restored, and he saw everything clearly" (Mark 8:23-25, NIV).

When I was in medical school, I was obnoxiously competitive. On one occasion, our class was sitting in the school auditorium, and I made a spectacle of myself when I saw my biochemistry test score. 83%! I was bowled over. As I sat there surprised and irritated, I reflected on how prepared I thought I was. I didn't even have to guess at the answers to most of the questions. Yet, my score, although not poor, was not what I expected.

Then, I looked again at the first page and there was a different student's name. I had been given another classmate's test paper. I yelled, "This is not my paper"," and ran from the auditorium. My test score was 94%, which was more in line with how hard I had studied. I was happy, but my classmates found my behavior excessive. My fellow students were my teachers on that day.

In the above scripture, Jesus heals a blind man. Before the blind man could see clearly, he had to take another look. There is a song that says, "Just one look that's all it took," but that is not necessarily true. Life situations may require more than one look before you can see God's hand at work in the midst of darkness. And, even if my score had been 83%, it wasn't the end of the world. Why did I awfulize the situation? I needed to take another look not just at the paper but at my response to the situation. We have to trust God in the midst of every circumstance and be thankful that our destiny is in God's hands, not humans.

"Getting wisdom is the wisest thing you can do! And whatever else you do, develop good judgment" (Proverbs 4:7, NLT).

February 24
Making a Living Versus Making a Life

In this highly sophisticated technological society, the question must be asked of young people, what will you do with the wealth of knowledge at your fingertips? If your answer is to make a living, then you have succeeded in understanding what a job means in America. Indeed, we do need to be able to make a living (cover the cost of a mortgage, car, college debts, entertainment, clothing, food, and social media technology).

But consider this, if the value for acquiring a wealth of knowledge is to earn a six-figure income, acquire a half-million-dollar condo, and a BMW is more than the value you place on yourself, then dig deeper. Jobs come and jobs go. Houses come and houses go. One day, you may be a successful businessperson, and the next, you may have no business, no family, and no meaningful life.

When your focus is on finding meaning in life, making a living becomes more purposeful. Making a life requires practice. For example, a physician practices medicine. To practice medicine effectively, she must continue to enhance her skillset to keep up with medical advances. In like manner, to have a life filled with meaning, you have to work on your human skillset.

Work on spending time alone in prayer and contemplation. Establish a relationship with an elderly person. They have a lot of wisdom to share. Be true to yourself. Stand up for what you believe in. Open your mind and heart to other people's perspectives. Both of you will be stronger. Speak kind or uplifting words to a stranger at the grocery store. Choose to take care of yourself. Choose to find your voice and the gift God has given you to serve humankind.

"Focusing your life solely on making a buck shows a certain poverty of ambition. It asks too little of yourself. Because it's only when you hitch your wagon to something larger than yourself that you realize your true potential."
  ~ Barack Obama

Mistakes, Mess ups, and Misbehaving

When I was about fifteen years old, my mother insisted that I cook the evening meal. While I was able to prepare a good tasting meal, I didn't want to, so, to get back at everyone, I was overzealous in the amount of salt I used. My father's response was not what I expected. He turned it into a joke. He said I had stumped my toe when I was shaking the salt. Both he and my mother knew but did not address my behavior. I deserved to be punished, but I wasn't. The 'baby' in the family gets away with a lot. About a year ago, I acknowledged this incident to my sister who listened without passing judgment. She is a true friend.

They say that just before a person dies, life events are rapidly reviewed before them. Who knows if this really happens? One thing is for sure, it seems to me that as I move through the seasons of my life, I am already starting to reflect or review my life to date. And, this is great because it allows me to ponder, to share if I choose, and to really be thankful for God's amazing grace.

For there were many times when I made mistakes, mess ups, and misbehaved not only during adolescence but throughout my seventy-one years. There were times I deserved to be punished. But through God's loving mercy, grace, and forgiveness, I have had more second chances than I ever deserved.

"The person who is incapable of making a mistake, is incapable of anything."
~Abraham Lincoln

February 26
Anniversary

Today I remember the love of my life because this is the day Cecil and I married. If he were alive, it would be year number thirty-seven. Several months before a sudden illness overpowered him, he would wrap me in his arms and kiss me like we did while we were dating. When I reflect on those kisses now, I believe he was kissing me good-bye. At the time it was happening, I didn't know what to think, but they were a lot of fun. Cecil had a way of always making me laugh. About a month after he passed, I dreamed he was kissing me and awakened from the dream laughing vigorously.

My birthday celebration four months before Cecil's transition is one I'll always remember. He presented me with the largest bouquet of flowers I had ever seen, and he selected three birthday cards. As I re-read those cards, the theme was the same in all, thanking me for sharing my life with him. The cards seemed to signal that his earthly journey was ending.

Enjoy your loved ones, your husbands, wives, children, mothers, fathers, cousins, and the entire human community. Every day is a gift. What will you do with your gift of today? Cherish, honor, respect, appreciate, and love this present day. Live this day like this is your second life, your second time around.

"So teach us to number our days, that we may apply our hearts unto wisdom" (Psalm, 90:12).

February 27
~~IM~~POSSIBLE

That's right! Strike through the first two letters in the word impossible. Now I'm ready to enter medical school. When I was accepted, I couldn't imagine where the money would come from. For my mother, the answer was simple. Just go! So, I took a leap on her faith, certainly not mine. She sacrificed and borrowed money on my behalf. I was able to obtain a partial scholarship and partial loan for tuition that allowed me to devote all my time to schoolwork.

During my second year, there was some reprieve for my mother. On honors day, I was awarded two scholarships. They were such a pleasant and needed surprise. In 1972, two-thousand dollars was a huge deal, and the awards did not come with specific stipulations on how the monies were to be spent. One scholarship came from a medical society in the District of Columbia and the other from an anonymous source in my home state of Florida. I sent one check home to my mother who had been going without to assist me. To this day, I remember the peace and joy in my mother's voice when she received that check.

Never underestimate the strength and endurance of a good mother. They know how to get a prayer through but can also work magic if necessary. If this isn't your experience, consider what kind of mother you can be to your own children, or nieces or nephews, or even the children in your community. Do you have faith that they can leap on? Are you willing to trust God enough to walk with them or show them God's way?

"We need women at all levels, including the top, to change the dynamic, reshape the conversation, to make sure women's voices are heard and heeded, not overlooked and ignored."
˜ Sheryl Sandberg

February 28
Divine Intervention or Coincidence

When my nephew was thirty-four years of age, a large mirror dropped from a wall onto his right foot causing a cut on the back of his foot. The wound was so deep, it severed and exposed the arteries, veins, tendons, ligaments, and bone. He needed the trauma team immediately.

When he arrived in the emergency room, three highly specialized transplant surgeons happened to also be there. They were waiting for a helicopter to arrive with donor organs for patients in urgent need of life-saving organs. The transplant physicians consisted of an orthopedic, vascular, and plastic surgeon.

While they waited, they heard the commotion about my nephew, saw there was a need, and went to work on Duane's foot. Their degree of expertise and precision enabled them to not only repair the damaged blood vessels and tendons and secure the bone but perform the necessary procedures expeditiously with time to spare before the helicopter arrived.

If these specialists had not been in the emergency room, it would have been near impossible to get all three there in a timely fashion. There is a real possibility that he would have lost his foot.

Was this a coincidence? Some might say so. Was Duane lucky? Some might say so. But those with faith are convinced that God used these physicians to not only save his foot but his life as well. God works in mysterious ways!

"Coincidence is God's way of remaining anonymous."
~ Albert Einstein

March 1
Life is in the Birds

In the middle of my medical career, I met a fifty-year-old man with advanced colon cancer. His special words have remained with me over the past twenty years. He is the reason I listen to the birds sing. I'll refer to him as John. John discovered he had colon cancer during an emergency room visit. He'd been having pain in his lower abdomen for a while, but his job and family responsibilities delayed him from taking any action until the pain became intolerable.

At the time of his diagnosis, the colon cancer was widespread, and there was no curative treatment. John shared how he used to work hard and when he finally got to bed, he would easily fall asleep because he was so tired. He knew it was time to get up when he heard the birds sing and used to dread hearing them. As John laid in the hospital bed waiting to be transferred to the hospice unit, he said heartwarmingly, "Now, I long to hear the birds sing."

John loved life and his family. He worked hard for them, so much so that he neglected himself. Could the birds singing be a metaphor for what we need to pay attention to in our lives? In John's case, the birds singing represented his family. But they also signaled things that needed his personal attention (the pain in his abdomen).

Can you hear the birds singing in your life? What is the melody? What are their lyrics? What is their message to you?

"Today, just take time to smell the roses, enjoy those little things about your life, your family, spouse, friends, job. Forget about the thorns-the pains and problems they cause you- and enjoy life."
~ *Bernard Kelvin Cline*

March 2
Marriage is Transformational

A well-known marriage story is found in the Gospel of John 2: 1-12. It's at a wedding reception where Jesus performs his first miracle. At the celebration, they run out of wine, and Jesus instructs the servants to fill six large pots with water. Then, the master of ceremony is asked to taste a small amount. He is amazed at the taste of the wine and surmises that the host has saved the best wine for last.

Jesus transforms water into elegant wine. This miracle represents overflow, radical change, and new possibilities. It's saying that you'll not run out of what you need. Your life story will never be the same. The sky is the limit. The best is yet to come! Transformation takes place when you taste the sweetness of Jesus. One scripture says, "O taste and see that the Lord is good" (*Psalm 34:8, NLT*).

In a similar way, marriage is a transformative life event that changes the lives of two human beings. At their wedding, there is an air of expectation as two lives miraculously change into one. At the end of the ceremony, the minister introduces the newlywed couple, signaling that the best is yet to come. The miracle of marriage represents good fortune, awakening, and promise. Yes, there will be high and low times throughout the marriage, but the miracle will have already taken place.

"To have and to hold from this day forward, for better, for worse, for richer, for poorer, in sickness and in health, to love and to cherish, till death us do part, according to God's holy law, and this is my solemn vow."
~ Book of Common Prayer

March 3
The Lenten Season:
A Time to Renew Our Divine Wedding Vows

"Therefore, since we are justified by faith, we have peace with God through our Lord Jesus Christ through whom we have gained access by faith unto this grace in which we stand" (Romans 5:1-2, NIV).

Do you remember when you committed your life to Jesus? Do you recall the time you made up your mind that you were going to serve the Lord? It was the beginning of an extraordinary and personal relationship similar to the beginning of a marriage.

As the above scripture points out, there were three components:

1. The proposal — "Behold I stand at the door and knock." Your response—Yes. God's response—you are justified.
2. The engagement — You receive your divine engagement ring. It's during this time that you make peace with God and God makes peace with you.
3. The marriage — You gain access to grace. You can come boldly to the throne of grace and see a glimpse of the glorious hope for what is to come.

Question: Are you still wearing your ring, or have you misplaced it? Have the cares of this world weakened your personal relationship with God? Do your eyes look more at the surrounding situations and less with eyes of faith? The Lenten Season is an excellent time to reflect on one's personal relationship with Jesus and renew your marriage vows to the Lord.

"As Lent is the time for greater love, listen to Jesus' thirst...'Repent and believe,' Jesus tells us. What are we to repent? Our indifference, our hardness of heart. What are we to believe? Jesus thirsts even now, in your heart and in the poor— He knows your weakness. He wants only your love, wants only the chance to love you."
~ *Blessed Teresa of Calcutta*

March 4
The Perfect Soul

I believe that the soul is the most vital part of us. It is our connection to God. "...God formed man of the dust of the ground and breathed into his nostrils the breath of life; and man became a living soul" (*Genesis 2:7, KJV*). One day while reading Isaiah 53, the word 'soul' captured my attention. Soul is mentioned three times.

We must offer up Jesus' soul

"When thou shall make his soul an offering for sin, he shall see his seed, he shall prolong his days and the pleasure of the LORD shall be in his hand" (*Isaiah 53:10, KJV*). Our soul is blemished. Jesus soul is perfect. Only a perfect soul can save us, connect us with God, and give us eternal life. Our new life begins when we say the prayer of salvation and offer up Jesus' soul for our sin.

The travail of his soul

"He shall see of the travail of his soul and shall be satisfied" (*Isaiah 53:11, KJV*). It was the intense pain on his perfect soul that brought him satisfaction. How did pain satisfy his soul? Only God truly knows the complexities involved in the plan of salvation.

He poured out his soul unto death

"...Because he hath poured out his soul unto death" (*Isaiah 53:12, KJV*). It takes a perfect soul to die for you and for me. Jesus had the power to give up his spirit, descend into hell, and then be resurrected with all power. It is virtuous for one human being to sacrifice their life for another. There are news reports about these extraordinary occurrences. Human beings can sacrifice their life but not their soul. Our souls are imperfect. Only a perfect soul can pour out their soul unto death. This is the heart of the Gospel of Jesus Christ.

Each time you participate in the Lord's Supper, offer up Jesus perfect soul. Be reminded of the satisfaction it brought him to die for us. Because he poured out his soul unto death, we have connection with God and eternal life in Jesus Christ.

March 5
Acrimony, Anger, Animosity

In the Academy Award nominated movie *Fences*, Denzel Washington plays a man named Troy. The movie is an adaptation of the play by American playwright August Wilson. It takes place in the 1950's when Jim Crow was at its peak. Troy's dream to become a baseball player never materializes, leaving him angry and bitter. Throughout his life, he expresses nothing but vitriol to his son whose dream is to play football. He discourages and bullies him every time his son mentions his desire to play football. Troy's relationship with his son deteriorates after they have an explosive encounter, and he dies a few years later, never reconciling with his son.

Although Troy talked boldly about death, God did not appear important in his life. Troy's life cycle was filled with bitterness. He lived in the past and not the present. Troy made excuses to satisfy and justify his reality: Everyone else was to blame. He was always right. No other options were possible. His vision was tunneled in one direction.

There are many Troys in society who are not willing to take ownership of their life and thus resort to a variety of crutches. An attitude of bitterness causes deterioration in family and community relationships. Like Troy, they seek outsiders to affirm their state of being. It's up to each individual to open their hearts and receive God's abounding love. God's love heals wounded hearts and brings new meaning and purpose to life.

"Let all bitterness and wrath and anger and clamor and slander be put away from you, along with all malice" (Ephesians 4:31, KJV).

March 6
Get Up and Start Moving

In Chapter 5 of the Gospel of John is a story about a man who had been paralyzed for thirty-eight years. He was one among a crowd of sick people who gathered daily around a 'pool' known to have healing powers. However, there was a catch. Healing depended on one's ability to be first in the 'pool' when the waters swirled.

Jesus learns that the paralyzed man lays around the pool day-after-day. When Jesus asks him if he wants to be made well, the man replies, "Yes, but...I have no one to help me in the pool...everyone else moves quicker and jumps in the pool before me."

Is this gentleman physically or mentally paralyzed? My instinct leads me to believe that this is not a physical disability. First, he says, "Others move quicker and jump in before me." One who is paralyzed is unable to use arms or legs or both. He continues, "No one was willing to help me." If that is the case, how did he get to the pool every day? If he was physically paralyzed, someone had to help him. Why wouldn't those who helped him get to the pool help him get in before the others?

Jesus confronts and then tells him to: "Rise, take up thy bed and walk" (*John 5:8, KJV*). And immediately the man gets up and starts to walk. The intervention he had with Jesus was transforming. Still, he had to generate the power from within himself to get up and walk.

Life situations are overwhelming sometimes. But excuses only justify, discourage, and cripple. Owning up to the situation empowers, liberates, and strengthens. Faith in God and faith in self changes the situation and transforms you.

"I can do all things through Christ who strengthens me" (*Philippians 4:13, NKJV*).

March 7
What a Difference a Deer Makes

Today, she is a young, vibrant engineer. Eight years ago, she was a homeless youth on the streets of Atlanta. Two incidents transformed her life. The first one occurred while she was lying in a park feeling the piercing pains of hunger when a deer appeared next to her with food in its mouth. The deer dropped the food at her side. She looked at it and when it did not appear that the deer had eaten the food, she devoured it. It was at that point that she started believing in God.

Shortly thereafter, she was invited to live in a homeless shelter for youth. She lived in the shelter for the next few years. With love, food, and a nurturing environment, she started to grow emotionally and spiritually. While living at the shelter, she was able to complete college and following that time, earned a graduate degree and is now working as an engineer.

The mystery of the Almighty Sovereign God is profound. God used the intuition and gentleness of a deer and the love of a homeless shelter to empower this young person to mature into the person she was already chosen to become.

"The LORD God is my strength, God will make my feet like hinds' feet, and God will make me to walk upon mine high places" (paraphrased Habakkuk 3:19, KJV).

March 8

The Spirit of Queen Esther

In the book of Esther, you meet Queen Esther, a woman who is in a position of influence. She was selected queen because of her remarkable beauty but hid her Jewish ethnicity. Upon learning that the entire Jewish population is about to be annihilated, Esther is asked to go before the king on behalf of her people to stop this action. But the only way to meet with the king is to be summoned by him; an unsummoned visit means death. Esther faces her dilemma and comes to terms with what she must do. She makes the decision to go before the king, saying, "If I perish, I perish" (*Esther 4:16, NIV*). After much prayer and fasting, Esther visits the king and is warmly received. The king responds with compassion to her request, and the Jewish people are saved.

Queen Esther's spirit is in every Christian. And, more often than not, God places us in a position of influence to make a difference. The position or job you have is not just so you can have a beautiful house, a nice car, or glorified status in the community. As a Christian, if something needs to be done to right a wrong, to inspire a discouraged heart, to share the love of Jesus, or to speak for the voiceless, you use your influence to help. The sovereignty of God abides over everything, but God uses us to effect change.

"You are the salt of the earth. But what good is salt if it has lost its flavor. Can you make it useful again? It will be thrown out and trampled underfoot as worthless. You are the light of the world—like a city on a mountain, glowing in the night for all to see. Don't hide your light under a basket! Instead, put it on a stand and let it shine for all" (Matthew 5:13-15, NLT).

March 9
Towards Optimal Spiritual Health

Forty-four years ago, I committed my life to Jesus Christ. This happened while in training to become an internal medicine specialist and after a rocky relationship left me feeling alone at the bottom of a well. A beautiful young lady with a heart of gold named Debbie entered my life. We both worked at the same hospital.

Debbie wore a beautiful smile every day. There was a peace I felt when in her presence. I soon learned that she had a personal relationship with Jesus Christ. I felt like this was exactly what I needed in my life.

The process was insidious. I can still picture in my mind and feel in my heart when God's word became alive to me. Every morning I woke up with God on my mind. I enjoyed reading the Bible. Gospel music had a much deeper meaning. The people, plants, and even the animals looked brighter. I fell in love with God.

Eighteen years later, I answered the call to the ministry to serve, teach, and preach the Word of God. God's purposes are not always clear or revealed in a way that we can understand, but our challenge is to trust God as Jesus did to help us discover the best direction for our lives. Have you committed your life to Jesus Christ? If you have not, I invite you to do so right now.

"If you confess with your mouth that Jesus is Lord and believe in your heart that God raised him from the dead, you will be saved" (Romans 10:9, NLT).

March 10
Stepping Out on Faith

I'm not one to take big leaps of faith, but I did at the turn of the century (2000). I closed my medical practice in Jacksonville, Florida to return to school. I sought counsel from two people—my husband (Cecil) and my mother who said follow your heart.

My leap of faith was amazing. The first year consisted of taking courses at a seminary in Atlanta, Georgia. The plans for my second year were to continue seminary classes but also start classes at Morehouse School of Medicine and earn a Master in Public Health (MPH). Because I was a physician, I was offered a position in the Morehouse School of Medicine Preventive Medicine program, and I accepted.

By taking this route, I received a salary, excellent health insurance, earned my MPH, and completed specialty training in preventive medicine. Blessings upon blessings!

After completion of the preventive medicine program, I joined a large medical group in Atlanta that was known for its preventive focus. Not only did I start practicing medicine again in one of their clinics, but I also served as physician program director for health promotion and disease prevention. Had I not stepped out on faith, none of this would have materialized.

As I started my journey, I had no idea what the future would look like. One thing for sure, I believed God was guiding my steps. Trust in God is the assurance that your life is in God's hands. Faith is the evidence that your future is secure not just for now but throughout eternity.

"I do not know how long 'twill be, not what the future holds for me. But this I know, if Jesus leads me, I shall get home someday.
~ *Charles A. Tindley*

March 11
Three Grandmothers

Growing up, we had one paternal and two maternal grandmothers. My biological grandmother was an unmarried teenager when my mother was born. During that time, unwed pregnancy was frowned upon, and my biological grandmother was taken to a country village in the outskirts of Bainbridge, Georgia, where my mother was born and adopted by a family in the village.

Throughout my life, I've always been amazed by my mother's stories about how divinely connected she felt to her adoptive mother. She described her as being a friend, teacher, and mentor with unending love for her family. Her love for her adoptive mother was evident in how she cared for her until she died.

While attending nursing school in Jacksonville, Florida, at age seventeen, my mother met her biological mother. Mama spoke of the joy she felt meeting her. The relationship started to blossom and extended to our entire family. We grew up sharing time with three grandmothers.

Mama had a keen interest in knowing her roots. In my mother's book, "*Waving from the Balcony*," she expresses gratitude for both mothers and honors their contributions not only to her life but to the larger community.

"From my perspective, God always moves according to what is best for us in the stream of human history. In my own life for example, nursing was not my first choice as a profession. But life experiences have taught me that God's choices and time are always at work to make our lives memorable and complete."
~ *Nan Campbell Fletcher (my mother)*

March 12
Two Gifts of Life: Wrapped in One Package!

How unusual is it to be diagnosed with leukemia and to also learn that a baby is on the way? Well, that's what happened to my cousin's husband, Gilbert. About thirteen years ago, Gilbert was diagnosed with leukemia. Shortly thereafter, they learned that his wife, my cousin, Monise was pregnant with their second child.

Leukemia is a cancer of the blood forming cells in the body and is very serious. Treatment for the leukemia required stem cell transplantation. The family chose to receive medical care at the University of Texas MD Anderson Treatment Center. This meant temporarily leaving their home in Miami and living in Houston for several months. Monise received prenatal care in two cities.

Perhaps at the time of his diagnosis, God was saying to Gilbert and Monise that everything would be all right. And to prove it, you are being blessed with a son. These life disruptions were challenging, but the outcome made life more meaningful. Gilbert had successful stem cell transplantation for leukemia and has been cancer free for thirteen years. Their son, Alexander who was delivered several months after Gilbert's treatment is now a bright and handsome thirteen-year-old adolescent.

Seasons of uncertainty occur in life. Burdens almost crush our bodies, minds, and spirits. We ask questions. Will this spirit of heaviness ever pass? Why is my burden so heavy? Even in the midst of uncertainty, God is present and working things out for our good. Remember Paul, "Three times I pleaded with the Lord to take it away from me. But he said to me, 'My grace is sufficient for you, for my power is made perfect in weakness'" (2 Corinthians 12:8, NIV).

"Therefore I will boast all the more gladly about my weaknesses, so that Christ's power may rest on me. That is why, for Christ's sake, I delight in weaknesses, in insults, in hardships, in persecutions, in difficulties. For when I am weak, then I am strong" (2 Corinthians 12:9-10, NIV).

March 13
The Quilt of Life

I had a memory quilt made from my late-husband's ties. As the project progressed, I thought about God as the ultimate divine quilt maker.

We are all tiny pieces in God's fabric. Each piece is essential and helps make God's quilt beautiful. God places each of us in the fabric in a specific place with a specific mission that no one else can fill. The quilt is dynamic. God continues to shape and mold us to fit into the fabric. Sometimes the shaping and molding can hurt, but it is always for our good.

Never think that you don't fit in God's quilt, or that what you do doesn't matter. Wherever you are, whatever you're doing, even if you're still searching, seek direction from God. "In all thy ways acknowledge him and he shall direct your path" (*Proverbs 3:6, KJV*). When you do, you will be in the right place at the right time growing spiritually and finding meaning and purpose in life.

Know this, there is nothing small about what you are doing. I never want to imagine what God's quilt would look like without you.

"Being confident of this, that he who began a good work in you will carry it on to completion until the day of Christ Jesus" (Philippians 1:6, NIV).

March 14
When Death Awakens

Everything we know about Jesus was written after he died. It was the impact of his death—the power of his death—that which happened at the cross that aroused people's consciousness and started people to talking and writing.

The events happening at the death of Jesus demonstrate the significance of his death: Darkness covered the earth for three hours. The holy curtain in the Temple tore in two. A large earthquake occurred. The bodies of Godly men and women rose from the dead.

Even with all these occurrences, the most paramount miracle at the cross happened to the Roman soldier who nailed Jesus to the cross; the man who observed him as he died. As Jesus dismisses his spirit, the Roman soldier's heart is changed. Suddenly, he becomes enlightened, meets Jesus face to face, and says with a loud voice, "Surely he was the Son of God" (*Luke 23:47, NIV*).

It didn't matter anymore that he worked for the government that sentenced Jesus to die. No longer was it important that he was the head of the execution team. The power of Jesus's death awakened his soul and changed his life forever.

The power Jesus has to change a life stands head and shoulders above everything else. The birth of Jesus is incredible, but it did not save. The miracles that Jesus performed are mind-blowing, but they did not save. Salvation is in the crucified Lord!

"At the cross, at the cross where I first saw the light, And the burden of my heart rolled away, it was there by faith I received my sight, and now I am happy all day!"
~*Isaac Watts*

March 15
A Mother's Wisdom

"History will judge us by the difference we make in the everyday lives of children."
˜Nelson Mandela

When I was in the sixth grade, I learned that certain students were handpicked to be in the 'best' sixth grade teachers' class. The selection was not based on merit but politics. Although, they didn't mean any harm, the selected students let the rest of us know how they had been chosen.

Well, I felt cheated since my parents were excluded from this matchmaking scheme. I believed I was missing out on the skills of a talented teacher. It also made me feel like my family was not good enough to be included. I shared my feelings with my mother, and she was understanding.

As a wise mother, she did not criticize anyone's actions. Rather, she assured me that my sixth-grade teacher was top notch and that when I left her class, I would be well-prepared for the seventh grade.

Indeed, my mother was right. I loved Mrs. Feacher and remember her to this day. In fact, she and the rest of my elementary school teachers kept up with me through my family. And, when I returned to my hometown to practice medicine, many of them entrusted the care of their health to me.

If you want to know God's will for your life, seek out guidance from special loved one's—your mother, father, or some other special person. God will speak through them and guide you to what is best for you.

"Motherhood is priced of God, at price no man may dare, to lessen or misunderstand."
˜Helen Hunt Jackson

March 16
Affirming the Children

"If children live with approval, they learn to like themselves."
~ *Dorothy Law Nolte*

I used to imagine how hard it must be for children growing up in today's society. After an aha moment, I realized children do not need my pity. They have one reality, the present moment. They did not live fifty or sixty years ago and are probably glad they didn't. In spite of the societal challenges facing young people, most are adjusting, achieving, and moving forward in a healthy and safe direction. Their success is most likely related to value-based living that never changes.

In 1972, Dorothy Law Nolte wrote a poem entitled "Children learn what they live." It is a poem that is as true today as it was forty-eight years ago. When I revisited the poem recently, I asked myself the question, "of all her verses, which is the most important for young people growing up?" As I write this reflection, I decided that it must be, "If children live with approval, they learn to like themselves."

A good starting place in life for children is to like themselves, to be comfortable in their own skin. When one cares about themselves, they are more likely to practice self-care. Self-care will extend to family, church, and community. If children are affirmed, approved, or accepted, they are more likely to be self-confident, engage in positive self-talk, be more resilient, and develop positive relationships. They are more likely to honor their parents, respect their teachers, improve their scholarship, and less likely to be ashamed of themselves.

Affirmations and words of approval should not just come from immediate family but extend to the church, community, and school. Remember, it takes a village to raise a child.

"There was a child went forth every day, and the first object he looked up and received with wonder or pity or love or dread, that object he became..."
~ *Walt Whitman*

March 17
Dignity and Self-Determination

I recall a ninety-five-year old lady God placed in my care a few years after entering medical practice. In spite of her age, she was alert and able to live independently. However, she had a heart condition that at times weakened her heart to the point that she would have to be hospitalized.

During an office visit, she asked if there were advanced treatments for her heart. This puzzled me since she was ninety-five years old and the heart weakens with age. I advised her to continue to eat healthy, reduce salt intake, and take her medications. This retired schoolteacher said vehemently, "If you can't help me, then send me to someone who can."

People want to live and feel good regardless of their age. It is a sign of self-respect and dignity when a person is able to make decisions about their health care. Health care providers have a responsibility to provide hope in spite of age, sickness, socioeconomic level or condition of the patient. Because of this wise woman, I learned to value self-determination and dignity at a much higher level.

Close to the end of my medical practice, one of my patients, an eighty-nine-year-old man wanted to have a colonoscopy to check for colon cancer. He had colon cancer ten years earlier and wanted to make sure the cancer had not come back. I referred him to a colon specialist. Because of his age, he was advised against being checked. My patient refused to accept this advice, and as a result of his persistence, the specialist gave in to his request. Sure enough, cancer was again discovered in his colon. Surgery was performed, and he had an excellent recovery. When it comes to health, it is each person's right to be included in the decision-making process.

Almighty God, because of your Word, I refuse to get rattled by what other people say or how they act. You have the final say in my life. My health is in your hands. My faith is first and foremost in you, and I love you with my whole heart. AMEN.

March 18
Becoming Deborah

The book of Judges, chapters 4 and 5, tells the story of Deborah. She was chosen by God to lead the Israelites through a major crisis. She was a woman with strong faith, foresight, courage, and organizational skills.

Time and time again, the Israelites turned away from God, choosing to follow after idols. When life became intolerable, they cried out to God who always sent a deliverer to get them out of their man-made predicaments. God called Deborah, and she was ready for the task. Like a military general, she knew the geographic area of operation, planned her mission, and gave instructions to Barak, her second in command. Barak was afraid to go without Deborah and cried out, "If you go with me, I will go, but if you don't go with me, I won't go" (Judges 4:8 NIV). Deborah went with him and guided him through a highly successful military journey delivering the Israelites from oppression.

How does a Deborah come to be? Deborah was one of the Israelites who listened and believed the stories about God's deliverance of the Israelites from Egyptian bondage and all the promises that followed. Unlike many of her people, she never turned away from God. She kept God's covenant. Her faith grew into wisdom, courage, and love for her people and their relationship to God.

Thank you, God. It is faith in you that sustains us from generation to generation. Help us to be like Deborah who listened and believed the generational stories about the God of our ancestors who is the same today as in past years. AMEN

"Ye have seen what I did to the Egyptians, and how I bare you on eagles' wings, and brought you unto myself. Now therefore, if ye will obey my voice indeed, and keep my covenant, then ye shall be a peculiar treasure unto me above all people: for all the earth is mine: and ye shall be to me a kingdom of priest, and a holy nation" (Exodus 19:4-6, KJV).

March 19
Success in God's Eyes

Everyone likes for success to be a part of their life story. People like to have a favorable outcome in any endeavor they undertake and avoid situations that might result in failure. When people feel victorious, you hear them speak boastfully about their success stories. *I have a 4.5 GPA. I have just been hired at my dream job. Our church has grown to 25,000 members. We have been married 45 years!* These are impressive achievements. But let's think about success on a higher level.

God's formula for success is measured by how we use our gifts to benefit the whole. It may or may not result in awards, recognition, fame, or power. Success in God's eyes is a call to be faithful to the mission of Jesus Christ. Every action he took was guided by unconditional love. A sure sign of godly success is giving care to those in need.

Jesus not only identifies with the poor, he says when you look at the poor, homeless, hungry, and oppressed, you will see me. And, when you refuse to help the least of these my brothers and sisters, you deny me. "For I was hungry, and you fed me. I was thirsty, and you gave me a drink. I was a stranger, and you invited me into your home. I was naked, and you gave me clothing. I was sick, and you cared for me. I was in prison, and you visited me" (*Matthew 25: 35-36 NLT*). These are measures of success in God's eyes.

Where does God fit in your life story? How faithful are you to God? How do you measure your success as a Christian?

"God has not called me to be successful; God has called me to be faithful."
~Mother Teresa

March 20
Happy Birthday to a Forgotten Hero:
A Man Who Answered Three Calls to the Ministry

On this day in 1939, Jonathan Daniels was born in New Hampshire. His first call to the ministry came during his freshman year at Harvard. After one year at Harvard, he dropped out and enrolled in seminary at the Episcopal Theological School in Cambridge, Massachusetts, to answer the call to ministry.

Soon thereafter, Daniels answered another call. This call came from Dr. Martin Luther King, Jr. King called on American clergy to respond to the injustice and violence in the deep south. Daniels joined the march to Montgomery and elected to stay and work to improve the deep racial divides. Not only was he called an "outside agitator" and a "white nigger," he was arrested during a protest in Fort Deposit, Alabama. After he was released from jail, he continued to walk the road for justice. Sadly, things turned dark when the third call came.

Daniels and a small group of Civil Rights workers entered a store. A part-time deputy sheriff aimed his gun at sixteen-year-old Ruby Sales. Daniels pushed her to the ground and saved her life. However, the bullet killed him instead. Martin Luther King, Jr. said, "One of the most heroic Christian deeds of which I have heard in my entire ministry was performed by Jonathan Daniels."

Daniels was an Episcopalian minister. A friend who is also an Episcopalian shared his story with me. It is amazing how there are so many hidden heroes within the various denominations. We can learn so much from each other when we share historical gems.

"Then said Jesus unto his disciples, 'If any man will come after me, let him deny himself, and take up his cross, and follow me. For whosoever will save his life shall lose it: and whosoever will lose his life for my sake shall find it. For what is a man profited, if he shall gain the whole world, and lose his own soul? Or what shall a man give in exchange for his soul'" (Matthew 16:24-26, KJV)?

March 21
A Higher Level of Being

"But who am I, and who are my people, that we should be able to give as generously as this? Everything comes from you, and we have given you only what comes from your hand" (1 Chronicles 29: 14 NIV).

In the above Scripture, David's godly wisdom is heard in a prayer he makes to the assembly as he petitions them to give wholeheartedly to the completion of God's Temple. David's prayer is filled with adoration to God as he acknowledges that everything we give to God already belongs to God. He acknowledges the omnipotence and omnipresence of God and that all wealth and honor are God given.

David prayed like someone who was aware of the confidence God has in human beings. "What is mankind that you are mindful of them, human beings that you care for them? You made them a little lower than the angels and crowned them rulers over the works of your honor. You made them rulers over the works of your hands; you put everything under their feet" (*Psalm 8:4-6, NIV*).

When we awaken fully to the reality of who we are and who we belong to, then like David, we will boldly live out our mission here on earth. This prayer is worth remembering and incorporating into regular meditation.

"Yours, O LORD, is the greatness and the power and the glory and the majesty and the splendor, for everything in heaven and earth is yours. Yours, O LORD, is the kingdom; you are exalted as head over all" (1 Chronicles 29: 11, NIV).

March 22
Faith of a Great Woman

Faith in the Almighty Sovereign God, plus a dream, and an intention, coupled with perseverance and the rest is history. That's the story of Mary McLeod Bethune, a woman who put theory into practice.

Bethune was the daughter of slaves and during her young life worked in the fields alongside her parents. When she learned to read, her total being changed, and she felt compelled to share this gift with others.

Mrs. Bethune's dream was to start a school for young women of African American descent. She wanted them to be able to develop spiritually, intellectually, and be good at home economics. She moved forward with this intention. And with perseverance, she endured. Starting out with $1.50 and five students, people from every race captured her vision.

What started out as Daytona Educational and Industrial School, in 1904, is today Bethune Cookman University with an endowment of forty-eight million dollars.

"The greatest power is faith in God. The second is faith in one's self."
~Mary McLeod Bethune

Worry: Trapped in My Own Head

In Michelle Obama's book *Becoming*, she describes a time when she was 'trapped in her own head.' On re-election night, anxious thoughts kept nagging at her—what if, not good enough, not enough hard work, deserved outcome. Everything she did that night while waiting for the election returns was controlled by her thoughts, and she was all wrong.

Indeed, I too have a tendency to let thoughts make life miserable for me. My husband used to say that I worried enough for both of us. Worry can make you sick, unhappy, and paranoid. It is a confidence robber and a major cause of insomnia. Worry will not add a day to your life. It will not add money to a bank account or take any from it. Although I have heard people say you can worry yourself to death, there is no death certificate that list the cause of death as worry.

If you've got a handle on the situation, then there is no need to worry. If you can do something about the circumstances, then do it. Say a prayer of thanksgiving for things just as they are and give your worries to God. Once you rise from your knees, don't take the worry back.

Faith in God is no match for worry. Worry will win every time, and here's why. Because God has given us free will. We can will to have faith in God, or we can worry.

"Do not be anxious about anything, but in every situation, by prayer and petition, with thanksgiving, present your requests to God. And the peace of God, which transcends all understanding, will guard your hearts and your minds in Christ Jesus" (Philippians 4:6-7, NIV).

March 24
Grief on the Loss of a Pet

"One day we will again see our animals in the eternity of Christ."
~Pope Paul VI

The death of a beloved pet is an upsetting life event. About two years ago, the New England Journal of Medicine reported the details of one such loss. A woman developed chest pains and shortness of breath after her dog died. Following multiple tests, she was diagnosed with stress cardiomyopathy also known as "broken-heart syndrome." With treatment, she recovered and shared that she was "close to inconsolable" after the death of her beloved Yorkshire terrier.

Comments about the loss of a pet are similar to those about the loss of a loved one: "It was the most tragic, traumatic, and emotionally devastating experience I had ever been through. I cried day and night... I never knew anything could hurt so bad. I hated myself for putting my pet to sleep."

Pet owners are embarrassed about the amount of grief they feel, so they hold their emotions inside. Additionally, the usual routine of the griever has been interrupted. The owner is no longer engaged in walking the dog, feeding the cat, spending time with other pet owners, or making visits to the dog spa. These feelings and disruptions may complicate the grief process.

Seek help when sadness and loneliness becomes unbearable. Talk to a counselor or therapist. There are bereavement groups for pet owners located in some animal clinics. Pet owners are most appreciative when friends, families, and communities recognize and honor the value that animals bring to their life. Finding ways to connect with them helps to heal their broken hearts.

"God made the wild animals according to their kinds, the livestock according to their kinds, and all the creatures that move along the ground according to their kinds. And God saw that it was good" (Genesis 1:25, NIV).

March 25
Wisdom: Knowing Who to Consult

"When the queen of Sheba heard about the fame of Solomon and his relationship to the LORD, she came to test Solomon with hard questions" *(1Kings 10:1, NIV).*

Knowing how to research, observe, consult, and listen to find answers is essential to wisdom. The Queen of Sheba was a woman in search of wisdom. Although there are a number of qualities that people with wisdom have, there are two that stand out as exemplified in the Queen of Sheba.

The first quality is determination. The queen left her home and traveled twelve hundred miles to gain insight and wisdom from the wisest man in the East. When you have determination, you go the extra mile. Determination is purpose driven. You can visualize the results before they are achieved. You put in the time or practice to become an excellent student, minister, writer, athlete, musician, scientist, attorney, dancer or whatever is your heart's desire. Obstacles are real, but determination is stronger. How far would you go to gain wisdom and understanding?

The second quality is curiosity. The Queen of Sheba was going to meet King Solomon. Yet, she was not afraid to ask him hard questions. When you are curious, you have a passion for learning. You learn with your heart and mind, and you listen attentively. As you study and read, you know what questions to ask. There is no such thing as a stupid or silly question.

On our Christian journey, Jesus expects us to seek, to search, and to dig deep as if we are searching for a pot of gold. That's exactly what we are in quest of!

"Ask and it will be given to you; seek and you will find; knock and the door will be open to you" *(Matthew 7:7, NIV).*

March 26
Today Will Be Your Best Day

"The supreme value is not the future but the present."
~ *Octavio Paz*

How often do your thoughts wander to things that happened yesterday, a week, a month, or even years ago? Or how often do you allow your thoughts to wander into the future? A trigger starts the tape playing in the mind. And before you know it, the scenario is as real as if it is happening in the present moment. If past events bring you joy, that's great. Most times, the events that plague our memory arouse anger, sadness, and gloom. The future you looked forward to having with a deceased loved one makes the future look bleak. The challenging situation on the job or even the loss of a job robs the possibilities available in the present moment.

Lyndon B. Johnson is quoted as having said, "Yesterday is not ours to recover, but tomorrow is ours to win or lose." Maybe it would be more fitting to say that today is ours to win or lose. We have no control over the past or future, but we do have control over the moment or hour in front of us.

The next time past and future thinking paralyze your behavior, affirm with power, "This is the day that the Lord has made, I will rejoice and be glad in it" (*Psalm 118:24, NIV*). It does not say that yesterday is the day or that tomorrow is the day. It says this is the day!

"Stop acting as if life is a rehearsal. Live this day as if it was your last. The past is over and gone. The future is not guaranteed."
~ *Wayne Dyer*

March 27
The Tougaloo Nine

"The reading of all good books is like a conversation with the finest minds of past centuries."
~ Renè Descartes

Libraries are foundational to our culture, and knowledge is power. Reading liberates and is transformational.

A group of young courageous students appreciated the value of books. They placed their lives at risk so that everyone would have access to information found only in libraries. The students are known as the Tougaloo Nine.

On March 27,1961, these nine students walked into the all-white Mississippi Public Library, staged a sit-in and were immediately arrested. The Black Public Library was ill-equipped for their creative curious intellect. They wanted people everywhere to have the opportunity to grow in knowledge. Their protests were a major contributor to the integration of public libraries in the Jim Crow South.

In 2011, the Mississippi Freedom Trail was created to commemorate people and places in Mississippi that played a pivotal role in the American Civil Rights Movement. In August 2017, a historical marker was created on that trail to honor the courage of the Tougaloo Nine.

"Read not to contradict and confute; nor to believe and take for granted; nor to find talk and discourse; but to weigh and consider. Some books are to be tasted, others to be swallowed, and some few to be read in parts, others to be read, but not curiously, and some few to be read wholly, and with diligence and attention."
~ Francis Bacon

March 28
The Power of Love

In the late sixties, Hal David and Burt Bacharach wrote the song, "What The World Needs Now Is Love." The lyrics speak of there being too little love in the world. The lyrics are just as true to life today as they were fifty-five years ago. And maybe even more today given the amount of schisms in the communities of the world.

There are communities, schools, families, work colleagues, and marriages at odds because of political ideology. This shouldn't be. First and foremost, human beings were created with an overabundance of love that is to be given away and not just to those we favor. Hear Jesus as he says, "And if you greet only your own people, what are you doing more than others? Do not even pagans do that" (*Matthew 5:47, NIV*)?

Here's a suggestion I read in Martha Whitmore Hickman's book, *Healing after Loss*. Offer a silent blessing to people you meet during the day—the barista in the coffee shop, your colleague at the water fountain, the postal clerk, the driver in the lane next to you or anyone you encounter during the day.

Prayer is powerful. Imagine what would happen if these gestures of goodwill were to catch fire. When you say silently, "May God bless you," a smile shows up on your face. It only takes a love spark to spread a fire of love.

"The best and most beautiful things in the world cannot be seen or even touched-they must be felt with the heart."
~ *Helen Keller*

March 29
A Blind Hurry

Slow down. Take time to smell the roses, listen to the birds sing, learn to enjoy early morning quietness. Go to the seashore, collect seashells, and place a shell on your ear to hear the sound of the ocean. Even when we stop, often times our minds are still on the move.

I am reminded of a story about a minister running late for his plane. To make up lost time, he breaks the speed limit to get to the airport. By the time he arrives at the gate, he is flustered and agitated. This is exacerbated when the attendant advises him he's too late to board.

He becomes belligerent and hostile, demanding the agent open the door, saying that he is to run a revival in a few hours. The agent yields to his powerful bully tactics and opens the door to the loading gate. As he looks for his seat, he discovers it has been given to another passenger and becomes more agitated.

To eliminate more confusion, the stewardess offers him an available seat in First Class. He thinks, *"The Lord is blessing me to ride in First Class."* As the plane moves down the runway, the pilot welcomes aboard their Jacksonville, Florida, passengers to Flight 537 four-hour nonstop flight to Albuquerque, New Mexico. The minister is flying to Dallas, Texas. He is on the wrong plane!

In his mind, getting on that plane was all that mattered. The minister was blind to everyone's concerns except his own. He risked his life and others' lives on the highway. He bullied the gate agent and flight attendant and the person sitting in his seat. Hopefully, his eyes will open on that four-hour flight and see that "Nothing good comes out of hurry and frustration, only misery" (Auliq Ice).

"I don't know why it is we are in such a hurry to get up when we fall down. You might think we would lie there and rest for a while."
~Max Eastman

March 30
No More of This: Don't Resist Anymore

As the Lenten season comes to a close, there is a scripture that's worthy of contemplation. In the book of Luke 22:47-53, Jesus is about to be arrested by the temple guards and priest. Anyone who is about to be arrested knows how ill at ease and apprehensive this moment is. The arresting officer tells you not to resist. Yet, the event triggers the body's flight fight phenomenon causing the heart rate and blood pressure to go up, muscles to tighten, and sometimes rapid and inappropriate talk. And, if there are loved ones at the scene, they are also excited and helpless.

In this scripture, Jesus' companions became defensive and asked permission from him to use their swords. One disciple impulsively wielded his knife and cut off a soldier's ear. Jesus remains calm and in control of the situation. He admonishes his disciples for acting violently and says, "No more of this." Immediately, Jesus touches the man and restores his ear, and Jesus is taken into captivity.

In a similar way, both Dr. Martin Luther King, Jr. and Mahatma Gandhi practiced nonviolence and encouraged others to do the same. Jesus said, "No more of this" or "Don't resist anymore." This must be the way of the Christian.

"Do not take revenge, my dear friends, but leave room for God's wrath, for it is written: 'It is mine to avenge; I will repay,'" says the Lord'" (Romans 12:19, NIV).

March 31
Love Never Ends

"Love never fails. But where there are prophecies, they will cease; where there are tongues, they will be stilled; where there is knowledge, it will pass away" *(1Corinthians 13:8, NIV).*

This day is the anniversary of my husband's death. As I grieved my loss, I used to wonder if the tears would ever end and the heartache would ever ease. In my daily meditation book by Martha Whitmore Hickman entitled *Healing After Loss*, she writes a meditation about the land of the living and the land of the dead and describes a bridge that connects the two. The bridge is love. In other words, love does not cease with the event of death. You will continue to connect because of love. As in 1 Corinthians 13, love never fails. Love never ends.

Ms. Hickman shares stories of persons experiencing a spiritual connection with their departed loved ones: warmly feeling their presence; seeing a vision of them; receiving a warning to avoid taking a specific trip. In one instance, a man heeded the warning. Sure enough, the plane crashed that he was forewarned not to take.

I am grateful for the love and the time that my husband and I shared. It is eternal and will last forever. The heart will eventually heal, but the love will remain. Just like nothing will separate us from the love of God, nothing will separate us from the love of our departed loved ones.

"We were together. I forget the rest."
~ *Walt Whitman*

April 1
Springtime Will Come

One of my favorite songs is "The Rose" written by Amanda Mc-Broom and sung beautifully by Bette Midler. When I first heard "The Rose," it warmed my heart and made me think more deeply about the song's message. I've sung it in church and on a cruise ship during karaoke time. Years ago, one of the physician assistant's brought his guitar to our clinic. Early one morning before patients arrived, he played along as I sang "The Rose." It was a great way to start the day.

"The Rose" is a song about love, but it's also a song about life. So even if you've never been in love, you've been in life. The song is about the heartbreak that sometimes results from being in love or the anguish that sometimes results from living.

We are vulnerable, exposed, defenseless creatures when we love or live. Both love and life can bring joy. Then, just when love or life is flowing along beautifully, something happens leaving an endless aching or a longing in our hearts. Until hope enters our hearts again.

Don't be afraid to love. Welcome life with open arms. Don't be afraid to give. Take a chance on love. Take a chance on life. No matter how lonely the nights are or how long the road seems, no matter how cold life gets, remember that winter does not last forever. Springtime will come again.

"Never cut a tree down in the wintertime. Never make a negative decision in the low time. Never make your most important decisions when you are in your worst moods. Wait. Be patient. The storm will pass. The spring will come."
 ~ *Robert H. Schuller*

April 2
A Warrior for Life

I read a story on social media about a young married mother of three young children diagnosed with a brain tumor. She shared how the tumor was discovered and that brain surgery was recommended to remove it.

She expressed terror at the idea of having her brain opened up with all the possible complications including death, even in the hands of a stellar brain surgeon. She worried most about her children and the precious time away from their lives this whole ordeal would cause.

She ended her writing with a specific request to pray for her calmness and that God be in the room with the surgeons to give them all the guidance, steadiness, and the confidence they needed; to pray for her safety during and after surgery and for her husband, to give him the courage and strength to wait patiently in the waiting room during her surgery.

Her story touched me. The first thought that came to my mind was that she is a warrior for life. A warrior fights, and she was fighting for her life. She demonstrated courage, forthrightness, confidence in her doctor, love for her family, but most of all, faith in God and the power of prayer. She asked social media to join with her in prayer. I can't think of a better way to use social media. Indeed, I added her name to my prayer list.

"Do not be anxious about anything, but in every situation, by prayer and petition, with thanksgiving, present your requests to God. And the peace of God, which transcends all understanding, will guard your hearts and your minds in Christ Jesus" (Philippians 4:6-7, NIV).

April 3
#Me Too—Two Close Calls

According to the CDC (Centers for Disease Control and Prevention), sexual violence is a serious public health problem that affects millions of women and men. In the United States, 1 in 3 women and 1 in 6 men have experienced sexual violence involving physical contact at some point in their lives.

In 2006, the "Me Too" phrase was coined by Tarana Burke, an American social activist and community organizer. Its purpose was to promote "empowerment through empathy" among women of color who had been sexually abused. In 2017, there were widespread media reports of sexual assault and harassment in places of employment. People were encouraged to use social media to share their experience using the hashtag #MeToo. The magnitude of the problem became evident through this platform. While writing my collection of reflections, I decided to share my own experiences for the first time.

There were two episodes in my life where I (miraculously) escaped sexual violence. The first occurred when I was a shy seventeen-year-old college freshman. I went to a house party with some dorm mates but otherwise did not know most of the people in attendance. Alcohol was served, and I recall getting tipsy. A tall older man who may not have been a college student took me by the hand and led me into a bedroom. There, he picked me up and was about to place me on the bed. Fear gripped my whole being. Fortunately, he stopped, and I was able to leave the room and return to the dormitory physically unharmed but very frightened and embarrassed.

The second episode occurred four years later. By this time, I had graduated from college and was living in an efficiency apartment. The efficiency consisted of one large room with a daybed and a separate bathroom. I was about to move back to Jacksonville for the summer and contacted a moving company to estimate the cost of moving my furniture. The male estimator arrived noonday and viewed the furniture. Then he sat on my day bed and stripped to nothing but his underwear. I looked at him but never said a word. He puts his clothes back on and told me the moving company would be in touch.

I did not report either incident, which is a common response. Many women and men do not escape the brutal attacks of sexual violence. I don't know why I was spared such emotional and physical turmoil. I thank God for grace. I identify wholly with my sisters and brothers throughout God's universe who have been physically and emotionally harmed by sexual violence.

April is Sexual Assault Awareness and Prevention Month. God is concerned about the safety, dignity and the humanity of every human being. Speak out, share information, and support victims. Contact www.rainn.org for more information on how you can help.

"If I take the wings of the morning and dwell in the uttermost parts of the sea, even there thy hand shall lead me, and thy right hand shall hold me. If I say, surely the darkness shall cover me; even the night shall be light about me. The darkness hides not from thee; but the night shines as the day: the darkness and the light are both alike to thee, but the night shines just as the day" (Psalm 139: 9-13, KJV).

April 4
Value-Based Living

Value-based living is living an abundant life. John 10:10 (*NIV*) says it this way, "The thief comes only to steal and kill and destroy; I have come that they might have life and have it to the full." Value-based living is living the best possible life in the midst of whatever circumstances we find ourselves in.

Too often, we place more focus on material things like houses, cars, highest paying job, the stock market, clothes, clubs, sororities, fraternities, and sporting events. After school and before homework, children attend ballet lessons, basketball practice, taekwondo class, camp, and the list goes on. There is not enough time to just enjoy each other.

The Scripture warns us to "Be on your guard against all kinds of greed; life does not consist in the abundance of possessions" (*Luke 12:15, NIV*).

Real life begins when we commit our lives to Jesus, when we begin to store up treasures in our spiritual bank account, when we take some of our spiritual investment and use it to spend time with family, to fellowship in the church, enjoy God's beautiful universe, and find ways to serve humankind.

"What good is it for someone to gain the whole world, yet forfeit their soul? Or what can anyone give in exchange for their soul" (Mark 8:36-37, NIV)?

A Divine Moment in Time
(Matthew 21:1-11)

The days before the crucifixion of Jesus Christ were filled with wonder and passion. It began with 'the triumphal entry,' Jesus entering Jerusalem on a donkey. This action was prophesied five-hundred years before Jesus was born. "Rejoice greatly, Daughter Zion! Shout, Daughter Jerusalem! See, your king comes to you, righteous and victorious, lowly and riding on a donkey, on a colt, the foal of a donkey" (*Zechariah 9:9, NIV*).

While Jesus did not have the appearance of a king, the people responded to him as if he did. When a king made a triumphal entry into a city, the people spread out their cloaks, cut palm branches from the trees and lay them on the road, erupting with festive shouts of adoration, joy, and praise. All of these things were done for Jesus.

There was nothing in Jesus' outward appearance that looked regal. In fact, just the opposite. He was wearing tattered apparel and riding on an ass. Yet, for a few divine moments, the crowd's eyes opened to the Shekinah Glory of God, and together, they proclaim, "Hosanna, blessed is he who comes in the name of the Lord" (*Mark 11:9, NIV*)! Soon thereafter, their spiritual eyes would close, and they rejected the one they had called king.

Jesus doesn't appear the way we have conjured him up in our minds. If you want to see Jesus, look for him among the poor, hungry, homeless, lonely, imprisoned, and the exposed. His presence is not spectacular and glamorous but paltry and unimpressive. Like the people on the road, when you see Jesus, divine moments in time will happen over and over again!

"I know that my redeemer lives, and that in the end he will stand on the earth. And after my skin has been destroyed, yet in my flesh I will see God; I myself will see him with my own eyes—I, and not another. How my heart yearns within me" (Job 19:25-27, NIV)!

April 6

Activate the Key

"I will give you the keys of the kingdom of heaven; whatever you bind on earth will be bound in heaven, and whatever you loose on earth will be loosed in heaven" (Matthew 16:19, NIV).

In the above scripture, Jesus tells Peter what's possible with these keys. With your keys come power and authority. Whatever you lock down here, I will lock it up in heaven. And, whatever you open up down here, I will open it up in heaven. All you need to do is activate your keys.

Jesus is talking about the power of the church: Love, healing, liberating, saving, and changing power! In other words, Christians have the power to kick defeat out of the door.

Use your key to lock up low self-esteem. *"I praise you because I am fearfully and wonderfully made." (Psalm 139:14, NIV).*

Use your key to lock up fear. *"The angel of the Lord encamps around those who fear him and delivers them." (Psalm 34:7, NIV).*

Use your key to lock up jealousy and envy. *"Love is patient, love is kind. It does not envy, it does not boast, it is not proud" (1 Corinthians 13:4, NIV).*

Use your key to lock up oppression. *"It is for freedom that Christ has set us free. Stand firm, then, and do not let yourselves be burdened again by a yoke of slavery"(Galatians 5:1, NIV).*

Use your key to open up to love. *"For I am convinced that neither death nor life, neither angels nor demons, neither the present nor the future, nor any powers, neither height nor depth, nor anything else in all creation, will be able to separate us from the love of God that is in Christ Jesus our Lord" (Romans 8:38-39, NIV).*

Use your key to open up to righteousness. *"Surely the righteous will never be shaken; they will be remembered forever" (Psalm 112:6, NIV).*

Use your key to open up to peace. *"Peace I leave with you; my peace I give you. I do not give to you as the world gives. Do not let your hearts be troubled and do not be afraid"* (John 14:27, NIV).

Use your key to open up to justice. *"When justice is done, it brings joy to the righteous but terror to evildoers"* (Proverbs 21:15. NIV).

Use your key to open up to liberation. *"Now the Lord is the spirit, and where the spirit of the Lord is, there is freedom"* (2 Corinthians 3:17, NIV).

You have the keys to the kingdom. How will you use the power you have in your hands and in your heart?

April 7
Metaphors in the Matrix

The Matrix, starring Lawrence Fishburne (Morpheus), Keanu Reeves (Neo), Carrie Ann-Moss, (Trinity) and Gloria Foster (the oracle), is one of my favorite movies. The first time I watched the movie was for an ethics class in seminary. What captivated me most was the symbolic use of Christian themes (liberation, savior, enemy, faith, redemption, death and resurrection).

The movie's major plot is about freeing the minds of human beings imprisoned by their own creation of intelligent robots. Morpheus, Trinity, and a few others were able to rebel and wage a war against the enemy. In order to win the war, they need a savior. Morpheus had faith and believed wholeheartedly that Neo is their savior. Does this sound familiar?

In the last major confrontation, the enemy kills Neo. After a kiss from Trinity, Neo is resurrected with unmatched power to control and defeat *the Matrix*. "Resurrected with unmatched power..." Who does this sound like? Our savior, Jesus, came to redeem lost human beings. He dies and is resurrected with unmatched power to free human beings! I'm not sure if the writer of *the Matrix* had this in mind, but for me it comes through loud and clear. If you look deep into movies, you can use some storylines as an impetus to discuss important spiritual principles.

Movies are about life experiences and the choices human beings make. Sometimes the scenes are exaggerated and outside the bounds of acceptable behavior. Regardless of the movie genre you're watching, if you're open, you may discover deeper meanings and answers that speak to your own life. Always keep in mind that your guideposts are Jesus, the Holy Spirit, and the Almighty Sovereign God.

"The real voyage of discovery consists of not seeking new landscapes but in having new eyes."
~Marcel Proust

April 8
Soul Food

"It is written. Man shall not live by bread alone, but on every word that comes from the mouth of God" (Matthew 4:4, NIV).

When I first committed my life to Christ, there was a surreal feeling of joy and peace that I wanted to last forever. God gave me my answer. I remember awakening early one morning and being directed to the scriptures about staying rooted and grounded in God's word.

In Luke 8, Jesus uses seed to symbolize God's word. Just like it is impossible for a plant to grow without seed, it is impossible for you to grow without God's Word. He says when seeds fall on a hard path they cannot grow. Have you seen bits of grass embedded in a driveway? That's a hard path. A hard path is like a hard heart. God's Word will only grow in a heart that's open and soft.

When seeds fall on rocky ground, the seed starts to grow but quickly dies for lack of depth. Shallow or rocky soil is like people who enjoy sermons and gospel music but as soon as life challenges happen, they fall by the wayside.

Then there is thorny ground. I had beds of flourishing lilyturfs planted around my house. The lawn service company failed to maintain my beds. Before long, thorns almost choked out the lilyturfs. Another company pulled out the weeds. Thorns are like the cares, persecution, and riches of the world that choke out quality time with God.

How do you produce a healthy crop? The grounds need to be fertilized, watered, and cared for. If you want to grow and stay strong in the Christian way of life, you will have to read and study the Bible on a regular basis and spend time in prayer and fellowship with other Christians.

"All Scripture is God-breathed and is useful for teaching, rebuking, correcting, and training in righteousness." (2 Timothy 3:16, NIV)

April 9
A Chain of Divine Reactions

"I could not run away from the situation. I had become, whether I liked it or not, a symbol, representing my people. I had to appear."
~Marian Anderson

Eighty-one years ago, today, Marian Anderson performed on the steps of the Lincoln Memorial before an audience of seventy-five thousand people. Millions more listened on the radio to this gifted contralto as she sang, "My Country Tis of Thee." Arturo Toscanini, Italian conductor and acclaimed musician of the nineteenth and twentieth centuries called her, "a voice such as one hears once in a hundred years."

The original intent of her sponsor, Howard University was for Ms. Anderson to perform at Constitution Hall, a venue owned by the Daughters of the American Revolution (DAR). However, they refused to allow her to perform in their space because of her race. In response, Eleanor Roosevelt resigned her membership with DAR and arranged for Ms. Anderson to sing at the Lincoln Memorial. Mrs. Roosevelt's resignation served as a catalyst for racism to gain national attention and set the stage for the civil rights era.

Ms. Anderson's gift was first noticed at the age of six when she started singing in her church choir. Her family and her church sacrificed to help perfect her voice. With assistance from the church, she was able to study under Giuseppe Borghetti, a respected voice teacher, and opportunities started to open up.

In 1928, she performed at Carnegie Hall. Ms. Anderson received a Julius Rosenwald scholarship that allowed her to tour Europe, and a few weeks following the Lincoln Memorial concert, she gave a concert at the White House where President Roosevelt was entertaining King George VI and Queen Elizabeth of Britain. In 1955, she sang at the New York Metropolitan Opera House, a first for any African American.

Ms. Anderson's gift made room for her and helped to open the door for many other African American artists. Her talent led to a variety of leadership roles and awards. Anderson served as a "goodwill ambassador" for the State Department. She sang at the March on Washington in 1963 and received many awards over her lifetime. Ms. Anderson was awarded the Presidential Medal of Freedom in 1953, the Congressional Gold Medal in 1977, the Kennedy Center Honors in 1978, the National Medal of Arts in 1986, and a Grammy Lifetime Achievement Award in 1991.

"Fear is a disease that eats away at logic and makes man inhuman. I forgave the DAR many years ago. You lose a lot of time hating people."
~Marian Anderson

April 10
Junior Guild

In my opinion, a community or village that reaches out to its children honors God and respects the nation. About sixty years ago, I grew up in a community that lived out this core belief. There were about twenty-five houses in our subdivision. During these years, teachers were among the most highly respected professions in the Jim Crow environment in which we lived, and several teachers lived in our neighborhood. Two teachers, Mrs. Mathis and Mrs. Terry formed an after-school neighborhood children's guild which they named, *Junior Guild*. Their mission was to help build self-esteem and pride in our rich black culture. Our parents knew we were safe with them.

I remember the times we spent sitting in their living rooms as they tutored and taught us lessons in etiquette. Under their guidance, we and recited poetry, the Books of the Bible, and songs about sharing and caring. At Halloween, they held fun activities and safe games like bobbing for apples and making candy apples in their homes. At Christmas, they chaperoned us as we went Christmas caroling around the neighborhood.

These two ladies were self-directed volunteers. They valued the lives of the children around them and helped to stimulate their present and future welfare. They also made a difference in the lives of all the children they touched. The primary responsibility of child development belongs to parents, but it also extends to the school, church, and community. Indeed, it does take a village to raise a child.

"Children have never been very good at listening to their elders, but they have never failed to imitate them."
~James Baldwin

April 11
The Final Act

The Gospel of Luke 23:39-43, tells what happened to the two criminals who were nailed to crosses alongside Jesus. No doubt their bodies were releasing plenty of stress hormones to help fight against their inevitable death. This is how the human body reacts during extreme stress. I suppose this body function kept them alive long enough to have a talk with Jesus. How did they use their time?

Both men knew about the good news Jesus preached, the mercy he showered, and the miracles he performed. They were given one last opportunity to make their peace. One man used his time to mock and sneer Jesus. He was about to take his last breaths on earth but all he could do was parrot the mean words of the mob that surrounded Jesus: "Aren't you the Christ? Save yourself and us" (*Luke 23:39, NIV*). As he did with the other mockers, Jesus did not respond and left him to his own demise.

The other man used his time for the highest good. He admitted his wrongdoing and then humbly asked for mercy, "Jesus, remember me when you come into your kingdom." This time Jesus responds, "I tell you the truth, today you will be with me in paradise" (*Luke 23:42-43, NIV*). I can imagine a song swept over his soul similar to the old gospel hymn, "At the cross at the cross where I first saw the light and the burdens of my heart rolled away. It was there by faith, I received my sight, and now I am happy all the day."

Jesus' final act on earth was to assure a place in paradise for a criminal. No one is beyond God's love and forgiveness. As long as we are on this earth, there is no time limit on believing and receiving salvation and eternal life. The decision is in our hands.

"For the Son of Man came to seek and to save the lost" (Luke 19:10, NIV).

April 12
Resurrection Faith

Easter is the most important event in the life of the Christian because it celebrates the resurrection of Jesus Christ from the grave. Easter Sunday is different from other Sundays. Church auditoriums are
filled to capacity on Easter Day. The congregants' voices pulsate with
vigor and energy. The children are adorned in colorful spring wear as
they hold on to their Easter baskets and bunny rabbits and recite their
Easter speeches. The preacher prepares to give the Easter sermon on
the resurrection. The people are filled with glee. What happens after
Easter Sunday? How is the resurrection lived out in your life?

When we walk in resurrection faith, we live every day believing
and acting like Jesus got up out of the grave. It is a walk by faith and
not by sight. It does not leave room for doubt. It is an expectant faith.
When Jesus and Mary were at the wedding in Cana and the wine had
run out, Mary expected an overflow. Hear her as she tells the wedding party, "Do what he tells you" (John 2:5, NIV). When Lazarus died,
Martha demonstrated resurrection faith when she said to Jesus, "But I
know even now God will give you whatever you ask" (John 11:22, NIV).

Resurrection faith empowers, liberates, and is filled with holy
boldness. Faith in the resurrection empowers us to witness about the
love of Jesus. It is not just talking the talk but walking the walk as well.
It matures through regular prayer, meditation, Bible study, fellowship
with other believers, and most of all being an instrument in God's
divine hands.

*"In their fright the women bowed down with their faces to the ground, but the
men said to them, "Why do you look for the living among the dead? He is not
here; he has risen" (Luke 24:5-6, NIV).*

April 13
Helen Keller

"Where there is great love, there are great miracles."
~Willa Cather

If there was an extraordinary life, it was the life of Helen Keller. At the same time, I would hasten to add that her teacher, Anne Sullivan was also exceptional. Up until the age of nineteen months, Ms. Keller was a bright and vibrant infant who was suddenly overtaken by a disease that left her unable to see, hear, or speak.

The first six years of Ms. Keller's life was like being trapped inside a body without having any thoughts or feelings. It was Anne Sullivan's endearing love and patience that gradually awakened Ms. Keller's soul. Once her soul awakened, her fervor for knowledge became insatiable. Ms. Sullivan was the catalyst used to illuminate Ms. Keller's gifts. She learned to speak, write in braille, and even use a typewriter. Her accomplishments were so noteworthy, she started touring the United States lecturing, visiting, talking, and praying for the handicapped.

Ms. Sullivan was the right person at the right time to help Helen Keller. She too was visually challenged and also grew up very poor. Her health and background helped her not only to be more compassionate and patient, but an innate divine power propelled her through her mission.

"As he went along, he saw a man blind from birth. His disciples asked him, "Rabbi, who sinned, this man or his parents, that he was born blind?" "Neither this man nor his parents sinned," said Jesus, "but this happened so that the works of God might be displayed in him" (John 9:1-3, NIV).

April 14

Acceptance

One of the things that keeps us frustrated and anxious is wanting conditions to be different especially when they are in disarray. Rather than living the best possible life in the midst of whatever life circumstances present, we spend too much time thinking about yesterday or focusing on tomorrow. When we live the best possible life, we accept people, situations, and circumstances as they occur with the expectation that God will make a way for us.

At this moment in time, everything is as it should be. It is the right time, the right people, and the right circumstances, but it may not feel that way. Uncertainty is all around. Our prayers are not being answered. To struggle against this moment is to weigh yourself down more. The starting place in the midst of adversity begins with your thoughts about your circumstances.

Stop trying to sort things out. First, observe the situation and accept things as they are. There is wisdom in uncertainty. If you can only see one possible solution, then you close the field of limitless possibilities in God. Now is the time to rest in the Lord and wait patiently for God to act. When you do, the peace of God that passes all understanding will soothe your heart and mind. When you come to this divine peace, you no longer have to understand.

"God grant me the serenity to accept the things I cannot change; Courage to change the things I can; and wisdom to know the difference."
~Reinhold Niebuhr

April 15
Chance of a Lifetime

One hundred-eight years ago today, the Titanic sank in the Atlantic Ocean. There were 2,200 passengers on board. 706 people survived the disaster. The notorious *Shipbuilder Magazine* called the Titanic unsinkable and indestructible. Because of its immense size, the passengers aboard the Titanic felt secure. No one thought the ship could sink.

The Titanic was beautiful and featured a heated pool, four restaurants, a state-of-the-art gym, and two barbershops. It cost $7.5 million to build which would be $400 million today. It was a chance of a lifetime cruise from South Hampton, England to New York City.

There were no passenger safety drills on what to do and which lifeboats to board should something happen. There were only twenty lifeboats available to accommodate about one-half of those on board. The ship had been given multiple warning messages about icebergs, and the officers made a few adjustments but kept moving at a high rate of speed until the ship hit a huge iceberg. Three hours later, the ship sank. In the twinkling of an eye, everything changed. As the ship sank, most onboard met their death.

Death is inevitable whether one dies alone or with a mass of people like on the Titanic. Jesus talked about death. He talked about his own death, which no disciple wanted to even imagine. But his conversations were about life after death. "The one who believes in me will live, even though they die: and whoever lives by believing in me will never die. Do you believe this" *(John 11: 25-26, NIV)*? Jesus didn't want anyone to miss the chance of a lifetime to spend eternity with God.

".... whoever believes in Jesus will not perish but have everlasting life" (paraphrased John 3:16, NIV).

April 16
Not One Faileth

Have you ever been reading the Bible and suddenly words or a passage seem to speak directly to you? It happens to me, especially when I have been praying about a concern, like when I was studying for my internal medicine board exams for the second time. Yes, I failed the first time, and I admit that I didn't put a lot of time or energy into studying. But I did the second time around.

In addition to reading a good portion of *Cecil's Textbook of Medicine*, I listened to tapes and attended multiple board review courses. Every evening before I started studying, I read scripture. It was my prep time. One day while reading in Isaiah, the words *"Not one faileth"* stood out. (*Isaiah 40: 26, KJV*) At that point, I knew that I would pass my boards. The internal medicine board exam is known to be difficult. It requires a great deal of focused study. Reading the Bible before I studied helped my focus and was a blessing from God.

The first few verses of Psalm 1 says reading and meditating on God's Word brings prosperity. "But whose delight is in the law of the Lord; and who meditates on his law day and night. That person is like a tree planted by streams of water, which yields its fruit in season and whose leaf does not wither—whatever they do prospers" (*Psalm 1:2-3, NIV*).

I passed and became a Diplomate of the American Board of Internal Medicine. It was one of my happiest life experiences. I owe it all to the Almighty Sovereign God.

"Lift up your eyes on high, and behold who hath created these things, that bringeth out their host by number: he calleth them all by names by the greatness of his might, for that he is strong in power; not one faileth" (Isaiah 40:26, KJV).

April 17
Care for Caregivers

Are you the primary caregiver for a loved one? Do you know someone who is a primary caregiver? Being a caregiver can take its toll on one's health, work, and relationships. A caregiver's body is more likely to stay in a high stress zone.

In response to stressful situations, the body releases large quantities of hormones and chemicals into the bloodstream. When this happens, the heart rate, blood pressure, blood sugar, and respiratory rate increase. This allows more oxygen to be pumped into the bloodstream to supply muscles with energy needed to respond to threat. If the stress is short lived, the chemicals return to normal levels. Under stress, these chemicals tend to stay at a high level. If these chemicals remain high, blood vessels become inflamed. Inflamed blood vessels shrink causing high blood pressure. Inflamed blood vessels, plaque and cholesterol build-up increases the risk for a heart attack or a stroke. Other factors that contribute to inflamed blood vessels include unhealthy foods, sleep deprivation, and physical inactivity, all of which are more likely to occur in caregivers.

Caregivers must attend to the health of their bodies, minds, and spirits. If not, caregiving may lead to anxiety, depression, sleep problems, and poor physical health.

Reach out to your family and friends for help. Research the internet for what services are available in your community. In Georgia, where I live, you can reach out to https://aging.georgia.gov/programs-and-services. This is a government funded program that should be available in every state.

"There are only four kinds of people in the world. Those who have been caregivers. Those who are currently caregivers. Those who will be caregivers, and those who will need a caregiver."
~ Rosalyn Carter

April 18

Lip Service

"Why do you break the command of God for the sake of your tradition?"
(Matthew 15:3, NIV)

Lip service is allegiance expressed in words, appearance, or tradition but not backed by deeds. Lip service blocks the Christian's primary mission to make disciples of all nations. Jesus warns against this action.

It was a Jewish tradition to perform a ceremonial handwashing ritual before eating. Jesus and his disciples broke with this tradition. The Pharisees and scholars looked at them with disdain because of this. Jesus admonished them by pointing out their worse hypocrisy. These men followed tradition to the point of not supporting their parents if it interfered with them giving to the church.

Traditions can become obstacles to the primary mission of service to humanity and discipleship. While it's not easy to identify with the ritual of handwashing in today's society, there are other traditions that impact our Christian walk.

Do you show disdain to some people in the church? Does their apparel offend you? To be sure, it does not offend God. God looks at the heart and not at clothing. How well do you know the Bible? Is this your measuring rod for what makes a good Christian? The Pharisees knew the Bible backward and forward, but they were mean, hypocritical, and self-serving. Remember, the church is not the building. The church comprises people from all walks of life. And like the people said years ago, some need Jesus for one thing and others need him for something else.

"These people honor me with their lips, but their hearts are far from me. They worship me in vain; their teachings are but rules taught by men." (Matthew 15:8, NIV)

April 19
Friendship Gone Awry (An African Folktale)

There is a story about two boys who were the best of friends. While still young, they committed to remain close friends forever. They grew up, got married, and built their homes facing each other. Only a narrow path formed a border between their farms.

Both young men were happily married and still the best of friends until a charlatan decided to play a trick on them. He dressed in a two-color coat that was divided down the middle. One side of the coat was red, and the other side was blue. The charlatan wore the coat and walked along the narrow path between their houses. He made loud noises to be sure the friends heard him.

At the end of the workday, they talked about the coat. One said, "Wasn't that a beautiful red coat?" The other said the coat was blue. Certain about the color of the coat, both became excited. They started insulting each other, and the name-calling ended in them fighting and shouting, "Our friendship is over."

The charlatan returned and started laughing at them. He showed them that his coat was red on one side and blue on the other. Then, the two friends turned their anger toward him, blaming him for their fight. But the charlatan replied, "I did not make you fight. Both of you are wrong and both of you are right. What each of you saw was true. You are fighting because you only looked at my coat from your own point of view."

How often does one's perspectives lead to division in relationships, families, and communities? Making a declaration that my way is right and other ways are wrong, moves away from healing and wholeness at every dimension of life.

"You have your way. I have my way. As for the right way, the correct way, and the only way, it does not exist."
~ Friedrich Nietzsche

April 20
What's in Your Salvation Bank Account?

Two stories in the New Testament describe what's at stake when you make a decision for Jesus Christ. One story describes a rich young ruler who bragged that he had kept every commandment since childhood. Then Jesus told him to sell everything he had, give it to the poor, and gain treasure in heaven. He said, "Come, follow me" (*Matthew 19:21, NIV*), but the man went away sad because he was very wealthy.

The other story is about a man who said to the Lord, "Look, Lord! Here and now I give half of my possessions to the poor, and if I have cheated anybody out of anything, I will pay back four times the amount" (*Luke 19:8, NIV*).

Jesus talks about the plight of the wealthy who seek salvation. "How hard it is for the rich to enter the kingdom of God. Indeed, it is easier for a camel to go through the eye of a needle than for someone who is rich to enter the kingdom of God" (*Luke 18:24, NIV*). At this point, the disciples were a bit disappointed. From Jesus' answer, it appeared as if no one can be saved. But Jesus responds, "What is impossible with man is possible with God" (*Luke 18:27, NIV*).

What's in your salvation bank account? Store up treasures in love, generosity, patience, peace, joy, forgiveness, and gentleness, and then leave the rest to the Almighty Sovereign God.

"No one has ever become poor by giving."
~ Anne Frank

April 21
A Story About Shame

To be ashamed of yourself is to lack confidence in the Creator God. Unfortunately, shame causes many people to spend most of their lives hiding their real identity, and after a while he or she can't remember who they really are.

Night School is a movie about a man (Teddy) who was ashamed of himself. Teddy was embarrassed because he did not complete high school. His life was filled with pretense and deception. For years, he was able to deceive people by driving a fancy car and dating a highly successful businesswoman.

Then his life started to fall apart after losing his job. Although he lacked confidence, he goes back to school to earn a GED. At first, he used the same tactics of deceit and pretense but these no longer worked. With the help of a teacher, he gains some self-esteem. It took him several tries, but he finally passed the GED examination and earned his high school diploma. He was invited to be the spokesperson at his graduation and used that opportunity to share his life story, one of embarrassment and deception. The audience, including his girlfriend, warmly received his message. This was his shining moment and changed his life from an inauthentic to an authentic existence.

Everyone has felt shame at various times in their lives. Something or someone makes us feel like we don't measure up and we take it to heart. If you're feeling this way, go to God in prayer. There, you will find confidence in God who created you. God has a plan for your life. God's plan is more powerful than all the shame and inadequate feelings you can ever have. The first step is to trust in the one who created you. God believes in you. When you believe in God, you will believe in yourself.

"For we are God's handiwork, created in Christ Jesus to do good works, which God prepared in advance for us to do" (Ephesians 2:10, NIV).

April 22
Sibling Violence

Sibling violence is a problem that is under reported. Unlike domestic violence, child abuse, and bullying by classmates, it is rarely talked about. More often, it is considered horseplay between siblings, but when a sister or brother causes harm and pain to another sister or brother, it is violence. This includes shoving, hitting, slapping, kicking, biting, scratching, and hair pulling. And, if it is found in the Bible, it can happen in families of today as well.

In the book of Genesis, there is the story about Joseph and his eleven brothers. Joseph was their father's favorite son and, for this and other reasons, they were jealous of him. Their jealousy led them to choose violent actions of the worst kind. They threw Joseph into a pit and later sold him into slavery for twenty pieces of silver. The brothers covered up their actions by killing an animal and placing the blood of the animal on Joseph's coat. They told their father Joseph had been attacked by an animal and showed him the coat as evidence.

The actions of Joseph's brothers were egregious. How on earth could they live with themselves after committing such an act? Their jealousy turned to cold-blooded hate. No families should experience violence of this magnitude, but it can happen. Parents and grandparents must monitor sibling rivalry so that it never slips into violence of any kind.

"At the end of the day, the most overwhelming key to a child's success is the positive involvement of parents."
~*Jane D. Hull*

April 23
Thankful Thoughts

Regardless of who we are or what we have, we can always be thankful. Use the first letter in the word Thankful and think about other words that are related to being appreciative and grateful. What happens when you are thankful? Here are my thoughts. What are yours?

- Thoughtful actions heal families and communities.
- Health is a great gift that cannot be purchased.
- Appreciation is gratitude in action.
- Never forget to be truthful and kind.
- Kindness is love in action.
- Freedom from sin is a blessing and possible only through Jesus Christ.
- Understanding means to stand under another person and see from their perspective.
- Love makes it easy to be grateful.

"Give thanks in all circumstances; for this is God's will for you in Christ Jesus" (1 Thessalonians 5:18, NIV).

April 24
Mirror Mirror on the Wall

Have you ever thought about how much focus society places on external beauty? Or why criteria for beauty is based on hair, body shape, eyes, lips, and age? After a certain age, people start getting Botox injections, face lifts, lip augmentation, hip implants, breast implants, tummy tucks, wigs, weaves, and eyebrows added and shaped. My pastor preached a sermon to the children in the church about external beauty, but it rang true for my ears as well.

He used the children's story, *Snow White and the Seven Dwarfs* to make his point. At age seventy-one, I had forgotten most of the story, but hearing it was refreshing. The focus throughout the story was the queen's fanaticism with beauty. She wanted to be the most beautiful person in the world, prompting her to approach her 'truth mirror' and ask the question, *"Mirror, mirror on the wall, who is the fairest of them all?"* She fumed when the mirror's response was Snow White instead of her. Because she was vain, being the most beautiful person was a matter of life and death. As a result, she made multiple attempts to kill Snow White, so she could regain this title. Her vanity cost her everything. She ended up losing her life trying to harm another.

Twenty-three years ago, I was diagnosed with Graves' disease. It caused my eyes to protrude, something I had to learn to live with. It wasn't easy, but God gave me the strength. Real beauty is not external but internal. Man looks on the outside, but God looks on the inside. *"Mirror, mirror on the wall, who is the fairest of them all?"* The answer is all those who seek godly wisdom, peace, joy, forgiveness, and love and use it to help bring God's kingdom a little closer to earth as it is in heaven.

"Charm is deceptive, and beauty does not last, but a woman who fears the Lord is to be praised" (Proverbs 31:30, NIV).

April 25
Good Will Win

There are several keys to overcoming resentment or removing that chip off of your shoulder. The main block is your ego. It will tell you all the reasons why you're right and they're wrong, and everything else that's annoying about a person or a situation.

When I was an intern, training to become an internal medicine specialist, there was one intern (Dr. X) who never wanted to carry his weight. We all had beepers and were expected to respond to being paged. Interns were called to do what was known as 'scut' work (draw blood, perform arterial blood gases, transfuse blood, remove impactions). We also worked nights, days, and weekends.

One day, I was scheduled to stay over and work the night shift, and throughout this particular day, Dr. X was paged several times to draw blood gases. He never answered any of his pages. At 5:00 p.m. when the night shift began, I was paged to do the work he did not complete during the day. As a young indignant doctor with a chip on my shoulder, I entered the unit and made a bad decision. I refused to complete the blood gases.

An attending physician observed my behavior. Although he did not say a word to me, he reported my lack of compliance to the Chairman of the Department of Internal Medicine. I had a teachable moment during my internship that helped me throughout my career. I am glad someone observed the situation and reported it. Our chairman reminded me of my call to care for the patient regardless of how any other physicians respond. It never happened again. Resentment is not a sustainable option.

"Do not be overcome by evil but overcome evil with good" (Romans 12:21, NIV).

April 26
Good for Evil (Genesis 39-40)

In an earlier reflection, I wrote about Joseph who was sold into slavery by his brothers. He was purchased by a man named Potiphar who was in charge of King Pharaoh's palace guards. It was there where Joseph was observed to be handsome, intelligent, kind, and filled with the Spirit of God. Potiphar placed him in charge of the entire household and all business dealings. Then, trouble began to stir. Potiphar's wife liked Joseph and tried to seduce him, but he declined her frequent advances.

Embittered from rejection, Potiphar's wife turned the whole story around and accused Joseph of trying to seduce her. Joseph was arrested and thrown into prison. In spite of this, he remained kind, helpful, and wise. His ability to interpret dreams eventually caught the attention of King Pharaoh who was having a difficult time understanding the meaning of several disturbing dreams. Joseph predicted seven years of abundance followed by seven years of famine. Not only did Joseph interpret his dreams but he made recommendations on how to handle the upcoming situation. The King was so enthralled by Joseph that he made him governor, placing him in charge of the entire land of Egypt.

During the famine, Joseph's brothers came to Egypt seeking assistance. Twenty-two years has passed since they last saw each other. Joseph recognized them but pretended he didn't. His heart was filled with generosity and love, but he held back his identity during the first two meetings. When he finally revealed himself, the brothers kept waiting for him to retaliate for the evil they had done to him. Joseph's response was powerful. "You intended to harm me, but God intended it for good to accomplish what is now being done, the saving of many lives" (*Genesis 50:20, NIV*).

"And when you stand praying if you hold anything against anyone, forgive them, so that your Father in heaven may forgive you your sins" (Mark 11:25, NIV).

April 27
A Near Fatal Voyage

Dwight L. Moody was a well-known evangelist who lived during the nineteenth century. He had a call to preach the word of God to the world. Initially, he was actively involved in Sunday school and YMCA. During a business trip, he was invited to fill a pulpit in England. The sermon was described to be spectacular. Following this, he became a full-time worldwide evangelist.

In 1892, Moody and his son boarded an ocean liner in England bound for New York. On the third day of the trip, the shaft of the vessel broke causing the ship to flood and begin to sink. The sea was too rough to place passengers on lifeboats. All they could do was assemble everyone in a central location and hope to be discovered by a passing vessel. Although the situation was unsettling for him as well, Moody helped to calm passengers with prayer. During this time, he had a defining moment with God.

Moody felt God confronting him to make a decision. He had been told by a doctor to slow down because of some heart irregularities. If he didn't, he would die early. He decided that if God would spare his life, he would work with "all the power that He would give me." And if he should die this year or next, that was in God's hand.

The next morning, a miracle happened. The ship was discovered and towed one thousand miles to safety. Following this, Moody traveled the world preaching the gospel with passion and fervor. It is reported that "thousands were converted to Christ."

While we may not be physically stranded on a sinking ship, some life experiences feel that way. Like Moody's experience, they may catch us by surprise. They're usually totally out of our control. When that happens, it's good to get quiet, sit still for a while, offer up earnest prayers, seek divine direction, and then wait on God.

"Let us hold unswervingly to the hope we profess, for he who promised is faithful" (Hebrews 10:23, NIV).

April 28
One Minus Ten

In the gospel of Luke Chapter 17:11-19, there is a story where Jesus heals ten lepers. Persons with leprosy were considered outcasts. No one wanted to be near a leper. They were forced to live in separate communities, usually on the outskirts of town. In this particular text, ten persons with leprosy 'stood at a distance' and cried out to Jesus for mercy. Jesus healed them and instructed them to, "Go, show yourselves to the priest" (*Luke 5:14, NIV*). [A priest had to certify that they were cleansed from leprosy.]

One of the ten men looked at himself, overjoyed to see that his body was healed. At this point, he could not contain himself. He started shouting, then turned around and kneeled at Jesus's feet, elated at the miracle that just took place. His gratitude was an expression of his faith in the One who changed his life.

Jesus asked, "Were not all ten cleansed? Where are the other nine" (*Luke 17:17, NIV*)? How often do we take our blessings for granted? When you really see your blessings, you will be like the man who couldn't go any further without expressing gratitude. Not only were his physical eyes opened, but his spiritual eyes as well. He experienced a double blessing. That is why Jesus' last words to him were, "Rise and go. Your faith has made you well" (*Luke 17:19, NIV*).

"There are two ways to live your life. One is as though nothing is a miracle. The other is as though everything is a miracle."
~*Albert Einstein*

April 29
Thank You, Doctor

On the tenth day of my husband's hospital stay, I started thinking about taking him home. My heart's desire was for him to reach a point where it was safe for him to be discharged. On the positive side, although he still required large amounts of oxygen, he had been weaned off the respirator. And on this particular day, he was sitting in a chair with his chin resting on his chest. He 'appeared' to be asleep when one of the specialists entered his Intensive Care Unit room and asked if I had any questions.

"How long do you think it will be before Cecil is able to go home," I asked. And the specialist answered cold and disrespectful as if Cecil was not in the room, could not hear, or was asleep. "I doubt that he will ever leave the hospital. He will be here a very long time. Most physicians will not level with you, but that's not how I operate." I thanked him for his directness and said I understood, which of course was not true.

As the physician was leaving the room, Cecil raised his head and spoke with strength in his voice like only Cecil could and said, "Thank you, doctor." Cecil made me feel so good that day. The scripture, "My grace is sufficient for you, my strength is made perfect in weakness" came to mind. The Almighty Sovereign God's anointing was all over Cecil.

This physician, intentionally or unintentionally, ignored the humanity of Cecil. I hoped Cecil's response would compel him to think before talking about a patient as if they were not in the room.

"Patients don't care how much you know until they know how much you care."
~ paraphrased from Teddy Roosevelt

April 30
Remember Who You Belong To

It is easy to get mixed up in this fast-paced technological society where up can seem down and down can seem up. If you turn on the news (which I seldom do), you'll hear about murders, economic downturns, volatile stock market, political steam, Twitter, Instagram, Facebook, etc. Don't spend too much of your time fretting about the news cycle. If you want peace, take a break from the news cycle and remember who you belong to.

You belong to the great I AM —the Creator of this magnificent universe. You are God's servant. You bow before God. You don't belong to the evil in the world.

How do you feel about the Almighty Sovereign God? The understanding that you have about who you belong to determines your outlook. If you feel good about belonging to God, then you will try to live a life that is pleasing to God. If you are excited about belonging to God, then your life will be lived expecting good things to happen. If you are proud to belong to God, you will spend your time sharing the love of God.

Don't live your life wishing you had different parents, a different pedigree, a different heritage, or a different set of circumstances. Things could have been better, but they also could have been worse!

We can only see a tiny part of the whole picture. Most of our parents raised us the best way they knew. Now it's time to let Jesus take over and pick up where they left off. Remember who you belong to.

"I make known the end from the beginning, from ancient times, what is still to come. I say, 'My purpose will stand, and I will do all that I please'" (Isaiah 46:10, NIV).

May 1
How Would You Act If You Were Invisible?

If you could be certain that your bad behavior would not be discovered – that you'd have no consequences - how would you act? There's a story found in *Plato's Republic* called "The Ring of Gyges." Following an earthquake, one of the king's shepherds finds an unusual gold ring. To his amazement, he discovers that he can disappear or reappear depending on how he positions the ring. He uses this power to take over the kingdom by seducing the queen and then plotting with her to kill the king. Why would he use this power to carry out evil acts?

This story has good insight. Your response to this question might be to say there are people who are visible and exhibit bad behavior. That is true. The question here is what would you do if no one could see you? Would your actions still be the same?

In Romans 8, Paul explains the situation human beings find themselves. "When I want to do good, evil is right there with me" (*Romans 7: 21, NIV*). The mind is powerful. We slip up and hope we don't get caught. Our ego convinces us that our behavior does not compare with people who lie, steal, cheat, and kill.

But all human beings fall short. "No one is right with God, no one at all. No one understands; no one trusts in God" (*Romans 3:10-11, NIV*). The only way to be freed from a life dominated by sin is through Jesus Christ. There is no magic wand that can be waved to change everything. It is a faith walk that you take when you accept Jesus Christ as your personal savior.

"So now there is no condemnation for those who belong to Jesus Christ" (Romans 8:1-2, NLT).

May 2
Giving—Who is Your Neighbor?

What would you do if you met someone in need, but she or he was of a different race, religion, or culture? Or maybe they were wearing a tee shirt or tattoo with wording you despise. Do you look the other way? Do you judge, curse, or harm them? Or, do you show compassion and help them?

The Good Samaritan story is one Jesus uses to show how to treat another human being. The man in the story has been beaten and wounded by thieves. The story does not describe the wounded person's race, ethnicity, or culture because the only thing that matters is he needs help.

There are three people who find him in this predicament; a priest, a temple assistant, and a Samaritan. The first two pass by without even looking his way. The person who reaches out to help, the Samaritan, is regarded as an outcast. But he is the one who shows what it means to be human. He attends to the injured man's wounds and then takes him to an inn where he continues to care for him. He even went as far as to pay the innkeeper for any additional expenses.

What is Jesus saying? Humanity is a spirit of inclusion. Race, culture, ethnic background, and belief systems are secondary. When a human being is in need, being kind, caring, and hospitable is the neighborly thing to do. Human beings must break through man-made cultural and racial confines. These boundaries invalidate and give excuses to look the other way when others are in need.

"And if you do good to those who are good to you, what credit is that to you? Even sinners do that" (Luke 6:33, NIV).

May 3
Happiness (based on an old folktale)

A physician begins to feel "on the job weariness." So, she decides to look for employment in a different health clinic. She seeks guidance from a wise woman. "What sort of people work here?" asks the physician. "What were the people like in the previous clinic where you worked?" replies the wise woman. "They were inconsiderate, unfriendly, lazy, indifferent, and lacked empathy. "Is that so?" replies the wise woman. "Well, I'm afraid that you'll find the same sort of people in this medical clinic."

Sometime later another physician hails the wise woman, and they stop to talk. "What sort of people work in this clinic?" she asks. Once again, the wise woman asks, "What were the people like where you've come from?" "They were the best people in the world: considerate, hardworking, friendly and compassionate. I'm sorry to be leaving them." "Fear not," said the wise woman. "You'll find the same sort of people in this medical clinic."

The easiest thing to do is to blame others for life challenges. We end up frustrated, and it shows up in our attitude and our spirit. The key is finding peace regardless of the external circumstances. Here are some thoughts to consider:

- Observe your emotional state. Are you angry or discouraged? When you are aware of your feelings, you are more likely to move away from negative self-talk.
- Practice being nonjudgmental. When you're hard on yourself, you're more likely to find faults in others.
- Try not to let others' viewpoints define your feelings toward them. Each person is the sum total of their background, family history, genetic make-up, culture, life-experiences, and more. Respect theirs and yours.
- Discover your identity with an all loving God through consistent prayer, meditation, and periodic fasting.

"A contented heart is a calm sea in the midst of all storms."
~ *Anonymous*

May 4
Job and The Sovereignty of God (Part 1)

The story of Job in the Bible is familiar to most Christians. Job was an extraordinarily wealthy man. If he were living today, he would be a multi-billionaire. In spite of his wealth, he loved God and had an enduring faith. God allowed Satan to take away Job's wealth, health, and even kill his children. His whole life and livelihood are shattered to pieces. In spite of this, Job remained faithful but still felt devastated and wanted to die.

Why would God allow Satan to wreak such havoc in Job's life and cause him to suffer so much? Forty-three years ago, Cecil Wayne Cone wrote an article, "Why Do the Righteous Suffer?", in which he said, "The Christian answer is one which can only be found through an encounter with God. When Christians encounter God, they are totally overwhelmed by him. And being overwhelmed with this God, they deny themselves, take up their crosses, and follow him wherever he leads." Job has such an encounter which seems to make all the difference for him. In my humble opinion, it wasn't the answers that Job received as much as it was being in the presence of a holy, all wise God.

Cone further says, "There are some things that cannot be brought to a rational understanding because they transcend rationality." Several examples come to mind. 1) God allowed Joseph's brothers to sell him into slavery. 2) The prophet Habakkuk asked God why he allowed the people of Judah to be captured and punished by the Babylonians. 3) God allowed Africans to be sold into slavery in the United States and remain in slavery for 244 years. 4) In the New Testament, "Jesus was led by the Spirit out into the wilderness, where the Devil tempted him for forty days" (*Luke 4:1-2, NIV*).

The sovereignty of God is beyond the intellect of human beings to understand. Even with all the outstanding accomplishments human beings have made down through the centuries, we are still perplexed by suffering and death. This is why this is a faith walk that is beyond our human comprehension.

"Oh, how great are God's riches and wisdom and knowledge! How impossible it is for us to understand God's decisions and God's ways! For who can know the Lord's thoughts? Who knows enough to give God advice? And who has given God so much that God needs to pay it back? For everything comes from God and exists by God's power and is intended for God's glory. All glory to God forever! Amen" (paraphrased Romans 11:33-36, NLT).

May 5
Job and Failed Friendships (Part 2)

Job had his livelihood, family, and health stripped from him. Triple trouble. How can anyone not be devastated, depressed, and feeling quite alone under these circumstances? There was no *Go Fund Me* page on social media and if there were, it could not help his distressful situation. The degree of his grief from the death of his children cannot be fathomed. Job's friends came to comfort him.

At first, Job's friends empathized quietly with him as sometimes saying nothing is the best thing to do. "...Mourn with those who mourn" (*Romans 12:15 NIV*). But after a few days, they could no longer hold their peace. They reasoned that he had been sinful and offended God at some point and that he needed to come clean. When Job denied their accusations, they called him a liar and insisted that he should stop trying to vindicate himself. His friends were now acting more like self-righteous judges than friends. There is an old saying, "With friends like these, I don't need enemies."

As time passed, Job's friends became more of a nuisance. They were like news pundits giving their perspective but not involved in the real-life situation. They had no clue about the relationship between God and Job. A true friend meets you on your terms. She senses your needs. She cries or laughs with you. She knows when to be quiet, when to speak, and when to intervene. In the next reflection, God's response to Job's friends is revealed.

"Friendship isn't about whom you have known the longest... It's about who walked into your life and said, 'I'm here for you and proved it."
 ~ Unknown

May 6
Job's Encounter with God:
Who Has the Final Say? (Part 3)

With all the negative talk coming from his friends, Job started to wonder why God was allowing this to happen to him. He reasoned that he had served God, strived for the right, and did not harm others. Indeed, this is a predicament we sometimes find ourselves in.

Then Job encountered the Almighty Sovereign God. When you encounter God like Job did, something happens. He was astounded at the meager limitation of his understanding and knowledge of God's greatness. He was overwhelmed and humbled at the extent of God's unlimited power and creation.

The Almighty Sovereign God was pleased with Job's response but angry at his friends for their behavior. God had them go back to Job, sacrifice a burnt offering, and have Job pray for them. The scripture then says, "Job prayed for his friends and the Lord made him prosperous giving him twice as much as he had before" (*Job 42:10*).

Job's friends accused and judged him harshly without having an inkling of what was happening between him and God. God directed Job to pray for his accusers and once he did, blessings overflowed.

Almighty Sovereign God, I thank you for my friends. You know what they need right now, and I ask that you shower them with your grace, mercy, and love. In Jesus name, I pray and thank you in advance. AMEN

May 7
Reverence in Meditation

"Let the words of my mouth, and the meditation of my heart be acceptable in thy sight, O LORD, my strength and my Redeemer" (Psalm 19:14, KJV).

Meditation is reverence to God in thought and heart. Psalm 19 crystalizes the reasons to meditate. Meditation converts the soul, rejoices and cleanses the heart, enlightens the eyes, and rewards the doer. Reverence for God in heart and thought enables you to see God's Hand in the daily affairs of life. Meditation changes one's perspective from a personal view to a God-view. It's so fulfilling, you will say like David, "My meditation of him shall be sweet: I will be glad in the Lord" *(Psalm 104:34, KJV).*

How does one reach this point? Expressions of faith through the practice of meditation cannot be forced. If it's your desire to spend more time in prayer and Bible study and delve more deeply into the scriptures and their practical application in your life, you have started the reverence of meditation.

There's a lot going on in our lives. There are mountains of issues that weigh down our heart. Flood waters drown out our ability to think clearly. What's needed is peace. God says, get quiet. "Be still and know that I am God" *(Psalm 46:10, KJV).* With meditation, you can move from a survive mode to a thrive mode. It takes time, but it is more valuable than any amount of money.

"The Law of the Lord is perfect, converting the soul: the testimony of the Lord is sure, making wise the simple.
The statutes of the Lord are right rejoicing the heart: the commandment of the Lord is pure, enlightening the eyes.
The fear of the Lord is clean enduring forever: the judgments of the Lord are true and righteous altogether.
More to be desired are they than gold, yea, than much fine gold: sweeter also than honey and the honeycomb" (Psalm 19: 7-10, KJV).

May 8
The Guiding Hand of God

Recently, a friend shared her personal health story with me. I'll call her Diane. Diane's mammogram screening was up-to-date and normal. One day while lying in the bed her hand just moved to her left armpit where she felt something. She checked her right armpit and didn't feel anything.

After contacting her physician, she had an ultrasound, MRI, and another breast mammogram. All tests were negative for any lumps in either breast. Then, she underwent a biopsy of the lump in the armpit and breast cancer was found. She is in the midst of undergoing chemotherapy and her outlook is phenomenal. Her face is radiant, and she speaks with holy boldness. She is ready to share her testimony and to tell women to add checking both armpits in addition to getting a mammogram and doing a breast exam.

There was no reason for her to check her armpits, but she did. It was the hand of God guiding her to the area in her armpit that needed immediate attention, Hear Diane as she says, "It is truly His hand that has guided my entire journey, and all glory to Him for all He has done for me. God is good, and I am good."

"If I rise on the wings of the dawn, if I settle on the far side of the sea, even there your hand will guide me, your right hand will hold me fast" (Psalm 139: 9-10, NIV).

May 9
The Poorest of the Poor

After reading *Mother Teresa, a Life Inspired,* I am in awe of her life. In my opinion, the Old and New Testament comes alive in her. When the Old Testament is carefully studied, the overarching theme is extending justice and righteousness to the very least in the community. Mother Teresa called it caring for "the poorest of the poor." In the New Testament, Jesus says, "When you refused to help the least of these my brothers and sisters, you were refusing to help me" (*Matthew 25:45, NLT*). Mother Teresa's devotion to God was demonstrated by this: to serve Jesus is to serve the poorest of the poor.

When she lived inside the Indian caste system, she lived among the people she served, known as the 'untouchables.' There, she opened up orphanages, hospices, medical clinics, and schools for this population of people.

Her worldview was to treat everyone as family. When asked what an individual could do to promote peace in the world, she answered, "Go home and love your family." After Jesus healed a mentally deranged man, he wanted to follow Jesus. Jesus replied, "Go home to your own people and tell them how much the Lord has done for you, and how he has had mercy on you" (*Mark 5:19, NIV*). In other words, love starts with family. When you are patient, generous, loving, and caring to your family, it will extend out into the community and nations of the world.

"All of humanity is God's people, and thus a commitment to God means a commitment to help the poorest and the most destitute of humanity, whoever and wherever they might be."
~ Mother Teresa

May 10
A Reflection on Motherhood

"She is clothed with strength and dignity; she can laugh at the days to come" *(Proverbs 31:25, NIV).*

When I recall the time I shared with my mother, I remember her courage, strength, nurturing spirit, intellect, and compassion. She believed in me 100% and if it were mathematically possible, more than one hundred percent. That's motherhood. That's womanhood.

Who does not feel the vibrations and vigor of a woman?

- Like the Queen of Sheba, she is wise.
- Like Deborah, she is courageous and saves the nation of Israel.
- Like Esther, she places her life on the line for her people.
- Like Mary McLeod Bethune, she inspects a field, buys it, and Bethune Cookman University is planted.
- Like Helen Keller, she takes the hand of life she is dealt and becomes a world renown activist and advocate for blind people worldwide.
- Like Mother Teresa, she extends a helping hand to the poor.
- Like Michelle Obama, her husband is well known and becomes the leader of the free world.
- Like Mary, her faith is the progenitor of Jesus Christ.

Almighty Sovereign God, thank you for the gift of motherhood. Indeed, they are closest to who God is. They bring life into the world, provide the first food for the newborn, give unconditional love, and minister and care to those in need. AMEN

"She speaks with wisdom, and faithful instruction is on her tongue" *(Proverbs 31:26, NIV).*

May 11
The Favor of God

When it comes to salvation, the Bible is quite clear. "...God does not want anyone to perish" (*2 Peter 3:9, NIV*). Hear Peter as he says, "I realize how clear it is that God does not show favoritism" (*Acts 10:34, NIV*). However, there are instances in the Bible where some persons have divine favor. One person was Moses. The Lord said to Moses, "I will do the very thing you have asked, because I am pleased with you and I know you by name" (*Exodus 33:17, NIV*). How did God's favor manifest itself to Moses?

Moses had a unique relationship with God and all the people could see it for themselves. Whenever Moses would consult God, a pillar of cloud would hover over their meeting arousing a spirit of reverence in the people. They knew that Moses's relationship with God was different. What was it about Moses that made him a favorite of God's?

Was it his humility? In Numbers 12:3, it says that "Moses was more humble than any other person on earth." Even though he grew up in King Pharaoh's house, he carried himself as one of low importance. He did not identify with the oppressor. Was it his fervor for justice? Moses passion was to make things right. He identified with the powerless and risked his life fighting the oppressor. Even when he enters unfamiliar territory, the first action he takes is to stop bullies from harassing sisters at a well.

What is your relationship with God? How visible is it to your family and community? Indeed, no one knows the mind of the creator God and why Moses was one of God's favorite people but humility, identifying with the poor, and becoming a drum major for justice goes a long way with the Almighty Sovereign God. There is a popular gospel song that asks the question, "Do you have favor?"

"May the favor of the Lord our God rest on us; establish the work of our hands for us— yes, establish the work of our hands" (Psalm 90:17, NIV).

May 12
What Are Your Prayer Requests?

Whenever we travel, we see road signs that provide information to road users. In a similar way, there are signs along life's highway that provide instruction for living a Christian life. One sign that's seen frequently is the sign of prayer. The signs read, it's prayer time...be constant in prayer...pray without ceasing...prayer is the greatest power on earth. And, if we stay within the boundary of prayer, we stay within God's safety zone. Sometimes we need to reflect on not just our prayer life but our prayer requests. King Solomon gives us some answers.

King Solomon was known to be the wisest man to ever live. In his young life, he recognized that he needed a whole lot of wisdom. And, when God appeared to him in a dream and said, "Ask for whatever you want me to give you" (*2 Chronicles 1:7, NIV*), Solomon asked for wisdom and knowledge that he might do God's work.

Solomon's prayer requests were not carnal (riches, honor, power). And, God was pleased with his request. God's response to his appeal was not only to give him wisdom and knowledge but to give him more riches, wealth, and honor than any previous king or any kings in the future.

To know what to pray for is powerful. Sometimes as it says in the Bible, we don't always know what to pray. That's when we can get quiet and let the Holy Spirit pray for us. As it is written, "the spirit intercedes for God's people in accordance with the will of God" (*Romans 8:27, NIV*).

Thank you, God, for the gift of prayer. Please keep me within the boundary of prayer for then I know that my view down the highway of life will become clearer, my challenges bearable, and my destination certain. In Jesus name, AMEN.

"Give ear to my words, O Lord, consider my meditation. Hearken unto the voice of my cry, my King and my God: for unto thee will I pray" (Psalm 5:1-3, KJV).

May 13
The Cost of My Praise

Each person's salvation experience is unique. An old gospel song explained it this way: *You don't know what the Lord has done for me.* A more recent song, "Alabaster Box," sings about the emotional cleansing one woman has after being forgiven of her sins. She showers Jesus with her tears and anoints him with oil to express her faith in him as her savior and healer (*Luke 7:36*). The salvation experience is tantamount to the depth of forgiveness one feels.

Jesus, the master of parables, asks the question. Two people owed a man money, one owed five hundred pieces of silver and the other owed fifty pieces. Neither could repay the money. He forgives both and cancels their debts. Who do you suppose loved him more after that? Most likely, the one who owed the most.

When I think about my personal life story, my own life experiences are the result of my choices. Some of my choices were productive and some were counterproductive. And to this day, some bring tears to my eyes. But like the lady in the "Alabaster Box," no one knows the cost of my praise. Regardless of what you think or how you look at me, I will pour out my praise and love to God for forgiving and healing me.

And Jesus said to the woman, "Your faith has saved you; go in peace" (*Luke 7:50, NLT*).

May 14
Divine Security: Psalm 91

When I first accepted Jesus Christ as Lord and Savior of my life, my mother shared that her favorite scripture was Psalm 91. If my mother loved it, I knew it was good. Not long afterward, using *The Living Bible*, I committed it to memory. It was a good Psalm to learn at the beginning of my faith walk because it introduced me to the one who I had placed my trust.

Psalm 91 is a profession of faith and my simple child-like faith took it all in. It's a declaration of God's abiding love, omnipresence, faithfulness, and security for a safe journey through the ups and downs of the cycle of life.

Psalm 91 can easily give the impression that Christians are fully protected from all hurt, harm, and danger. One has to be careful not to misuse the command of the words as if they have fairylike power. This is why it is important to study the Bible in its entirety.

In Luke 4 :9-12, Satan quotes scripture from Psalm 91 to tempt Jesus to jump off the high Temple roof, "For God orders angels to protect you wherever you go. They will steady you with their hands to keep you from stumbling against the rocks on the trail" (*Psalm 91:11-12, TLB*). Our response should be the same as Jesus' response, not to put God to a foolish test for our own benefit.

It is putting God to a foolish test if one's rent, car note, or some other bills are due and no provisions have been made for debts to be paid, or, refusing to take important medications because of your certainty that you are healed from a "deadly disease." Further, it's a foolish test when one expects superior academic grades but have not put in quality study time.

But when we trust God regardless of life situations, we are assured that nothing will ever separate us from the love, faithfulness, and security of God.

"The Lord says, "Because she loves me, I will rescue her; I will make her great because she trust in my name. When she calls on me, I will answer; I will be with her in trouble and rescue her and honor her. I will satisfy her with a full life and give her my salvation" (paraphrased Psalm 91:14-16, TLB).

May 15
Resilience

Resilience is the ability to adapt well in the face of difficult conditions. How do you bounce back when your starting point is at the bottom of a well? In the movie, *Fences*, Rose played by Viola Davis answers this question. Even before her life becomes more disruptive, Rose and her husband lived in a ghetto on the meager salary of a garbage collector.

Rose manages to rise up after her soul is ripped into tiny pieces. Her fifty-three-year-old husband of eighteen years impregnates another woman who dies in childbirth. To add insult to injury, Roses' husband asks her to help raise his newborn daughter, Raynell. She accepts Raynell as her daughter and finds the way of escape through the love she gave and received from her.

Even more compelling was that she took ownership of her life choices. She stopped finding fault with her husband. As a result, she did not live the rest of her life filled with blame and regrets. She was no better off financially, but her outlook on life became rich and wholesome. Through her new perspective, she was able to see the good qualities in her husband. He died six years into his new daughters' life, and by that time, Rose had built a solid relationship with Raynell. That is resilience!

"...Just like moons and like suns, with the certainty of tides, just like hopes springing high, still I rise."
~*Maya Angelou Still I Rise*

May 16
God's Formula for Success (Part 1)

After the death of Moses, Joshua was appointed to be the new leader of the people of Israel. Joshua was to take them across the Jordan River and conquer the enemies in the land God promised them. It was an incredibly challenging job. I don't believe Joshua would have been able to begin this task had he not been an outstanding follower. Before you can become a successful leader, you must be able to follow.

Joshua was Moses' assistant. He learned from a great leader. Joshua observed how Moses moved, his prayer life, communication with God and with the people. He was obedient and had a good attitude. Moses critiqued and encouraged Joshua who welcomed his comments. Joshua saw a vision of success, not a vision of failure. He was courageous and demonstrated positive thinking. When Moses sent agents to scout out the land, only Joshua and one other came back with a positive report: We will enter into our new land and conquer it.

What is your formula for success? Does it include God, followership, courage, optimism, hope, and the ability to accept constructive criticism? Or, are you working toward achieving these characteristics? If yes, you are on the road to success, and I am sure you have already encountered roadblocks, detours, had an accident or two and been slowed by a lot of traffic. But with the kind of faith you have, there is no stopping you.

"In everything you do, put God first, and God will direct you and crown your efforts with success" (Proverbs 3:6, TLB).

May 17
God's Formula for Success (Part 2)

The second component of God's formula for success is effective communication with God and with people. This is demonstrated superbly through Joshua's listening skills (the most important part of communication). The first chapter of Joshua begins with a message to Joshua from God. God spoke, and Joshua listened. Not once during the communication did Joshua speak. God told him everything he needed to know in order to accomplish his goals. Listening is most important.

Joshua listened as the Almighty Sovereign God made bold promises to him: The land is now yours. You do not have to fear the dangers of the day or night. I am your shelter. It will require you to be strong, courageous, and obedient. And, it will require you to meditate and maintain a prayer life. Throughout this conversation, God kept talking and Joshua kept listening.

Throughout the book of Joshua, you will find the passage, "The Lord spoke to Joshua," or "The Lord told Joshua to move this way." God was guiding his every step. Joshua had a very close relationship with God and spent many days and nights meditating on God's word.

In this highly technologically advanced society, the Bible might appear to be outdated and useless. But if you examine books on effective leadership, you'll find the same qualities emphasized in Joshua. When these principles are learned directly from the Bible, it helps both your work and your family life too. When you learn about them in books or seminars, you can attest to their power because they are Bible based.

"For the word of God is alive and active. Sharper than any double-edged sword. It penetrates even to dividing soul and spirit, joints and marrow; it judges the thoughts and attitudes of the heart" (Hebrews 4:12, KJV).

May 18
An Unclean Woman (Luke 8)

When it comes to healing, Jesus used his health-giving power regardless of Jewish law or custom. For example, one Jewish law considered a woman ceremonially unclean if the menstrual flow of blood lasted beyond the normal period. There was a woman who had been bleeding for twelve years, and according to law, any contact between her and Jesus would have made him unclean. Jesus knew this as well, but to him, healing always rose above the law. The woman also knew the law and before her encounter with Jesus had sought healing through many physicians until her money ran out.

This might explain the reason she hid among the crowd and reached to touch just the fringe of Jesus' robe. But when she did, the Bible says she was instantly healed, and the bleeding stopped. Although the touch was ever so light, Jesus knew someone had touched him and wanted to know who. It was not to shame her or to admonish her for breaking the law, but to bless her for demonstrating great faith. Hear Jesus as he says to her, "Daughter, your faith has made you well. Go in peace" (*Luke 8:48, NIV*).

There is no wound that Jesus can't feel or heal. Facing the wounds and hurts in our lives by letting Jesus shine God's light on the dark corners of our lives will not crush us. Instead, it will open us up to a deeper and wiser understanding of our wounds, their cause and effect, and lead to healing and wholeness.

"*Come ye disconsolate, where'er ye languish, Come to the mercy seat, fervently kneel, Here bring your wounded hearts, here tell your anguish: Earth has no sorrow that heaven cannot heal.*"
~ Thomas Moore

May 19
Surprise After Surprise (John: 4:1-28)

Jesus spent his time on earth breaking down walls between human beings. It was considered scandalous for people of Jewish descent to socialize with Samaritans. Not so for Jesus.

In the above text of scripture, Jesus meets a Samaritan woman at a well. He has one purpose in mind—the salvation of her soul. It surprises her that someone of Jewish ethnicity would talk to her. First, he asks her for a drink of water. He uses water, something most meaningful to her since she had to draw water every day. What does he mean that if I drink this water, I'll never be thirsty again? You might say he is wetting her spiritual appetite. She decides to stay around to see what he has to say.

She is surprised at his insight about her life. There is no judgement in his conversation and no disdain in his body language. She recognizes him to be a prophet. Then, she changes the conversation to the religious differences between the Samaritans and the Jews. This becomes the inroad for Jesus to talk about true worship—neither what the Samaritans or Jewish people practice. "God is spirit, God's worshippers must worship in spirit and truth" (John 4:2,4 NIV). Once again, his answer surprised her. A sudden feeling of divine wonder comes over her being. She realizes that he is the Messiah! She runs away excited and returns to her village to tell everyone who she has met. As a result, many other Samaritans became believers.

Jesus' ministry was all-inclusive. No one was out of the reach of his unconditional love. In essence, Jesus was saying to the Samaritan, your life is more important than any disagreements between my people and your people. Where you spend eternity is what matters. Now is the time for all of us to stop the pretense and the arguments and move to a higher level of living.

"There is neither Jew nor Gentile, neither slave nor free, nor is there male or female, for you are all one in Christ Jesus" (Galatians 3:28, KJV).

May 20
David's Confession

"Behold, thou desire truth in the inward parts, and in the hidden part thou will make me to know wisdom" (Psalm 51:6, KJV).

Psalm 51 is about the sins of King David and the forgiveness of God. The actual story is found in 2 Samuel where King David misused his power to sexually exploit a married woman named Bathsheba. David's act spirals out of control, and Bathsheba becomes pregnant. To cover up his grievous deeds, he has her husband killed. It is only when Nathan a prophet comes to confront him that he confesses to his heinous actions.

David was carrying around an awful secret. I think he was already close to a breaking point when Nathan challenged him because he confessed immediately. He did not incriminate Bathsheba saying that she tempted him. He did not justify his actions by telling an untruth about her husband, that she was the wife of an abusive man or glamorize his actions by saying it was love at first sight. Still, a cloud of gloom surrounded David's family because of his actions.

David's toughest punishment was being out of relationship with God. God never left him. David left God, and as he confesses in Psalm 51:6, God desires truth in the inward parts, the secret part. Other than God, only the individual knows the secrets in their heart. It is the sinful secret parts that separates one from God.

David's confession started the restoration process. With his confession, the heaviness in his soul gradually lifted. It was the wisdom that he gained from his mistakes that kept his heart and mind turned to God. Honesty with God is a sure pathway to forgiveness, deliverance, and reconciliation with God.

"Create in me a clean heart, O God; and renew a right spirit within me. Cast me not away from thy presence; and take not thy Holy Spirit from me; Restore unto me the joy of thy salvation; and uphold me with thy free spirit" (Psalm 51:10-12, KJV).

May 21
A Birthday Worth Remembering

Today is my husband's birthday. At the time I write this reflection, thirty-four months have passed since Cecil made his transition. I miss him just as much today as I did back then. It's the memories that hold my heart together.

Three months after our first date, he wanted me to meet his mother. So, we flew to Pine Bluff, Arkansas, and spent Thanksgiving with her. "Son, marry her. She is the one." That's what Cecil told me his mother said.

Cecil was intelligent, witty, and a great storyteller. I loved to hear stories about his life as an adolescent and young man. His father died years before we met, but I knew him because of the stories Cecil shared about his dad.

Cecil believed in me and was sensitive to my feelings. If he sensed something was not going well in my spirit, I'd come home to beautiful flowers and a huge stuffed animal. He was never too busy to stop and listen.

Cecil loved his three children. Whatever amount of time he spent with them, he embraced it as if it were a gazillion hours. I was blessed to witness the unspeakable joy they brought to his life and to see and feel his endearing fatherly love and dedication.

I am so thankful to the Almighty Sovereign God for the blessing of marriage. I was thirty-five years of age when I married but was still able to share thirty-five years of life with the man of my dreams.

"Every hour has sixty minutes with sixty seconds in it; that's a lot of time to share and time to show that you care. Don't abuse it or you will lose it; a friendly smile to a little child and hug to the elderly; life can be better all around; so keep your feet on solid ground."
~Nan Campbell Fletcher, my mother

May 22
Power in Weakness

"Some women were there watching from a distance, including Mary Magdalene, Mary the mother of James the younger, and of Joseph, and Salome" (Mark 15:40, NIV).

What else could these dedicated women do as they watched Jesus die? The disciples had all fled, but they too would have been helpless at this point. Even though these women had no physical power to change the outcome, God used them in a mighty way. They became witnesses to Jesus's death. Had they not remained at the cross, the naysayers could have come up with all kinds of conspiracy theories. He didn't really die. We saw them take him down and he was alive.

There is a gospel song that asks the question, *"Were you there when they crucified my Lord?"* These women can answer in the affirmative. *"Were you there when they laid him in the tomb?"* These women were heartbroken and filled with grief, but their devotion and love for their savior remained steadfast as they watched a stone being rolled against the entrance of the tomb where his body lay.

When our hearts and minds are open, God can use us for divine purposes. Two thousand plus years ago, there were no cell phones, iPads, social media, television, radio or video to authenticate occurrences. All news was delivered by word of mouth. These ladies were used to get two decisively important messages out: Yes, Jesus did die on a cross at Calvary. Be that as it may, Jesus has been raised from the dead. Now, that's the best news anyone can spread!

"He 'rose, He 'rose, He 'rose from the dead. He 'rose, He 'rose, He 'rose from the dead. He 'rose, He 'rose, He 'rose from the dead. And the Lord shall bear my spirit home."
~ *Traditional Spiritual*

May 23
Aging Gracefully

"Aging has a wonderful beauty and we should have respect for that."
~ Eartha Kitt

Thirty years ago, the Americans with Disabilities Act (ADA) was passed by Congress to ensure individuals with disabilities were not discriminated against in all areas of public life. Forty-one million persons are living with a disability in the United States. Indeed, this was a welcomed civil right for persons living with disabilities. Reading about the ADA made me think about our aging population.

Although many Americans age sixty-five and over may not have disabilities, they may start to develop physical inconveniences that impact their quality of life. For example, as one ages, reading small print is more taxing. If you develop programs or bulletins for a large group of people, I recommend using at least a size 12 font.

Knee and back arthritis weaken the muscles in the lower body. This makes it difficult to raise up out of chairs. Hand bars and higher toilets ought to be considered for all public bathrooms.

One in three individuals between the age of sixty-five and seventy-four have some hearing loss. When entering into a conversation with a person with a hearing loss, it helps to start the conversation with their name, face them directly on the same level and in good light, speak clearly and slowly, but naturally. Avoid shouting and/or talking from another room.

As the population moves down the seasons of life, it's good to be reminded about ways to assist our senior population.

"Christ has no body now but yours, no hands, no feet on earth but yours; yours are the eyes with which he looks compassion on this world."
~ Teresa of Avila

May 24
The "Ifs" in Life

Don't let the if's in life become a distraction

In the center of the word life is the word *if*, and there are *if's* in the heart of our lives that often depress, discourage, and demean us, halting forward momentum. If I had not listened to him... If I could right this wrong... If we had waited to buy the car... If I can get this job... If I had not gotten into debt... If I had not entered into that relationship... Things would be different.

Most of the *if's* in life are mundane, temporal, secular, and carnal. And we might end up repeating them multiple times. The reason they are if's is because they don't bring true meaning to life.

In the book of Ecclesiastes, King Solomon seems to make all of life seem meaningless, but as you read carefully, you can see a purposeful and divine message. Regardless of being rich, poor, wise, foolish, powerful, weak, happy or sad, it is all meaningless unless one fears God and obey God's commands. Simply put there is "one" gift in life that is worth negating with abandonment - if only I had given my life to God. Remove the "if" and commit your life to God.

"If it had not been for the Lord on my side, where would I be? Where would I be?"
~ *Margaret Douroux*

May 25
"Laughter and Health"

I once heard a woman with breast cancer share her method for dealing with cancer. She committed to be cheerful throughout her treatment period. She and her husband would regularly watch comedy films that would give rise to hilarious laughter. Laughter increases the flow of antibodies to the immune system. A strong immune system protects the body under stress. This lady fully recovered from breast cancer. While the laughter didn't kill any cancer cells, her immune system was better able to defend her body during this stressful time.

Sometimes, it's hard to laugh. Just as laughter strengthens our immune system, sadness from major life events can suppress it. The death of a loved-one and the grief that follows is a prime example. One's broken heart can result in depression, illness, and even death. During this time, most people do not feel up to taking deliberate actions similar to the lady with breast cancer.

Family and friends can be most helpful during these times. Try to be more observant of a loved-one who is suffering. Encourage them to seek professional health if you observe alcohol or drug abuse, notice difficulty functioning in daily life, neglecting personal hygiene, suicide talk or constant speaking about death. A medical check-up with their physician is recommended even if warning signs are not present. WebMD's special report about the stages of grief has a lot more information about grief and the negative health effects. While there are times in life that make us sad, God wants us to experience joy as often has possible. The Bible has been advocating for joy for thousands of years: "The joy of the Lord is our strength" (Nehemiah 8:10, NIV). "...weeping may stay for the night but rejoicing comes in the morning" (Psalm 30:5, NIV).

"A cheerful heart is good medicine, but a crushed spirit dries up the bones" (Proverbs 17:22, NIV).

May 26
My Way or the Highway

Some stories are worth repeating because they remind us there are almost as many ways of viewing life situations as there are people.

Many people know the story about the six blind men and the elephant, but it's worth contemplating once more. Six blind men were told that an elephant was in their village. They had no idea what an elephant was, so they decided, "Even though we will not be able to see it, let us go and feel it." All of them went to where the elephant was.

Each one touched the elephant. "Hey, the elephant is a pillar," said the first man, who touched his leg. "Oh, no! It is like a rope," said the second man, who touched the tail. "Oh, no! It is like a thick branch of a tree," said the third man, who touched the trunk of the elephant. "It is like a big hand fan" said the fourth man, who touched the ear of the elephant. "It is like a huge wall," said the fifth man, who touched the belly of the elephant. "It is like a solid pipe," Said the sixth man, who touched the tusk of the elephant.

An argument ensued because each man was adamant that he was right. Fortunately, a man of great wisdom heard the argument. He acknowledged their viewpoints with attentiveness and respect, and then calmly explained, "All of you are right. The reason every one of you is telling it differently is because each one of you touched a different part of the elephant. So, actually the elephant has all the features that each of you mentioned."

The human mind is not capable of understanding life situations fully. The whole picture is not at our disposal. We see only a reflection as in a mirror. But one day we shall see perfectly clear, know and understand fully, even as God knows and understands us.

"Change the way you look at things and the things you look at change."
~ *Wayne W. Dyer*

May 27
Standing on the Edge of a Miracle
(Joshua 3:1-4:18)

In the book of Joshua, the people of Israel (led by Joshua) are about to enter the promised land. Joshua's faith was strong. He stayed in deep communion with God who guided and reassured him. In a similar way, Joshua gave the people direction and reassurance, and they respect and trust him.

To enter the land, they have to cross the Jordan river. This does not appear to be the best time to attempt this feat because the river is overflowing at its banks. Joshua remembered the story of the Exodus event and knew God as the way-maker and the deliverer. He was not afraid to move forward.

As the children of Israel prepare to cross over, they demonstrate absolute obedience to leadership, and fear dissipates.

God directs them to cross the Jordan at flood stage. Yet, there is no complaining or grumbling. And sure enough, as soon as the priests carrying the ark reach the Jordan and their feet touch the water's edge, the water from upstream stopped flowing and piled up into a heap a great distance away. And the Israelites safely crossed the Jordan to reach the land granted to them by God.

As we move through life, we will face flood waters. Not only must we pray for spiritual leaders like Joshua, but we must, as he told the people of Israel, consecrate ourselves to God's service through prayer, obedience, and worship. When we do, fear will dissolve, and the waters will recede.

"When you pass through the waters, I will be with you; and when you pass through the rivers, they will not sweep over you" (Isaiah 43:2, NIV).

May 28
A Setback is a Setup for a Comeback!

Run, Baby! Run, Baby, Run! That's the cheering sounds of a mother running beside her eleven-year-old son when he played on a Pop Warner football team. He had just caught a pass, turned up field and was sprinting for the first touchdown of his life. His mother, Etta was there on the sideline cheering with great emotion like a typical mother.

Her son went on to play professional football. Etta was still there praying and encouraging him. When he was hospitalized for complications from appendicitis, she was at his bedside twenty-four hours a day, praying and reading her Bible. When his condition started to deteriorate, she went on a God directed warpath advocating for her son. Etta pressured the hospital staff to bring in a team of specialist. Medical experts came and saved his life.

After several football injuries, he became very depressed and lost faith in himself. But his mother kept on praying and encouraging him with inspirational scripture and messages. She told him, "Don't you know, son, that a setback is nothing more than a setup for a comeback?" His faith in her finally kindled belief in himself. When this happened, his career reached a level of success he had never imagined.

Without his mother, Jimmy Smith would not have been a four-time Pro Bowl wide receiver for the Jacksonville Jaguars. In fact, without his mom, he might have died. To be sure, human beings will find themselves facing setbacks. When this happens, we need someone who will listen, someone who will encourage us through these setbacks. Know this. God will not leave you alone. A setback is nothing more than a setup for a comeback.

"But they that wait upon the Lord shall renew their strength; they shall mount up with wings as eagles; they shall run, and not be weary; and they shall walk, and not faint" (Isaiah 40:31, KJV).

May 29
Power and Fear in the Same Man

Have you ever been threatened with revenge because of something you said or did? Well, that's what happened to Elijah, one of God's prophets. God anointed Elijah with so much power he called down fire from heaven to show all Israel that the Lord indeed is God. At the same time, he ordered 450 of the enemy's prophets to be put to death. Because of this action, Queen Jezebel threatened Elijah's life by saying, "May the gods deal with me, be it ever so severely, if by this time tomorrow I do not make your life like that of one of them" (1 *Kings* 19:2, *NIV*).

Jezebel scared the living daylights out of Elijah, and he did what many of us would do. He ran away. During this period, he was isolated. After a while, he became depressed and felt abandoned by God. He was so mixed-up, he wanted to die, thinking thoughts like, after all I had done for the Lord, God's enemy is about to kill me. Where is God?

God sent Elijah to the Mountain of God where he finally heard God in a gentle whisper. The Lord told Elijah that earthquakes, wind-storms, and fires will happen in your life. Their purpose is to get your attention and draw you back to me. Then, when I speak, you can hear me.

How often have you taken matters into your own hands? At first, it seems like smooth sailing ahead. Then, suddenly, the situation chang-es. No longer are things in your favor. God seems far away. And just like Elijah, despondency and fear start to weigh you down. It's time for some serious quiet time with God. Once you humble yourself before God and trust God to make a way, you will discover the path that has already been laid out.

"There hath no temptation taken you, but such as is common to man; but God is faithful, who will not suffer you to be tempted above that ye are able; but will with the temptation make a way of escape that ye might be able to bear it" (1 *Corinthians* 10:13, *KJV*).

May 30
A Story About Grace

For the Christian, grace is defined as the unmerited favor of God. Whether we are Christians or not, we have all had experiences during our lifetimes when we miraculously escaped a close call.

The author of the following story is unknown. It takes place during a time when pharmacist had apothecaries inside their homes and doctors made house calls.

A doctor makes a house call to attend to a very sick lady cared for by her devoted husband and family. He makes a diagnosis and writes a prescription, and the father has his son take the prescription to the home of the pharmacist. By the time the son arrives, it is quite late, and the pharmacist is groggy. He makes up the compound ordered by the physician and gives the medication to the son. The son is happy and skips home with the medication. The pharmacist easily falls back to sleep.

Shortly thereafter, the pharmacist awakens gripped with fear because he realizes the compound he made was incorrect and would cause harm to the patient. What could he do? He did not have transportation and the young son was probably well on his way. He started to pray fervently seeking direction from God.

Soon afterwards, he heard a loud knock at his door. It was the young lad apologizing. He explained that as he was skipping, he dropped the bottle and it broke and asked if the pharmacist would refill the prescription again.

How many times in your life have "broken bottles" saved you from embarrassing situations? Broken bottles are God's grace. I definitely have had my share.

Thank you, God, for your unmerited favor and grace that miraculously changes life's outcomes. AMEN

May 31
Misty Copeland (Life in Motion)

Life in Motion is the story of Misty Copeland. The title fits her life story. During childhood and adolescence, Misty experienced frequent moves. The worst episode was living in a crowded run-down motel where they all slept on pallets. These disruptions were taxing on Misty. It's hard to imagine how her vision to become a ballerina survived a childhood filled with disorder and unpredictability.

The culture of ballet is for rich girls, and Misty's family was extremely poor. Most children begin ballet training between the ages of four and eight. Misty started studying ballet at age thirteen, and the odds were stacked against her. Her first mentor observed her talents on a school drill team and told her, "You are going to be a star. You are God's child," predicting that she would dance before kings and queens. Everyone who observed her talent wanted to help her dream of becoming a ballerina materialize.

Misty was graced with natural talent. Most individuals practice for months to years to develop flexibility of limbs that was effortless for her. She could master techniques that took others months to accomplish in mere minutes. Before completing high school, she was already spending summers at well-known ballet institutes.

Off stage, Ms. Copeland was insecure and sometimes misunderstood. On stage, she was a natural who literally came alive with excitement and confidence. Blossoming over the years, with God's guidance and her extraordinary talent, she achieved her dream of becoming a principal ballerina with the American Ballet Theater.

"Don't let them take your over. Walk into the room knowing you are the best. Shoulders back, chin up. Their attitudes will totally change."
~ Arthur Mitchell, cofounder of Dance Theatre of Harlem

June 1
Rejected: A Poor But Wise Man

In the book of Ecclesiastes 9:13-16, King Solomon, a man filled with wisdom, demonstrates through a story that wise actions from a poor person are undervalued, underestimated, and ignored.

A 'poor but wise man' used his acumen to rescue a town from a powerful king and his army. In spite of his success, he received no recognition or credit. In fact, he was not even given a second thought. King Solomon reasoned that although wisdom is better than strength, those who are wise will be despised if they are poor.

While what King Solomon says has merit, I believe this 'poor but wise man' looked at his actions differently. To be sure, human beings have a great need to be loved, recognized, and appreciated and do their best to earn these accolades, but some actions are not done to earn earthly glory.

This man used his gift of wisdom to save his town. And in so doing, although this happened long before the coming of Jesus Christ, he was identifying with Christ.

When a Christian experiences rejection, they identify with Christ at the most significant point of his earthly existence. Christ was not acknowledged. He was rejected and despised. The glory and power of God was hidden on the cross and covered with shame and humiliation.

This 'poor but wise man' who saved his town will receive his glory in eternity. And, that is where it counts most.

"Only one life, yes only one, Soon will its fleeting hours be done; Then, in 'that day' my Lord to meet, And stand before His judgment seat; Only one life, 'twill soon be past, Only what's done for Christ will last."
~ *C.T. Studd's poem, "Only One Life, 'Twill Soon be Past"*

June 2
Sleepless Nights (Insomnia)

Insomnia is defined as difficulty falling or staying asleep. It is most frustrating when it happens over and over again. When I practiced internal medicine, patients described this problem frequently and indeed there are some health issues that can affect sleep. It could be something as simple as too much caffeine or lack of exercise. It could be related to depression, anxiety, or chronic illness like diabetes. My first recommendation with respect to sleep problems is to check in with your primary care doctor to determine if there is a medical cause.

If there are no medical reasons, I'd like to recommend a strategy that I find quite helpful. Quiet your mind by meditating on scripture, in particular the twenty-third Psalm. Most people know this Psalm from memory, and if you don't, it's easy to memorize. It contains very reassuring, calming and tranquil words. I've included the first few verses along with helpful thoughts to enlighten their meaning (*Psalm 23, KJV*):

"The Lord is my Shepherd; I shall not want." With God, I have everything I need. Worry keeps a lot of people up at night. Trust God. Let God do the worrying.

"God makes me lie down in green pastures." When David wrote Psalm 23 as a shepherd boy, the terrain was rocky, and the grass grew only in tiny sprigs. He led his sheep to these small sprigs, and it would be just enough to satisfy their hunger. One thing for sure, not unlike the shepherd guiding his sheep, God will guide us to the sprigs of green pastures and get us what we need right now. Picture God guiding you to green pastures.

"God leads me beside still waters." David knew his sheep did not like rough waters, so he went ahead and found waters that flowed very slowly and calmly. God knows that in the midst of the hustle and bustle of life, we need stillness in our lives to soothe and restore us. Let your body relax as you think about God's still waters setting you at ease.

"God restores my soul." The shepherd provides all the sheep needs to sustain their lives. God provides all we need to keep our souls alive. My soul is my connection to God. As Mary said, *"My soul doth magnify the*

Lord" (*Luke 1:46, KJV*). Likewise, hear David, "*My soul shall boast in the Lord*" (*Psalm 34:2, KJV*).

Read the twenty-third Psalm in its entirety until it is ingrained in your being. Then, let the words flow quietly on your heart and mind. Before long, you will be soundly asleep. Sweet dreams!

"Surely goodness and mercy shall follow me all the days of my life" (*Psalm 23:6, KJV*).

June 3
The Courage to Be

I have never been a fighter. You might say, I was a scaredy-cat growing up. When I was ten years of age, one of my classmates took advantage of my fear demons. I was walking home from school and about four hundred feet away from our doorstep when Carolyn seemed to appear out of nowhere. She used her fist to pound my back and then pulled out a wad of my hair. I used my arms to guard further hits, and the patch of my hair ended up in my hand. I finally made it home, tearful and frightened holding on to my hair. I have no idea how my mother knew where she lived, but she went to her home and discussed the situation with her mother. Carolyn didn't bother me anymore, neither did we speak again.

This incident surfaced in my thoughts while reading Rosa Parks memoir entitled *My Story*. Unlike me, Mrs. Parks was not afraid. This was evident during her childhood long before she refused to give up her seat on that Montgomery, Alabama bus. Even as a child, she was not afraid to confront Caucasian children who bullied her. In her book, she describes several encounters with bullies, but not once did she freeze. Instead, she challenged them back. Her family always tried to discourage and warn her to avoid such encounters realizing the possible consequences including being lynched. But this did not frighten her. In her memoir she writes, "I wanted to be awake to see any action."

Mrs. Rosa Parks had God-given courage most evident on December 1, 1955 when she refused to give up her seat on a segregated bus. Her actions prompted a one-year bus boycott that ended when the Supreme Court ruled segregation of buses unconstitutional.

"I have learned over the years that when one's mind is made up, this diminishes fear; knowing what must be done does away with fear."
~ Rosa Parks

June 4
The Word Becomes Flesh

In the Gospel of John, chapter 1, the apostle John writes that the Word became flesh and dwelt among us. This passage refers to Jesus. When you read the stories about Jesus and how he walked among the people, performed multiple miracles, broke down barriers between ethnic groups, it's easy to understand what the *Word becomes flesh* means.

In today's society, we associate the Word with the preached sermon, and indeed it can be healing and joyful to hear a good sermon. But the Word is more healing when we see it in action. This is why Jesus' first message in Luke says what is most important: "The Spirit of the Lord is upon me because he has anointed me to proclaim good news to the poor; He has sent me to proclaim freedom for prisoners and recovery of sight for the blind, to set the oppressed free, and to proclaim the year of the Lords favor" (*Luke 4:18-19, NIV*). After Jesus spoke these words, they came alive. He went about the countryside doing the work of God.

Through Jesus, you see good in action. He spoke powerful words of wisdom, and his words were always backed up by action. When you observe hands (Words) in action, there is no misjudging, missing the point, or misunderstanding about what it means for the Word to become flesh or what it means to be a Christian.

"I'd rather see a sermon than hear one any day! I'd rather one walk with me than merely show the way."
  ~ Edgar Guest

June 5
Where There's A Will, There's a Way

In Luke 19:1-10, Zacchaeus is described as a man of short stature, of Jewish descent, who worked for the Roman government. Zacchaeus became very rich using bully tactics to force poor people to pay taxes. Jews despised him for doing this and called him a sinner. In spite of his work, Zacchaeus heard about Jesus and wanted to see him. But being short in stature, the crowd blocked his view. Zacchaeus figured out a way to overcomes these obstacles. He ran up a tree and got a bird's eye view of Jesus. Jesus spotted Zacchaeus and told him to come down, which he did. Jesus invited himself to his home for dinner and says, "Today salvation has come to this house, because this man, too, is a son of Abraham" (*Luke 19:9, NIV*).

Zacchaeus refused to let anything hinder him from seeing Jesus. Little did he know, Jesus had already spotted him. He paid no attention to those speaking ill. He utilized a strategy to overcome the crowd and his short stature. Zacchaeus was ready to receive Jesus. "And without faith it is impossible to please God, because anyone who comes to him must believe that he exists and that he rewards those who earnestly seek him" (*Hebrews 11:6, NIV*).

Are there obstacles blocking your view of the Lord? Zacchaeus knew what he needed to do. If you have not given your heart to the Lord, God is speaking to you today. If you have a relationship with the Lord, are there things hindering your spiritual growth? A bird's eye view of Jesus has saving power, changes attitudes, behavior, and your relationship with Jesus and other people. Jesus extends to every human being the gift of eternal life.

"For the Son of Man came to seek and to save what was lost" (Luke 19:10, NIV).

June 6
What is Your Raison d'etre (Reason for Being)?

It is a blessing when you feel you are fulfilling your purpose in life. With a life purpose, you don't have to feel sorry for yourself or be jealous of what other people are doing. With a life purpose, you live with passion, joy, and confidence. How do you discover your purpose? It's not always clear, but here are three human beings who discovered their reason for being.

Dr. Martin Luther King, Jr. had a 'defining moment' that occurred just before the Montgomery Bus Boycott was to start. After a threatening phone call, fear gripped King, and he began to question his work. Then, he heard an inner voice say, "Martin Luther, stand up for righteousness! Stand up for justice! Stand up for truth!" Fear faded into the background and from then on, King moved with boldness and purpose. And the rest is history!

Mary McLeod Bethune had a vision to start a school for young women of African American descent. Although her funds were limited, she moved forward with powerful intention, perseverance, and hard work. In 1904, it started out as Daytona Educational and Industrial School. Today, it is Bethune Cookman University with an endowment of forty-eight million dollars.

John the Baptist was thought to be the Messiah. But he paid no attention to flattery. His words leave no doubt: I am here to prepare the way for him—that is all. John the Baptist had a purpose driven life, and nothing would move him away from his reason for being.

Faith in God, purpose driven vision, courage, humility, and self-confidence were evident in these three individuals, and I would venture to say is present in all people who have discovered their God-given reason for being.

"A person can receive only what is given them from heaven" (John 3:27, NIV).

June 7
Relationship Building

What causes people, communities, and nations to set up boundaries against one another? Why are differences in people's appearance,
ideology, religion, social status used to exclude, degrade, or even kill
other human beings? I can't think of a time when division did not exist
in some form or another: race relations in the United States, religious
wars between Christians and Muslims, ethnic wars in the Middle East,
Africa, Asia, and Europe, and the Holocaust in Germany.

The church is supposed to be free from discrimination but sometimes people get preferential treatment based on their social or financial status. The Bible speaks to this: "If you show special attention
to the man wearing fine clothes...have you not discriminated among
yourselves and become judges with evil thoughts" (*James 2:3-4, NIV*)?

In John 4, Jesus shows that it is time to cross boundaries, not
construct them. Enmity had existed between Samaritan and Jews for
centuries. For instance, Jews would travel extra miles to avoid going
through Samaria. Not so with Jesus. He was compelled to go and do
the unthinkable. Jesus met and talked with Samaritans. As a result,
many Samaritans were saved and received the gift of eternal life!

How often have you changed directions or looked the other way to
avoid talking to someone? How about voting against someone seeking
membership in your fraternity or sorority because they didn't meet up
to your standards or agree with your perspective?

Jesus made it possible for reconciliation to take place. He nailed
divisiveness to the cross. Every time we make or defend boundaries
between human beings, we take the nails out of Jesus' hands and give
evil the victory.

*"Some people build fences to keep people out...and other people build fences to
keep people in."*
~*August Wilson*

June 8
Humility

My husband defined humility as standing before God's divine mirror and measuring oneself against God. When I do, I am "weighed in the balance and found wanting." Let's take the letters in the word Humble and see what words help us to be more humble.

- Honesty in my inward being is what God desires from me.
- Understanding means to stand under another person and see from their perspective.
- Meek is unconditional love in action.
- Benevolence refreshes and rewards.
- Love never fails.
- Empathy is a source of grace to both the giver and recipient.

"Humility is the fear of the Lord; its wages are riches and honor and life" *(Proverbs 22:4, NIV).*

June 9
The Widowhood Effect:
What do you have to give?

There are 13.6 million widows in the United States, and every year, 700,000 more women become a widow.

Poverty is a significant problem among widows. According to the Social Security Administration, the rate of poverty among elderly widows is three to four times higher than that of their married peers. Even during biblical times, poverty and widowhood was a problem. In 2 Kings 4:1-7, there is the story about a widow whose husband had died and left she and her sons with an abundance of debt. The law required that debts be paid by selling the deceased's property and make the sons' slaves. The family would be left with nothing.

The widow seeks help from the prophet Elisha. He asks her, "What do you have in the house?" In other words, what can you use? She had only one flask of olive oil. Elisha instructed her to borrow as many empty jars from friends and neighbors as she could. Then, she was to take her one flask of oil and start pouring it into the jars. As she started pouring, the oil kept replenishing. She kept telling her sons to keep bringing the jars until they told her there were no more. Elisha told her to sell the olive oil and pay off her debts and use the rest of the money to live on.

The Almighty Sovereign God is concerned about our total welfare. God's question to this widow through the prophet Elisha was, "What do you have in your house?" In other words, what do you have to use? No matter how small it might appear, God's ability to bless you is greater than your capacity to receive what God has in store for you.

"God is able to do immeasurably more than all we ask or imagine, according to his power that is at work within us" (Ephesians 3:20, NIV).

June 10
The Heart of a Woman

Recently, I became familiar with poet, playwright, and novelist Georgia Douglas Johnson, a distinguished figure of the Harlem Renaissance. Mrs. Johnson was born twelve years after slavery ended and lived a full eighty-nine years. Here is her poem, "The Heart of a Woman." I tried to imagine her thoughts as she wrote this poem. My thoughts are found just below the poem.

> The heart of a woman goes forth with the dawn,
> As a lone bird, soft winging, so restlessly on,
> Afar o'er life's turrets and vales does it roam
> In the wake of those echoes the heart calls home.
>
> The heart of a woman falls back with the night,
> And enters some alien cage in its plight,
> And tries to forget it has dreamed of the stars
> While it breaks, breaks, breaks on the sheltering bars.

The heart of a woman respects the gift of time. She knows that time is priceless. She spends her time with God and her family first, and the rest falls into place. The heart of a woman values her oneness, being mysteriously connected into the divine web of God's universe. As she travels the journey and uncertainty of life, she walks by faith and waits patiently to hear the voice of God. The heart of a woman surrenders freely to God. Surrender brings freedom even in bondage. Her heart, protected by God, never gives up. Even when she appears to be caged in, the heart of a woman knows that a breakthrough is just a matter of time.

"You may write me down in history with your bitter twisted lies,
You may trod me in the very dirt but still, like dust, I'll rise."
~Maya Angelou

June 11
Cold Hands

(I wrote this about two years before my husband passed.)

Cecil's hands are bitterly cold, especially during the winter. Oftentimes, during a playful moment, he will partially close his hands and touch my back with fingers that literally feel like ice. Too often, I'll say to Cecil, "Don't touch me with those cold hands" and my loving husband's response is so gentle. "Just think, I have to live with them every day." We laugh, change the subject, no longer touching, and move on to something else.

A few days ago, a thought came to me about death: when the breath of life is taken away; almost immediately the entire body becomes COLD- *hands, feet, face, legs...* As I reflect on the finality of death (should Cecil precede me) when earthly interactions are no longer possible between us, I certainly wouldn't want to think that I spent any precious moments saying to my beloved, "Don't touch me with those cold hands."

If I must view Cecil in a casket and place my hands on his cold body, cold forehead, and cold hands, I want to be able to smile and remember how we embraced regardless of whatever physical changes affected our bodies (cold hands, edentulous mouth, bed sores, memory impairment) as we moved down the cycle of life.

Life is too short and beautiful to be miffed by worldly things. Every moment is precious together especially with loved ones. From this day forward, I will forget the cold hands. So, my darling Cecil, touch me with your cold hands. Let my body warm your hands. Touch my face. Touch my neck. Touch my chest. Touch me... Touch me... Touch me...

"Only the Almighty Sovereign God knows the end from the beginning and from ancient times things that are not yet done" (paraphrased Isaiah 46:10, KJV).

June 12
Double Vision

Double vision means a person sees a double image when there is only one. It is a serious medical condition and should promptly be addressed by a physician. I'm not referring to this medical condition in this reflection. I am referring to spiritual and physical eyesight in which case it is a blessing to have both.

In the Gospel of John chapter 9, Jesus heals a man who was born blind. In biblical days, persons born with a condition like blindness were said to be born in sin and not considered to have much value. As such, this man was referred to as a blind beggar. Not so in Jesus' eyes. Jesus massaged his eyes and they opened to the world. Imagine how excited and humbled he must have been to suddenly be able to see. This man's total being gradually changed as he processed what had happened to him.

The religious leaders displayed scorn and indignation. Instead of rejoicing with this man, they threw him out of the synagogue when he dared to speak as one who saw the reality of Jesus. From their distorted way of looking at reality, Jesus could not possibly be from God since he healed on the sabbath. The religious leaders could see physically but not spiritually.

Jesus finds the man who has been thrown out of the church and completes his transformation by introducing himself as the Messiah. The man believes and immediately worships Jesus. By faith, he receives his spiritual sight. Not only were this man's eyes opened physically, most importantly, they were opened spiritually. Now, he has double vision!

"I have come to judge the world. I have come to give sight to the blind and to show those who think they see, that they are blind" (John 9:39, NLT).

June 13
What's Your Reason to Love?

Two women were involved in car accidents. The first woman had just married, and a few weeks after the wedding, she has a car accident that caused severe facial disfigurement. Even though she was barely recognizable, her husband lovingly cared for her. It was her inner beauty and sweet attitude that he loved most about his wife.

The second woman who had an accident was in a long-term happy relationship, but she was not married. One day while driving alone, she had an accident that also caused severe facial disfigurement. When her boyfriend saw her after the accident, he cried and told her his feelings for her had not changed. While she was still in the hospital, he proposed to her and she accepted. About a year later, she gave birth to their beautiful daughter.

What's your reason to love? Is it a person's physical traits or socio-economic status? Is loneliness the reason? Or is it because the person looks healthy and has just received a clean bill of health? One thing for sure, life circumstances can change quickly.

These two men expressed the kind of love that comes from God. For them, appearance was not their reason to love. God's love is even more powerful, unconditional, and everlasting. It is not based on appearance, attitude, emotions, or behavior. There is nothing that can separate you from God's love.

"For I am convinced that neither death nor life, neither angels nor demons, neither present nor the future, nor any powers, neither height nor depth, nor anything else in all creation, will be able to separate us from the love of God that is in Christ Jesus our Lord" (Romans 8:38-39, NIV).

June 14
Amazing Grace

John Newton wrote "Amazing Grace" two-hundred sixty-six years ago. The story behind the hymn is uniquely linked to African American and American history because the author had been the captain of a slave ship.

Throughout his early life, Newton was described to be reckless and wretched. He trafficked thousands of men, women, and children from Africa to the US slave auction blocks. In 1748, after he nearly lost his life in a violent storm at sea, he started to change. He began to feel the malevolence of the inhumane treatment of those held in bondage. Around 1750, he started preaching and was subsequently ordained by the Anglican church. "Amazing Grace," describes his life before and after Jesus Christ touched him. As his life transformed, not only did he renounce slavery, he started working to abolish it. He wrote a treatise known as "Thoughts upon the African Slave Trade" that included eyewitness accounts of the appalling conditions on slave ships and the brutal treatment of the enslaved.

On June 26, 2015, President Barack Obama sang "Amazing Grace" at the funeral of Reverend Clementa Pinkney. He was the pastor and one of nine victims of the church massacre at Emanuel African Methodist Episcopal Church in Charleston, South Carolina. The assassin was a young white supremacist, Dylann Roof, who could easily fit the pre-conversion character of John Newton.

The story behind this great hymn is a valuable life lesson that ought to be shared each time the hymn is sung. Only God knows how many John Newtons are out there waiting for life transformation from the touch of Jesus Christ. I believe it could have made a difference in the life of Dylann Roof.

"Amazing Grace! How sweet the sound, That saved a wretch like me! I once was lost, but now I'm found, was blind but now I see."
~John Newton

June 15
Faith Versus Reason

Faith is the substance of things hoped for, the evidence of things not seen (*Hebrews 11:1, KJV*). Faith begins the Christian journey. Our walk is not totally blind. By faith, we are guided by the light of God's Word, "a lamp unto my feet, and a light unto my path" (*Psalm 119:105, KJV*). By faith, we receive blessed assurances from the Bible, messages through the preached word, and divine blessings along the way.

By faith, we willingly do fulfilling and joyful work for God. When sadness and trouble enters our lives (and it will), by faith we go to God in prayer and thanksgiving. It is our faith in God that brings comfort in the midst of sorrow. By faith, we believe that God will make a way when one doesn't seem possible.

Faith can be easily unsettled by reason. That is what makes us human beings. The same God who accepts our faith has given us a free will that oftentimes overshadows our faith. We start trying to reason things out.

In a society filled with capitalism and its rewards of jobs, houses, bank accounts, investments, cars, bills, bills, and more bills, reason trumps faith. Case-in-point, the stock market was volatile the last three months of 2018. As a retiree, with retirement funds in the stock market, I found myself panicking as the market took huge drops day after day. I made some personal decisions which helped to reduce my anxiety. But as I looked at myself in the mirror, I realized how reason and fear made my faith appear weak even while spending thirty to forty minutes in prayer and meditation every day.

Here I stood, blessed beyond measure while some people cannot make ends meet from one day to the next. Material things weakened my faith. I realize that as long as there are earthly necessities with financial ties linked to a national and global market, there are going to be stressors. No amount of preparation can block this from happening.

I pray that the next time the storms start to rage, and the world (and me) is being tossed about like a ship, my heart will not faint but speak and act like I am victoriously confident by faith that "My father is rich in houses and lands, and the wealth of the world is in God's hands." (John B Summer)

"On Christ, the solid rock, I stand; All other ground is sinking sand, All other ground is sinking sand."
~Edward Mote

June 16
Afraid to Ask: Fear of the Unknown

"...The Son of Man is going to be betrayed into the hands of men. But they did not understand what this meant. It was hidden from them, so that they could not grasp it, and they were afraid to ask him about it"(Luke 9:44b-45, NIV).

Have you ever felt something wasn't quite right? Something is bothering you in your body, at work, or in a relationship. Yet, you fear going to the doctor, addressing the work-related issue, or asking hard questions to your partner. You're afraid to ask, prefer not to know, or hope the concern will just go away.

You have a vision to do something extraordinary. You're afraid to step out for fear of being rejected. A college student avoids asking questions in class or even making an appointment with the professor. He is afraid he will appear inarticulate. In each of these instances, there is fear of the unknown.

If you had a crystal ball, would you want to see your future? Would that erase your fear, or would you spend your time trying to control the outcome? While Jesus knew his future, the events still had to happen. Jesus had the power to control his outcome, but that was not a part of God's plan. He walked by faith and so must we. And it was far from easy. Still, he was confident that God's plan was best and would bring him through.

God has a plan for your life. You don't have to be afraid of what you might discover along your life journey. God's plans for you are for your good. God's gift of life will have struggles. Struggle is one of the by-products of being alive. But as your faith grows in God and in yourself, you'll come to understand that God's plan is better and bigger than any uncertainty, concern, or obstacles that you will ever face on this earth.

"I know the plans I have for you declares the Lord, plans to prosper you and not to harm you, plans to give you hope and a future" (Jeremiah 29:11, NIV).

June 17
Forgiveness Is the Pathway to Love and Healing

On this date in 2015, a twenty-one-year-old man walked into a Bible Study group at Mother Emanuel AME Church in Charleston, South Carolina. He was graciously welcomed. At the end of the benediction, he murdered nine of the twelve participants. He stated he wanted to start a race war.

Two days after the massacre, it was reported that the survivors had found in their heart to forgive the shooter. A question raised by many was this, "How could they find the power to forgive such a cruel and heartless act?" I found an interview they did in the fall of 2018, where they discussed their feelings about forgiveness. The interview was entitled "Finding Forgiveness."

The survivors gave responses that are instructive and powerful to all of us as we face discord and even hatred in the United States. First of all, they are not living in denial or trying to be saints. They are real human beings:

"Somedays you can conquer the world, other days you just want the day to hurry up and go away."

"You know you always want to forgive because that is what we are taught, but sometimes I teeter totter."

"When I think about the father-daughter dance my girls will miss—daddy won't be there to walk them down the aisle. But then I know the right thing to do is forgive."

The survivors had a faith in God long before this merciless act. Why do I say this? They shared how they saw God's hand moving in the midst of terror:

"The lights in the room were off, but there were two different lights shining— the laser on the gun and the other light like you were in a different world, like the Twilight zone. I have no doubt that God was in the room with us."

Like Peter and the disciples seeing Jesus in the midst of the storm, people with strong faith see God in the midst of life's storms. Their struggles with the loss of loved ones led to godly answers:

"I said to myself, Felicia has lost a son. If she can forgive, why are you so hardhearted you can't forgive?"

"Forgiveness is like you think you are letting someone else off the hook. But you are actually letting yourself off the hook. Because if you keep it, there is no healing. "You have to love each other. That is the second commandment."

Most people will not experience trauma and violence inside a church sanctuary. God spoke through all of them. It was their immediate desire to follow God's command to forgive that was most humbling. I appreciated their honesty, willingness to share, wisdom, and most of all their faith in God. Their expressions of faith are a testament of the love of God manifested even in the darkest hours of life.

"Darkness cannot drive out darkness; only light can do that. Hate cannot drive out hate; only love can do that."
 ~ Dr. Martin Luther King, Jr.

June 18
Touch Down Every Morning

When I was in high school fifty-five years ago, one hour of exercise every day was a school requirement. During physical exercise class, we changed into matching white gym apparel and started warm-up exercises to inspiring music: *"Touch down every morning. Not just now and then. Give that chicken fat back to the chicken and don't be chicken again. No... don't be chicken again."* Then, the girls would participate in a variety of sports. I remember volleyball because it was a competitive team sport, and I found it exhilarating.

One hour of physical exercise every day at school helped to strengthen our minds, bodies, and spirits. Not only was it a break from the rigor of classwork, it taught us the value of exercise. It gave us a chance to play, and it kept our blood pressures, heart rate, and respiratory rates in a normal range while keeping obesity to a minimum. After one hour of physical exercise, we were ready to tackle the rest of the school day with vigor and vitality.

The health benefits of exercise are better known today than they were when I was in high school and include increased concentration, improved healthy growth and development, improved self-esteem, and opportunities to socialize.

Is exercise a part of your regular routine? If yes, keep up the great work. If no, start with small goals and gradually build up. If you have some physical limitations, consider chair exercises. I found some chair exercises on television that helped me. What motivates you to get up and start moving? That's what you should do. How does exercise make you feel? Remember, physical exercise helps to reduce stress. Make a list of how you feel after exercising. Review that list every day.

"In my judgment, physical fitness is basic to all forms of excellence and to a strong, confident nation."
~ *Robert Kennedy*

June 19
The Right Place at the Right Time for Healing

I love the story in Luke 13:10-13, where Jesus breaks customs, traditions, and laws to heal a crippled woman on the sabbath in the synagogue. For eighteen years, she was not able to stand straight and had
to walk bent over. Some women develop curvature of the spine from
a condition known as osteoporosis. In this illness, the bones become
fragile from hormone loss, calcium, and vitamin D. My medical knowledge tells me this is probably what this woman was suffering from.

This poor lady was weak and frail but still managed to come to
church Sunday after Sunday. The compassionate eyes of Jesus observes
her frail condition and beckons her to come to him. When he touches
her, she stands up straight and immediately begins to praise God!

Instead of rejoicing at her healing, the leader of the synagogue
becomes indignant that Jesus would heal on the sabbath. Jesus' answer
shamed them when he reminds them of how they provide care to their
animals if the need arose on any day including the sabbath. In other
words, is an animal more valuable to you than a human being?

A new decade is here. Who gets medical care in our society? Why
are some people indignant about the idea of healthcare for all? What
do your eyes see and how does your heart feel when you think of people going without needed healthcare? When Jesus saw the helpless, the
blind, and the sick, he moved and acted with compassion.

*"We must learn to regard people less in the light of what they do or omit to do,
and more in the light of what they suffer."*
~ Dietrich Bonhoeffer

June 20
God's Divine Table

"If you're not at the table, then you are on the menu."
~*Anonymous*

I was listening to a progressive radio talk show one morning and heard a politician use the catchy phrase, "If you're not at the table, then you're on the menu." The moderator had raised the question about jobs. The quote is known to mean if you're not represented at the decision-making table, you get left out, or you get eaten up.

The politician was referring to the limited voice that union workers have at the decision-making table. Who is there to negotiate the working person's dilemma? Although there are more jobs, the standard of living has declined. Wages are less. Health care costs are increasing. People have to work multiple jobs to make ends meet. Family time is markedly reduced. The most important value—time spent with family especially children is lacking due to long work hours. It was apparent that the radio talk show host and the prominent spokesperson wanted to do what was just but neither of them had the solution. How do you negotiate nutrition, housing, and your health?

I couldn't help but think what matters is who's at this table from a God-fearing perspective. Psalm 23:5 says *"Thou preparest a table before me in the presence of mine enemies."* For the Christian believer, we must never stop believing that God is always present at the table. What is needed at the decision-making table are people God can use to move the moral universe toward social justice.

At the table should be those with the boldness and brilliance of Dr. Martin Luther King, Jr. who speak in defense of the have-nots and guard their destiny. At the table should be people with the spirit of Esther, not afraid to use their influence to ensure that justice is served. At the table should be people with the spirit of Harriet Tubman who have been successful but are not satisfied until the standard of living is raised for the masses. At the table should be people with the spirit of Rosa Parks who got tired of hearing 'not yet' and decided to take a stand. Most of all, at the table emanating from all of them is the love of Jesus Christ who died that we all might have abundant life.

The table has been set. The host of the table is Jesus Christ. Once enough of us grasp the truth that everyone is invited to this table and that there is more than enough to go around, the standard of living will rise for everyone!

"The thief comes only to steal and kill and destroy; I have come that they may have life and have it to the full" (John 10:10, NIV).

June 21
Irreplaceable- A Reflection Especially for Men

Men and boys, you are God's chosen vessels—chosen to protect—chosen to teach—chosen to provide—chosen to be helpmates—chosen to serve and worship God in every aspect of your life. No one can take your place. It is not easy assuming this God-given responsibility. But know this, God who is all faithful will supply you with everything you need for the job you have to do. If you don't do it, it will not get done.

Every creature of God has a unique contribution to make toward building the community of God. God came in Christ Jesus to save the whole world, to redeem the entire human race, and to affirm the hope that the human family can indeed become a genuine community.

Our personal, family, church, community, nation, and the whole world will move to a higher level of existence when we value the life of every human being. One of the hallmarks of the ministry of Jesus was that he never lost sight of what his disciples could become. He knew they had a specific job to do. He had to get them ready. So, he encouraged them by demonstrating through his life how to do this great work. I believe Jesus expects us to do the same. It's not easy, but it is the way Christians are to live.

Thank you, God, for the gift of manhood. You identified wholly with men when you sent your son in the likeness of a man to be our savior. You implanted in men the seed to produce life without which life cannot continue. Not unlike Adam, Moses, David, and Solomon in the Bible, sometimes men make huge mistakes even in the midst of a life also filled with good. But the good is what keeps life moving. Thank you, God for providing unending unconditional love to our men and boys. In Jesus name, AMEN.

June 22
Starting Afresh

Monday *is an awesome day to start afresh. Activate the letters in the word* Monday *to make it a great day!*

If it's a Monday when you read this, that's great. If it's not a Monday, set it aside for Mondays or read it on any day you choose.

May God grant you your heart's desire and fulfill all your plans for today.

Once in a lifetime. Today will not return. Make it a great day.

Nothing is impossible with God (*Luke 1:37, NLT*).

Declare war on doubt and dare to believe. Toss doubt in the garbage can.

And focus your attention on today because this will be the best day of your life.

Yesterday is over and worrying about tomorrow blinds you for what God has in store for you today.

"The best preparation for tomorrow is doing your best today."
~ H. Jackson Brown, Jr.

June 23
Overcoming Billows of Gloom

"I would have despaired unless I had believed that I would see the goodness of the LORD In the land of the living" (Psalm 27:13, NASB).

People describe depression and anxiety in many different ways: I had grown weary. I am starting to feel uneasy. I am scared. My heart is pounding. My courage has dwindled. I feel anxious. I am depressed.

The mind is a powerful and unique part of our being. Thinking, perception, memory, intellect and a thousand thoughts cross our minds on a regular basis. It is natural for humans to be at risk for feeling fainthearted.

There are ranges or levels of emotional upset. And on any given day, most people have felt a little sad or anxious that passes almost as quickly as it started. After prayer and meditation, or hearing an encouraging word or cheerful song, doing a good deed, watching a spellbinding movie, or receipt of an unexpected gift, suddenly the uneasy feelings vanish.

When I practiced internal medicine, I reminded those under my care about the mind, body, and spirit connection. The best health outcomes occur when all parts are being cared for and in balance. Symptoms of anxiety and depression include feelings of impending doom, helplessness, heart palpitations, weight loss or weight gain, difficulty sleeping, and feelings of sadness. If feelings of emotional stress persist, professional help may be needed.

Depression and anxiety are common. They can occur separately or together. They have nothing to do with you being weak in strength or faith. They are part of being human and when necessary can be treated with medications and/or counseling.

"Just when the caterpillar thought the world was ending, he turned into a butterfly."
~ *Anonymous Proverb*

June 24
Looking Radiant

"Those who look to God are radiant; their faces are never covered with shame"
(paraphrased Psalm 34:5, NIV).

One of the most beautiful sights to behold is to witness a congregation worshiping the Almighty Sovereign God. Some have closed eyes or tears streaming down. Others have smiles as wide as their faces. Their arms swing and bodies move to the beat of the music as if the whole thing has been choreographed. Others raise their arms in praise and thanksgiving. From an outsider looking in, it might appear that these people don't have a care in the world. But that's not the case. In spite of what your eyes may see, these people have personal stories that are hard to imagine. They battle with disappointments, shame, obstacles, failures, illness, and death. But they don't look like what they have been through or what they are facing at this moment in time. What accounts for their appearance?

First of all, their beautiful appearance is not the result of an excellent hair stylist, lustrous eyelashes, dyed hair, high fashion clothes, and the gift of rhythm. No doubt, these features make people look good. But these beautiful countenances and harmonious body movements come from the Holy Spirit dwelling within.

The Holy Spirit dwells within believers every day. In their daily lives, they have seen God open or close doors, whichever was needed. And their faith experience led them to believe that God would continue to do the same today and tomorrow. On Sunday morning, the saints commune together. They look good with heads held high to God. They expect great things in the worship experience and in their lives. "Those who look to him for help will be radiant with joy; no shadow of shame will darken their faces" (*Psalm 34:5, NLT*).

"But thou, O Lord, art a shield for me; my glory, and the lifter of my head"
(Psalm 3:3, KJV).

June 25
Telling Your Story

Every human being has a life story. Whether we realize it or not, we tell our story every hour we live. Although our story is guided by our beliefs, family upbringing, politics, community, and nation, in my opinion it is the choices we make that reveals the most about one's storyline. And that is the good news. We can change our story at any time by making different choices.

In Deuteronomy 30:1-20, Moses gives his farewell address to the Israelites. He makes a final and earnest appeal to the people of God to change the direction of their lives, to change their story. At the time of the address, the people were in a quandary. They had already wandered in the desert for forty years and were now in exile. In spite of all the blessings and divine miracles, they were still unable to grasp and accept the power of God over their lives. Now, they were feeling hopeless, disconsolate, and fearful. Moses knew what they needed and appealed to their best nature. Hear him as he speaks.

"Now, listen! I am giving you a choice between prosperity and disaster, between life and death" (*Deuteronomy 30:15, NLT*). Choose to love, obey, and commit your life to God. He challenged them to make a choice between life and death, between blessings and curses. Walk out on faith. Hold to God's unchanging hand. Allow God to be the center of your life.

How central is God in your life story? Have you placed God in a category? —Sunday is for God. Weekdays are for work and school. Evenings are for happy hours, TV, social media, and politics. Saturdays are for shopping, cleaning, and partying. Or, is God more holistic—shaping and guiding all of your life and family decisions? Who is responsible for your life story?

"This is my story, this is my song, praising my savior all the day long; This is my story, this is my song, praising my savior all the day long."
~*Fanny J. Crosby*

June 26
Sisterhood and Friendship

Today is my sister's birthday, a great time to ponder about meaningful moments in our past and present. One such time was my sister's wedding in 1968. Cassandra was twenty-one years of age. She has now been married fifty-one years.

My sister's wedding was an exciting time, not just for her but for our entire family and friends. It was a major community event and turned out perfect. She was marrying a physician, which seemed to arouse everyone's interest. Bridesmaids flew in from across the country. Multiple bridal showers were given in her honor, and the wedding gifts were innumerable. The reception was held in our remodeled home in the comfort of central air conditioning, which we added for the wedding. No one would have guessed that we were a family with limited assets. Our God focus, family unit, cultural, and community ties added value that far exceeded monetary value.

Although there was an air of expectancy about the upcoming wedding, I experienced a high level of anxiety. My sister and I grew up very close even amid sibling rivalry. We shared the same bedroom and slept together in a double bed until we left for college. We wore similar clothes, took dancing and swimming lessons together. When she and Alan flew off to New York City for their honeymoon, I wondered what would happen to our relationship.

Indeed, our sisterhood weathered the change. Back then, social media technology was not even thought of. But we stayed connected through visits, phone calls, and old-fashioned letter writing. I watched my sister mature into a brilliant linguist and lover of the arts. We celebrated the gift of their daughter (Ayanna) and the many commemorations that followed as she too grew into adulthood.

Not only are we sisters, we are best friends. She has always been there for me. While my mother still lived, each summer we all spent a week on Amelia Island. We continued this tradition after Mama passed.

We have long telephone conversations almost every day. Thanks to Ayanna, we use our smart phones and watches to share exercise data and send fun congratulatory messages when we reach our daily exercise goals.

My worries were for naught. Through sickness, joy, heartache, death, and celebration, we have been together to support each other. I am so thankful to God for the gift of sisterhood and friendship.

"Sister is probably the most competitive relationship within the family, but once the sisters are grown, it becomes the strongest relationship."
~ *Margaret Mead*

June 27
Blessed Assurance

"Oh, what a happy soul I am although I cannot see. I am resolved that in this world contented I will be. How many blessings I enjoy that other people don't; to weep inside because I'm blind I cannot, nor I won't."
~Fanny J. Crosby

The above poem was written by a blind six-year-old girl named Fanny Crosby. She and her mother had just been told by an eye specialist that she would never be able to see. As an infant in 1821, she developed an eye infection and was treated by a charlatan posing as a doctor. He placed a harsh substance on her eyes causing blindness. Although her physical sight was lost, she gained miraculous spiritual insight that to this day comforts Christians around the world.

Ms. Crosby had an unusual memory. She was able to listen and commit to memory many books in the Bible. She used her familiarity with scriptures and love of nature to write poems and hymns effortlessly. It is reported that by 1906, hymnals with her music sold over fifteen million copies across the world. She donated all her royalties to a collection of charities and seminaries and died with only two thousand dollars in her estate.

In 1873, something miraculous happened. Her best friend played a beautiful melody on the piano but could not think of lyrics to match. Ms. Crosby wrote the words and entitled it "Blessed Assurance," the well-known church hymn still sung regularly by choirs and congregations. The words are powerful, soul stirring, and filled with expectancy.

"Blessed Assurance, Jesus is mine! O what a foretaste of glory divine! Heir of salvation, purchase of God, born of His spirit, washed in His blood. This is my story. This is my song, praising my savior all the day long."
~Fanny J. Crosby and Phoebe Knapp

June 28
Shield of Prayer

Jesus' disciples asked Jesus to teach them to pray. Jesus used the Lord's prayer as his guide. The Lord's prayer teaches us how to live the best possible life: (1) a life that respects and fears God, (2) a life that desires God's will, (3) a life that asks God for its daily sustenance, (4) a life that asks and gives forgiveness, and (5) a life that seeks deliverance from evil. In other words, prayer must become alive in our daily living. Prayer is a powerful activity, and even though it feels like there are a hundred competing priorities, taking time to pray is a wise choice.

How do we know that God hears us? Our faith in God assures us. In Psalm 5:1-2, David begins a prayer, "Give ear to my words, O Lord, consider my meditation. Hearken to the voice of my cry, my King and my God; for unto you will I pray." In one breath, David ask three times for God's ear. He does not ask for any material items, just for God's attention.

Is there a best time to pray? Anytime with the Lord is good, but peace and quiet helps. In this Psalm, David appears to believe that God will hear him in the morning, "My voice shalt thou hear in the morning, O Lord; in the morning will I direct my prayer unto you and will look up" (*Psalm 5:3 KJV*).

Prayer is a good time to pour out adoration. Prayer that includes praise and adoration for God's faithfulness, mercy, and grace is rewarding. God does inhabit the praise of His people, but it helps us the most.

How do we continue a meaningful prayer life in this fast-paced society? The more you commune with God, the more your faith strengthens. The more your faith strengthens, the more you want to commune with God. Communion with God leads to blessings, favor, direction, and protection.

"For thou Lord will bless the righteous, with favor will thou compass her as with a shield" (Psalm 5:12, KJV).

June 29
The Humanity of Jesus (by Cecil Wayne Cone PhD)

I found this writing among my late husband's papers. Please allow me to share it with you. Cecil was a theologian, philosopher and preacher. In this writing, his focus is on Jesus's humanity.

Often the divinity of our Lord is emphasized in such a manner that his humanity is diminished. However, our salvation is dependent upon both. Jesus's divinity is his point of contact with God, but his humanity is his point of contact with people, with us. As Christ, Jesus is God. As Jesus, he is a human being.

Jesus came into the world as a baby born to a very poor dark-skinned unwed peasant girl. He entered the world at the very bottom of the social ladder. At this level, his humanity left no one out.

He demonstrated his humanity in the garden of Gethsemane, a time when far-reaching decisions had to be made; the cross and all its shame are clearly revealed; "He began to be troubled and deeply distressed" (Mark 14:33, NIV). He was filled with horror, appalled and agitated; and for a moment he shrinks and hesitates: "Father, if you are willing, take this cup from me; yet not my will, but yours be done" (Luke 22:42, NIV). It is only by earnest prayer that his will is brought in complete harmony with the Father's.

Nowhere does the humanity of Jesus come through more than on the Cross. There is a man on that cross. Six hours have passed, his closest friends, his disciples are nowhere to be found. Death is staring him in the face. The state of the physical pain is enough, but the state of psychological pain, the emotional trauma is unbearable. His is a very lonely existence. It is as though God has turned away from Jesus as he cries, "My God, my God, why have you forsaken me (Matthew 27:46, NIV)? His cry is a very human cry, a cry of loneliness and despair. This is the humanity of Jesus.

"But he was wounded for our transgressions. He was bruised for our iniquities; The chastisement of our peace was upon him. And by his stripes we are healed" (Isaiah 53:5, KJV).

June 30
Hidden Messages

Time and again, when Jesus shared his salvation message with people it was misunderstood. People used human reasoning when listening to him. Jesus told Nicodemus, "Unless you are born again, you cannot see the kingdom of God" (*John 3:3, NIV*). Nicodemus thought the idea of returning to his mother's womb sounded ridiculous.

The crowd that Jesus fed was not able to comprehend Jesus' declaration, "I am the bread of life" (*John 6:35 NIV*). Their stomachs were full, and that's all that mattered. When he invited the Samaritan woman to drink from the well of living water, she took it to mean she would never have to return to the physical well to draw water again. When human beings search for God using human reasoning instead of faith, they miss the message.

In Luke chapter 9, Jesus calls a man to be his disciple. The man agrees but first wants to return home to bury his father. Jesus answered, "Let the dead bury the dead" (*Luke 9:60, KJV*). I've heard some say that Jesus was a bit harsh to this man. The text is not clear if the man's father had died. However, for centuries, it was considered a sacred duty to bury one's father. So, if his father was dead, why wasn't the man there tending to this sacred duty? Further, Jesus is omniscient and knows the man's heart and the father's present situation.

Today is the day that the Lord has spoken. Time is of the essence. Don't waste the opportunity when you hear Jesus call or knock on the door of your heart. Tomorrow may well be too late. When the heart is open to God, the message becomes clear.

"You may delay, but time will not."
~ *Benjamin Franklin*

July 1
Gratitude for Food

Gracious Lord, make us truly thankful for the food we are about to receive. This is a common prayer believers recite before a meal. What does it mean to be truly thankful for a meal? My parents used to tell us to eat everything on our plate because there were so many people starving in the world. My friends shared how their parents gave them similar advice. As a young person, this made no sense to me. How could eating food on my plate help someone else who was starving? Typical young people thoughts...

There are people with plenty of food and money but are unable to eat because of illness. Either they have lost their appetite for food, can only eat a tiny amount at any given time, or are unable to swallow food or liquids. During the time I practiced medicine, I had the privilege of caring for a very nice lady who had been treated for throat cancer. The surgery removed the cancer, but she was no longer able to swallow. While she was healthy otherwise, she required a feeding tube in her stomach only allowing liquid nutritional supplements. She would never be able to enjoy the taste of food again.

Forty-two million people struggle with hunger in the United States. Of this number, thirteen million are children and more than five million are senior citizens. While my parents and other elders did not know these facts, they may have experienced hunger growing up, knew someone with a major illness that affected their ability to swallow, or perhaps just had godly wisdom about the problem of hunger in the world.

Having a warm meal is a blessing that should not be taken for granted. So, this prayer about gratitude becomes more meaningful when you reflect on food from a global perspective.

Gracious Lord make us truly thankful for the food we are about to receive, for the nourishment of our bodies, for Christ sake. AMEN

July 2
Believe in Yourself

"When the going gets tough, the tough get going"
~*Joseph P. Kennedy*

The Almighty Sovereign God gives human beings a powerful will that we sometimes use haphazardly. Here's the story of a lady who used her will and determination to improve her health.

A seventy-two-year-old widow (I'll call her Mrs. C) was diagnosed with diabetes at the age of sixty-two. At the time, she weighed 250 pounds, had high blood pressure, and severe arthritis in both knees. She required pills and insulin for diabetes and pills for blood pressure. Because of severe knee pain, both knee joints were replaced. After surgery, she developed blood clots in both legs and a stomach ulcer. She gradually recovered and acknowledged her weight to be a major contributor to poor health.

Mrs. C used her God given will to make changes. She joined a nationally acclaimed weight management program and used her stationary bicycle to exercise regularly to gradually lose weight. It was a slow process but over a four-year period, not only did she reach her goal weight of 165 pounds, but her blood pressure and diabetes came under excellent control.

Under my guidance as her physician, she no longer required blood pressure or diabetes medications including insulin. Until I retired from practicing medicine, I was able to observe her health as she moved into her fifth year of success. Of course, there will always be the challenge of making unhealthy choices, but now she is determined to apply her innate capabilities to healthy living.

"Decision is the spark that ignites action. Until a decision is made, nothing happens...Decision is the courageous facing of issues, knowing that if they are not faced, problems will remain forever unanswered."
~*Wilfred A. Peterson*

July 3
Celebrating the Success of Others
(Matthew 20:1-16)

Have you ever thought you worked harder than someone else but received less reward?

The Lord appeared to a hardworking farmer and granted him three wishes with the condition that the Lord would give his neighbor double his gifts. The farmer agreed. His first wish was for a hundred cattle. Immediately, he received a hundred cattle, and he was overjoyed until he saw that his neighbor received two hundred. Next, he wished for a hundred acres of land, and again he was filled with joy until he saw that his neighbor received two hundred acres. Rather than celebrating God's goodness, the farmer felt jealous and slighted because his neighbor had received more than he. Finally, he stated his third wish, that God would strike him blind in one eye. And God wept.

One thing for sure, we don't know why life appears to go better for someone else. It's better to trust God and lean not to our own understanding. What makes it easier for us to look at someone else's misery and say, "Except for the grace of God, it could be me." In those instances, we choose to feel grateful. The same way we look at someone else's misery and feel grateful, we should look at someone else's blessings and celebrate with them. Gratitude is the best response. Gratitude always changes one's response to the experience. Gratitude takes away feelings of resentment and removes chips off shoulders.

"Everything comes from God alone. Everything lives by God's power. And, everything is for God's glory." (Romans 11:36, TLB)

July 4
A Healthy Soul

It is well with my soul
~ Horatio G. Spafford

The story behind the great hymn "It is well with my Soul" demonstrates the power of grace in weakness. The author, Horatio G. Spafford was born in 1828. Mr. Spafford was a successful lawyer, wealthy, highly intelligent, and deeply spiritual. He was married and had four daughters. Although he lived in Chicago, most of his time was spent around the world supporting renowned evangelists. In 1871, the Chicago fire destroyed his real estate and landholdings. To ease some of the anxiety from the devastation, he sent his wife and four daughters on a European cruise liner headed for Great Britain. The ship was struck by another vessel causing their ship to sink and all four daughters drowned, only his wife survived the horrific ordeal.

Mr. Spafford left by ship to join his wife, and the story goes that as he passed the area where their daughters had drowned, he wrote these words to express his grief, "When sorrows like sea billows roll, whatever my lot God has taught me to say, it is well, it is well, with my soul." A few years later, the Almighty Sovereign God blessed the Spafford's with two more daughters, and their dream of visiting the Holy Land became a reality. While there, they decided to live in Jerusalem and establish an American Colony which cared for the sick and destitute.

In the hour of trial, a spirit of wavering sometimes tries to grip our being. But as we hold to God's unchanging hand, God's peace fills us. Before long, we can sing with Mr. Spafford, "It is well with my soul."

"I would go to the deeps a hundred times to cheer a downcast spirit. It is good for me to have been afflicted, that I might know how to speak a word in season to one that is weary."
~ Charles Spurgeon

July 5
Attitude Determines Altitude

"For there is nothing either good or bad but thinking makes it so."
~William Shakespeare

James Baldwin, the late prolific writer, playwright, poet, and social activist was once asked to interpret the lyrics of a song written in 1927 by Bessie Smith. Ms. Smith was the most popular American blues singer in the 1920's and 1930's. Although it is not mentioned in the song, she appears to have survived a major hurricane that demolished her home, rendering her homeless. Thousands of others lost their homes as well. Ms. Smith sings the blues, but according to Mr. Baldwin, there is a message of hope in her words:

"What struck me is her singing [as you say], about a disaster which almost killed her, and [yet] she accepted it and was going beyond it." In other words, the starting place [after a misfortune] begins with your perception of your circumstances. Bessie Smith says there are important actions that must be taken to move forward in a crisis: observation and acceptance. She observes her situation (my house is toppled) and accepts what she cannot change (it is not livable).

How you think about experiences determines how we move forward. Will the event paralyze your thinking? Or, will you use the crisis as an opportunity to do something different? Once you come to terms with reality, you are ready to think beyond your present circumstances. When this happens, you will be able to see the ocean of possibilities in God's universe.

"God grant me the serenity
To accept the things I cannot change;
Courage to change the things I can;
And wisdom to know the difference."
~Reinhold Niebuhr

July 6
Forgiveness and Public Platforms

One of the most powerful stories in the New Testament is about a woman caught in adultery. It is a story about judgment and forgiveness and as such never grows old. Her accusers (religious men) use a public platform to judge, shame, and castigate her. They justified their actions based on the Mosaic Law.

Jesus does not respond to their hate filled voices. Instead, he takes two actions: 1) He challenges those without sin to throw the first stone. Each one of them walk sheepishly away. 2) He offers grace and mercy to a human being about to be cut off from society, and she gladly accepts.

In today's society, social media is a huge public platform. It is said that the pen is mightier than the sword, and on social media, the pen has impaled many individuals to tatters for human weaknesses we all have. Like the religious zealots, the loudest and harshest voices on social media are voices of condemnation.

How do you respond to stories on social media that expose the frailties of human beings? Would you use a public platform to exploit another's weakness, justify your political view or berate a religious perspective? I love the response Jesus gave. While she stood exposed on a public platform, he treated her with human dignity and respect.

"If you can't say something nice, don't say nothing at all."
~ Thumper's rule

July 7
An Affirmation for Children and Adolescents

There is a parable in the book of Judges about a young man named Abimelech (uh-BIHM-uh-lehk), one of the many sons of Gideon.

While the rest of Gideon's sons were from his many wives, Abimelech was Gideon's son by his concubine. Abimelech was ashamed of his mother and hated his half-brothers. His thinking became so distorted and evil he arranged for his half-brothers to be killed and then made himself king. God intervened causing the people to revolt against Abimelech. His tumultuous and stormy reign lasted a mere three years. He died when a woman threw a deadweight and crushed in his skull. As Dr. Martin Luther King, Jr. said, "Hate begets hate; violence begets violence."

How often we find ourselves trying to be different from who God created us to be? [My friend's mother has it altogether. My family doesn't fit in. My hair is not right. My skin color is too dark. My lips are too big or too small. My nose is too wide.] And sometimes we harm others with words and even weapons to get what we think will make us happy and more powerful.

Abimelech felt he had no purpose in life, so he tried to create one by killing others. When you know your mission and purpose in life, you won't spend time finding ways to destroy others, so you can get to the top.

"In the long run, we shape our lives, and we shape ourselves. The process never ends until we die. And the choices we make are ultimately our own responsibility."
~ Eleanor Roosevelt

July 8
Imagination is Everything

"Imagination is everything. It is the preview of life's coming attractions."
~Albert Einstein

Whatever the mind can conceive, and the heart truly believes, under God you can achieve, if you are willing to work for it. This was the mantra my husband expressed to the faculty and students at a college aspiring accreditation for the first time in its 113-year history. He was appointed college president to accomplish this mission. The bankrupt college had been written off as a hopeless case and nothing short of a miracle would enable the institution to become accredited.

My husband rolled up his sleeves and went to work. Before long, the attitude on the campus changed to a "believe mode" mindset. Full accreditation required hiring professors with terminal degrees (PhDs). Using his gift of persuasion, he hired professors who were willing to take huge cuts in salaries and join in the college's mission. As a result, the college met the standard for the number of professors needed with terminal degrees.

The college needed a well-equipped library. He convinced a contractor to renovate a 113-year-old building scheduled to be demolished. After renovation, the building housed the new library - another standard met. The college needed 50,000 volumes of books added to the library. Mission was accomplished.

Not only did this change the attitude on campus, but the civic and business community became involved helping to raise funds needed to assure the accrediting board of community support and financial stability. Two years after my husband arrived at the college, it was fully accredited as a four-year college by the Southern Association of Colleges and Schools for the first time in its history.

"Whatever the mind can conceive and believe, the mind can achieve."
~Oliver Napoleon Hill

July 9
Empathy

In the 1990's, I was a fitness fanatic and spent an excessive amount of time at the gym. I wanted my patients to spend time exercising and tried to convince them how it would improve their health. Most of them always had an excuse, but I wasn't buying any of them. Many of them probably would have come around if I hadn't pushed so hard. One day, I got a dose of my own medicine. I developed an overactive thyroid gland. The condition affected my strength and heart. This limited my ability and desire to exercise. I became more empathic to the physical challenges that affect one's ability to exercise.

When office visits occurred near a death anniversary, my patients often used up their time sharing memories. Before my own losses, I was ready to move away from the topic. After my losses, I felt what they felt. Empathy or compassion is a powerful virtue because it can lead to healing demonstrated best by Jesus. "When the Lord saw her, his heart overflowed with compassion. Don't cry, he said" (*Luke 7:13, NLV*). Then, he healed her son.

What is the difference between sympathy and empathy? Sympathy sparks us to administer "thoughts and prayers." It is short-lived. A person who demonstrates empathy understands the emotions of another person and feels what others feel.

Jesus was always sensitive to the plight of others. He was perfectly able to do this; "Because God's children are human beings—made of flesh and blood—the Son also became flesh and blood" (*Hebrews 2:14, NLT*). He understands our weaknesses and feels our pain. He used gifts of humanity (kindness, benevolence) to lift the spirt of the disheartened, heal the sick, empower the weak, and feed the hungry. We too have these same gifts. It is up to us to use them.

"Share each other's burdens, and in this way obey the law of Christ. If you think you are too important to help someone, you are only fooling yourself. You are not that important" (Galatians 6: 2-3, NLT).

July 10
Prevention: A Fence or Ambulance?

One of my favorite poems is "The Ambulance Down in the Valley," also known as "Avoiding Accidents at a Cliff." It was written by Joseph Malins in 1895. In his poem, Malins argues persuasively for applying a proactive approach rather than a rescue approach to life's circumstances. Malins writes, "Why not put a fence around the edge of a cliff rather than have an ambulance in the valley?" In other words, why not aim for prevention rather than spend time and money repairing consequences that result from the lack of prevention. Take a look at both approaches with respect to colon cancer.

The Proactive Approach (The Fence around the Cliff)

It is well documented that screening for colon cancer saves lives. Screening allows physicians to find cancers or precancerous polyps before symptoms start. The costs of screening are far less than the cost of treating cancer. Moreover, the cost of treating cancer at an early stage is less costly than when diagnosed at a later stage.

Additionally, there are lifestyle factors that help lower one's risk for colon cancer. Namely, reducing alcohol use to no more than three drinks a day for men, and two drinks for women, discontinuing cigarette use, weight management, and regular exercise. So, there are multiple opportunities for building a strong fence around the edge of life's cliff.

The Rescue Approach (Ambulance in the Valley)

Awakening from a colonoscopy with news of having advanced colon cancer is an alarming discovery. Besides coming to grips with the diagnosis and sharing the news with family, the person's future usually consists of multiple visits to various specialists, blood tests, CAT scans, PET scans, chemotherapy, and surgery. Depending on location of the cancer, some people may need a "colostomy bag" for a period after surgery. Some may require a permanent colostomy.

With advanced surgical techniques and highly specialized cancer drugs, there are people diagnosed with advanced colon cancer who have successful responses to treatment. Still, while every life is precious, these are rescue approaches that are extremely costly to the individual and to the health care system, particularly when there is a preventive and safer approach.

"Then an old sage remarked, it's a marvel to me that people give far more attention to repairing results than to stopping the cause when they'd much better aim at prevention."
~ The Ambulance Down in the Valley, Joseph Malins (1895)

July 11
A Pondering Heart

Some things are just too valuable to be shared with others. It's usually hard finding the right mix of words or the right time. Sometimes others cannot grasp the deeper meaning and misunderstand what you are saying. Or may not be able to hear you with the many challenges in their own life. Perhaps, it was meant for your ears only.

That's what Mary did after she delivered baby Jesus into the world. Her world had been turned upside down when the angel, Gabriel, informed her that she would be the mother of Jesus. Fortunately, God gave her Elizabeth as a confidant to share in her joy and a fiancée to stand by her side. Even still, she had to face the scrutiny of neighbors and the community about her status as an unwed mother. The world would never understand, so she held this treasure in her heart.

Then, the baby was born. Wise men and shepherds came to worship Jesus. Some in the community were in uproar, already plotting his death. While others were happy and in awe of his birth, Mary lay in peace, similar to any woman who has just given birth. The miraculous pre-events and what was about to happen in her son's life made it so different. What words were there to express how she felt? I can only imagine that her heart was overflowing with love and praise to the God she loved so much. But she remained still because some situations in life have to be quietly treasured in the heart and mind.

"But Mary kept all these things in her heart and thought about them often" *(Luke 2:19, NLT).*

July 12
A Special Tribute

One of my favorite musicians is Andraé Crouch. I was introduced to his music when I first committed my life to Jesus Christ, and it helped strengthen my faith. Not only did he and his twin sister, Sandra have anointed voices, they wrote songs on solid biblical precepts. I knew his music by heart, attended his concerts, and even met him on one occasion. I read his memoir in the 1970's, and what stood out most in his book was the strong calling on his life. In his book, he wrote that God called him by name as a young boy. This reminded me of how God called Samuel by name at the age of twelve (*1Samuel 34, NIV*).

Mr. Crouch was a gifted musician, lyricist, and minister. He wrote and sang many beautiful songs including his masterpiece, "My Tribute," which is now included in Methodist hymnals. The story behind the song is inspiring. He had befriended an ex-prisoner (Larry) at a local teen center. Larry told Mr. Crouch that he dreamed Andraé would write a song that would gain worldwide popularity and be his most successful song. Larry told him to read chapter 17 in the gospel of John, and Mr. Crouch followed his advice. The next day, Mr. Crouch woke up with glory to God on his heart. Ten minutes later, he had written "My Tribute."

The contributions of Andraé Crouch to music and ministry are innumerable. When I listen to the words of his music, my relationship with the Lord becomes more intimate. He died January 8, 2015, but his footprints will go far in music halls around the world.

"I was at a picnic, and there were a lot of songwriters. I remember praying, 'God I wish you would give me a song.' About five minutes later, my ears popped, and I saw everybody in slow motion. Nobody knew what I was experiencing."
~ Andraé Crouch

July 13
A Mother's Love Makes All the Difference

My niece, Tasha, suffered one of the greatest losses a person can experience; her daughter died. A few years later, she discovered her other daughter (Meri) had a learning disability. Her kindergarten teacher recommended transferring her to the slow-learners group. After feelings of guilt and disappointment waned, Tasha chose to rise to a higher level of thinking about the situation.

She considered the possibility that Meri's learning disability was similar to her own and invested in a variety of books, applying her own learning style to help her daughter. The extra schooling was done after work and allowed them to enjoy each other while Meri learned. Tasha soon discovered that not only did Meri have an amazing capacity to learn, but she had an intense fervor for knowledge.

Before long, she was reading, doing simple mathematics, and using adjectives, nouns, verbs, and adverbs in sentences. After about two months, Meri's kindergarten teacher observed her gifts and talents. She excelled when given advanced assignments. Her classmates were not able to keep up with Meri. Soon thereafter, Meri took the gifted test and scored in the 99.9 and was skipped to the second grade. Tasha took advantage of every special education accommodation available throughout all of Meri's school years including college. Now, Meri is a senior in college, has a talent for art and wants to be an art therapist.

How many children with learning differences do teachers give up on? Unconditional love stimulates children to achieve, to be the best they can be, to discover their talents for making their contribution to the universe.

"When you love someone, you will be loyal regardless of the costs. You will always believe in her; always expect the best from her, and always stand your ground in defense of her" (paraphrased 1 Corinthians 13, TLB).

July 14
The Power of the Spoken Word

"And God said, let there be light and there was light" (*Genesis 1:3, NIV*). Speaking life into existence is inconceivable. It takes faith to believe the power of God. Even if you don't have faith to believe, perhaps you'll agree that the ability of the human tongue to articulate speech makes it powerful and miraculous.

There are multiple biblical references to its power:

When Isaiah's life changed, the angel anointed his tongue, and said, "See, this coal has touched your lips. Now your guilt is removed, and your sins are forgiven" (*Isaiah 6:7, NLT*).

In Luke 1:20, the angel blocked Zacharias' ability to speak because he did not believe that his wife, Elizabeth, would become pregnant in her old age. After the baby was born, he was able to speak again.

In the Book of Proverbs there are over one hundred wise sayings that reference the tongue: "The tongue has the power of life and death, and those who love it will eat its fruit." (*Proverbs 18:21, NIV*). "Too much talk leads to sin. Be sensible and keep your mouth shut" (*Proverbs 10:19, NLT*). Growing up, my mother warned me that my mouth would get me in trouble. And, my father's favorite quote was, "If you can't say something nice, don't say anything at all." Indeed, their words came to my mind on those occasions when I reaped the consequences of not following parental advice.

What better way to use the power of the tongue than to be a mouthpiece for Jesus? That's how it all started when we confessed our faith in Jesus Christ. Sharing the gospel, bringing good tidings and encouraging words to friends and acquaintances follows. Spread the word about who is in charge of your life. There is power in the spoken word.

"Timely advice is lovely, like golden apples in a silver basket" (*Proverbs 25:11, NLT*).

July 15
Maggie Lena Walker: A Hidden Figure

Today is the birthday of Maggie Lena Walker, a humanitarian, teacher, visionary, and businesswoman. Born in 1864, in Richmond, Virginia, her mother was a freed slave and her father was of Irish descent. Her parents met on the estate where her mother worked.

In 2017, a towering bronze ten feet tall statue of Mrs. Walker became a focal point in her hometown of Richmond, Virginia.

Mrs. Walker taught school for a few years, but most of her work was accomplished through an organization known as The Independent Order of St. Luke. This society was dedicated to the financial and social advancement of African Americans. Under her leadership, the organization founded a newspaper and a department store providing work opportunities, particularly for women.

Most notably, Mrs. Walker was the first woman to establish a bank, St Luke's Penny Savings. The bank gave loans to black business owners and residents at fair rates. She managed to keep the bank alive during the Great Depression by merging with two other banks in 1929. Happy Birthday to a remarkable woman!

"Let us put our money together. Let us use our money out at usury among ourselves and reap the benefit ourselves. Let us have a bank that will take the nickels and turn them into dollars."
~Maggie Lena Walker

July 16
"This Little Light of Mine"

Everyone knew that "This Little Light of Mine" was my mother-in-law's favorite song. Her life reflected the lyrics in every way. In her home, God's light was bright. When I visited her home, I left more enlightened about the power of God and family. She led the prayers around the dining table, and everyone enjoyed sharing memories about her husband who had died fourteen years earlier. Her laugh was infectious, saturating the air with joy.

Whatever she did, it was done with vim and vitality. Similar to the lyrics, Mrs. Cone was lively and had an unquenchable thirst for knowledge. After her three sons graduated from high school, she returned to high school at the age of forty-three and continued her education, achieving her college degree at the age of forty-nine. Then, she started teaching school.

She never stopped letting God's light shine in her life. She made her transition on March 23, 1996, at the age of eighty-four. It was a blessing to have known her for twenty-three years. When I arrived at her home to attend her funeral, it was in impeccable order as if a housekeeper had been there. All the laundry including her sneakers had been washed, dried, and folded. It was as if she was expecting her house to be filled with guests. To be sure, we had come to celebrate the life of a beautiful Christian.

"You are the light of the world. A town built on a hill cannot be hidden. Neither do people light a lamp and put it under a bowl. Instead they put it on its stand, and it gives light to everyone in the house" (Matthew 5:14-15, NLV).

July 17
Spiritual Health

Throughout his ministry, Jesus met experts in religious law who looked with disdain on certain people in the community. They frequently questioned the motives of Jesus who would minister to those considered outcasts. They asked the question. "Why does he eat with tax collectors and sinners?" Jesus responded, "It is not the healthy who need a doctor, but the sick" (*Mark 2:16-17 NIV*). Here, Jesus is talking about spiritual health and not physical health, but it applies to both.

The Pharisees considered themselves "spiritually healthy" since they knew and upheld the Mosaic Law. In their minds, they had reached the pinnacle of religious fortitude. This attitude filled them with pride and disregard for other human beings. At the heart of their religion was a wall that excluded certain people. In their opinion, they needed nothing more. As a result, they would never grow beyond their wall. Jesus's ministry broke down walls and included everyone. It's no wonder they challenged him at every turn. Jesus's demonstration of love was in sharp contrast to their lack of the same.

No one exists outside of the boundary of God's love. Both the physical and spiritual frame is frail. We all need to heed the call he gives to the spiritually sick. As long as we are here on earth, we will need healing from the Great Physician. The word of God is medicine that strengthens our minds, bodies, and souls, healing our families, marriages, communities, and nations of the world. If you think your position of spiritual growth is above others, you will miss God's continuous flow of love and mercy.

"...I have come to call sinners, not those who think they are already good enough"
(Mark 2:17, NLT).

July 18
Saint Katharine Drexel: Miracle Lady

Saint Katharine was an American nun who descended from a very wealthy family. In spite of her wealth, in 1889, she took her vows of poverty, chastity, and obedience and entered a convent. In addition to these vows, she added a fourth: To be the mother and servant of the Indian and Negro races."

Two years later, she founded the order of the Sisters of the Blessed Sacrament, dedicated to serving African Americans and Native Americans. Many believe she started the Catholic Church in America on the road toward racial integration. In 1915, Drexel and her order opened Xavier University Preparatory School in Uptown, New Orleans. Ten years later, Xavier University became a reality with the creation of the College of Liberal Arts and Sciences. Years later, after her death, her divine power started to surface.

In 1974, one fourteen-year-old adolescent, Robert Gutherman became deaf from a severe infection. He had served as an altar boy in one of her orders. The family started praying for Sister Katherine's intercession. One month later his hearing was fully restored. In 1994, two-year-old Amy Wall was deaf from nerve damage in both ears. She too had a miraculous recovery through Katherine's intercession. This was the healing that led to her sainthood.

St. Katherine is a miracle herself. Not only did she walk with God, but she listened to God. She demonstrated that not only are our ears for physical hearing but also for spiritual hearing. When we listen and follow God's direction with our spiritual ears, there is no secret what God can do through us.

"If we wish to serve God and love our neighbor well, we must manifest our joy in the service we render to Him and them. Let us open wide our hearts. It is joy which invites us. Press forward and fear nothing."
~ St. Katherine Drexel

July 19
Thoughts of Praise

<u>God of care</u>—Has the burden of worry and fear ever felt insurmountable? Have they paralyzed any actions you were considering? A soft inner voice says, "Cast your care upon me." Then, out of nowhere peace enters your soul. You take one step and God does the rest. God's care is over the top.

<u>God of comfort</u>—As a part of a volunteer advocacy program for young persons under child protective services, I had the opportunity to observe a judge interact with young people in his court room. The judge deliberately engaged with each child in a warm and gentle way. The children's body language spoke volumes. He made each child feel special. The God of comfort used this judge to comfort these adolescents who were probably feeling confused and alone without their parents of origin. When our heart is willing, God will use us.

<u>God of death</u>—We are familiar with the God of life. But when we experience death, God may seem obscure or absent. Still, God makes this challenging time bearable. For me, from the time my husband transferred from the hospital to hospice, I witnessed one miracle after another that let me feel the powerful presence of God in death.

<u>God of love</u>—The love of God is all-inclusive of every human being, animal, plant, vegetation, and every resource on this magnificent universe. No one or nothing is out of the boundary of God's love. God would never say, "I am full. My love cannot include anyone else. Enough is enough." "God gives sunlight to both the evil and the good and sends rain on the just and the unjust" (*Matthew 5:45, NLT*).

Thine, O Lord is the greatness, and the power, and the glory, and the victory, and the majesty; for all that is in the heaven and in the earth is thine; thine is the kingdom, O Lord, and you are exalted as head above all. Both riches and honor come of thee, and you reign over all; and in thine hand is power and might; and in thine hand it is to make great, and to give strength unto all (1 Chronicles 29:11-12, KJV).

July 20
Healed and Ready to Serve (Luke 4:38-39)

The scriptures noted Peter's mother-in-law was suffering from a high fever. A high fever needs to be lowered as quickly as possible. Forty-four years ago, during my internal medicine specialty training, a young man was brought to the emergency room with a temperature of 108 degrees. This is a medical emergency. When the temperature is this high, the person is usually in a coma and near death. To recover under such dire circumstances is a miracle. God gave us wisdom and skill to lower his temperature to normal. He was able to be released from the hospital after a two to three-day observation period.

Peter's mother-in-law was very sick from this high fever. There was no mention of her talking. I suspect she was in distress and possibly in a coma. If she was to survive, the high fever needed to be brought down quickly. The family asked Jesus to help her, and Jesus wasted no time. The Bible says, "Jesus bent over her and rebuked the fever, and it left her" (*Luke 4:39, NIV*). What happened next was just as amazing.

Not only did the temperature return to normal, she regained her strength. She got up at once, walked into the kitchen, and prepared a meal for everyone. Where earlier, she had been sick unto death. After, Jesus healed her, she wasted no time expressing thanksgiving to Jesus and her entire family for her miraculous healing.

There are a multitude of ways to express your gratitude to God. Don't sit around trying to figure out what to do. The power of your healing includes immediate power and readiness to use your talent to serve.

"Each of you should use whatever gift you have received to serve others, as faithful stewards of God's grace in its various forms" (1 Peter 4:10, NIV).

July 21
A Divine Garden

Where are you at this moment in time? Is it morning, afternoon, or night? Regardless of the time, I encourage you to have some private moments with the Almighty Sovereign God. Walk into your imaginary divine garden. Water your garden with a song, dance, or words of praise. Moments of silence work as well. As you water your garden, your soul will be filled with Living Water.

These few moments I reference are not your usual prayer time. These are added bonuses. You might compare them to the short breaks taken on your job. God is giving you a gift of valuable time right now. Relish these moments. Just for now, let go of worry and doubt. God speaks to the heart. Listen to God with your heart. If you feel led to capture these moments, write a few notes down. Keep your notes to reflect upon on a day you may be feeling low.

Every now and then you need time for moments of clarity. Precious moments in time. Away from social media, radio, and television. Time spent in your divine garden will add value to all the other moments in your day.

"You make known to me the path of life; you will fill me with joy in your presence, with eternal pleasures at your right" (Psalm 16:11, NIV).

July 22
Step Over Yourself

In the Gospel of Luke 5:17-26, Jesus heals a paralyzed man. There are several themes in this story, but my point of reference are the four men who carried the man. Jesus was in a crowded house, and everyone wanted to be near him. If you hadn't arrived early, the likelihood of getting close to Jesus was slim. Four men arrived carrying a paralyzed man on a mat. They find it impossible to get anywhere near Jesus, so they revise their plan.

They decide to go up on the roof, move some tiles, and lower him down on his mat right in front of Jesus. Jesus was so amazed at their faith, he spoke the word, and instantly the man was healed.

In our lives, there will be obstacles along the way. In this man's situation, the faith and determination of his friends stepped up on his behalf. Indeed, it is a blessing to have friends like these four. But most times, it won't happen that way.

I attend a wellness center on a regular basis. One day, my coach gave me some new exercises. My first thought was 'no way.' They were more challenging, and I didn't want to risk failure. But then I heard an internal message that I needed to step over myself. And, when I did, I performed the new exercises with ease.

Sometimes you will have to step over yourself. Step over your fear, hesitation, doubt, or anything that obstructs your progress. Step out of your way and accomplish new goals.

"You gain strength, courage, and confidence by every experience in which you really stop to look fear in the face. You are able to say to yourself, 'I lived through this horror. I can take the next thing that comes along.'"
~ Eleanor Roosevelt

Temptation and Doubt (Luke 4:1-13)

Before Jesus started his earthly ministry, he had an encounter with Satan in a desert. The most interesting part of this story is that Jesus was led into the desert by the Holy Spirit to meet up with Satan at his weakest moment. He is alone without food, water, bathroom, or sleeping quarters.

Forty days and nights of fasting have passed, and he is famished. Satan tempts him with things any human being would want, particularly at a point of desperation: food, godly protection, and money.

Satan's goal was to turn Jesus away from his mission, to sidetrack and deter him. But Jesus was not sidetracked. He had faith in the Almighty Sovereign God, and he trusted himself.

I believe this encounter is similar to the kind of conflicts human beings face. Sometimes these temptations occur just after we give our hearts to Jesus. The temptation may be external to the church or it may arise in the church. It could be an illness, a job termination, or a job action where you're asked to take a stand.

We will not be perfect like Jesus and handle every situation miraculously. He is our model to trust. The lyrics of a Donnie McClurkin song says, "We fall down, but we get up." And, it was Paul who said, "I press on toward the goal to win the prize for which God has called me heavenward in Christ Jesus" (*Philippians 3:14, NIV*). We are on a faith journey. When we look for lessons learned and search for meaning in experiences and conflicts, not only does our trust in God grow, trust in self grows as well.

"The encounter of the Almighty Sovereign God and the encounter of one's self is one and the same. You cannot encounter God without discovering one's self and know yourself without encountering God. To know yourself is to know God!"
~ *Cecil Wayne Cone*

July 24
Cliffhanger

My pastor told a story during Bible study about a man walking along a cliff who lost his balance that made me burst out laughing. Falling, the man was able to grab and barely hold on to a tree limb. After a short while, he cried out, "Help, help." He heard a voice say, "This is God. I can help you. Trust me and let go of the limb." The man cried out again, "Is there anybody else up there who can help me?"

The pastor used this story to demonstrate how hard it is for us to trust God and tithe. This story holds true for many life situations that keep us barely hanging on. Credit cards, unhealthy overeating, substance abuse (alcohol, cigarettes, marijuana, vaping, illegal drugs), overindulgence of TV, texting, internet, and grudges are a few.

While this story is comical, it is true to life because it is hard to let go of harmful habits. We want God to help but when the message is to face a challenge, we look for a more comfortable option.

"Have I not commanded you? Be strong and courageous. Do not be afraid; do not be discouraged, for the LORD your God will be with you wherever you go" (Joshua 1:9, NIV).

July 25
A Father's Value to His Son

"To everything there is a season and a time to every purpose under the heaven"
(Ecclesiastes 3:1).

I read a story about a father who became annoyed with his son because he wanted to know how much money the dad made per hour. The father believed the question was too personal. As children do sometimes, he asked a second time. The father agreed to tell provided he kept it a secret. The son responded with joy, "I promise." The father stated he made $150.00 an hour. Upon learning this, the son asked to borrow twenty dollars. This question irritated the father even more, accusing him of using trickery to get money. The son burst into tears and ran to his room.

After the father calmed down, he went to his son's room to ask why he needed the money. The son took his piggy bank and counted out $130.00. The father was amazed and couldn't understand why he needed an additional twenty dollars. The son's response, "Then, I would have enough money to pay for an hour of your time."

Based on this man's salary, his job was probably quite time consuming not leaving much time for his son. His cross attitude suggested the job was also nerve racking, and he took out his frustrations on his son who just wanted to spend time with the most important person in his life. Time with dad was more important than all the money he had saved.

To be sure, our time on this earth is measured regardless of our age. How we spend that time impacts us as well as those we love.

"Fathers, do not exasperate your children; instead, bring them up in the training and instruction of the Lord" (Ephesians 6:4, NIV).

July 26
Forgiveness is Divine

There is a parable in Matthew 18:23-35 about divine forgiveness. In this story, the king orders a man and his family sold to repay the millions of dollars he owed. In fact, there was no way his debt could be repaid. The man begs for forgiveness and the king shows mercy and cancels his total debt. No sooner than he is forgiven, he finds a man who owes him a small amount of money. He threatens him while the man begs for a chance to pay him back.

The king learns of his unforgiving attitude and reneges on canceling his debt. He is ordered to be arrested and tortured. The parable ends by Jesus saying, "This is how my heavenly Father will treat each of you unless you forgive your brother or sister from your heart" (*Matthew 18:35 NIV*).

If the king symbolizes God in this story, is God taking back forgiveness? Some Bible scholars try to ease this interpretation by saying that verse thirty-five was not part of the original parable. This may or may not be true. However, including this scripture seems to align with God's message of forgiveness. It would seem that after being forgiven for such a hefty amount, your time would be spent making amends and letting go of small debts. The actions of the king says that unforgiveness is a detestable action.

The man who threatens the life of the other man because of a small amount of money is likened to substandard cheap grace. Cheap grace is an abomination in God's sight. His debt symbolizes the debt of sin. No amount of money can pay off this debt. It can only be canceled or forgiven. It requires GRACE from God. The cost of GRACE is incalculable. It costs Jesus his life.

"We must develop and maintain the capacity to forgive. He who is devoid of the power to forgive is devoid of the power to love. There is some good in the worst of us and some evil in the best of us. When we discover this, we are less prone to hate our enemies."
~ *Dr. Martin Luther King, Jr.*

July 27
The Call to Help

Have you ever wondered what God wants you to do in a particular situation? Pondered if you're making the right decision? Or questioned why it feels like you are not getting anywhere? If the answer is yes, know this, you're having normal human thoughts and feelings.

In the book of Acts chapter 16, Paul finds himself in this dilemma as he begins his second missionary journey. First, he had planned to travel with Barnabas but that didn't work out, and he ended up traveling with Silas and Timothy. Next, it was his intention to take a similar course to see how the converts were doing, but the Spirit intervened several times, closing the doors to Asia Minor. Nothing seemed to be working right. Although Paul was a little frustrated, he continued to follow the Spirit's direction.

Paul discovers why the Spirit kept changing his direction: He has a vision of a man in Northern Greece urgently pleading with him to, "Come over to Macedonia and help us" (*Acts 16:9, NIV*). The man crying out to Paul is on the European side of the Mediterranean. Paul is now convinced that God was calling them to proclaim the Good News there and Paul and his companions have the privilege of spreading the gospel across the sea from Asia to Europe. This particular mission was one of the most significant events in the history of the church.

Let us pray to grow and become more like Paul. He was a bit frustrated when roadblocks kept showing up. But Paul did not give up and say, "I did my best. It just didn't work out." He kept working, moving, and seeking God's direction and will.

"We can make our plans, but the Lord determines our steps" (Proverbs 16:9, NLT).

July 28
The Power of a Smile

"Sometimes your joy is the source of your smile, but sometimes your smile can be the source of your joy."
~Thich Nhat Hahn

There is an old African folktale about a little girl named Aïwa who had the unfortunate experience of losing her mother during Aïwa's birth. That didn't stop her from being a beautiful and sweet child. Aïwa was known to smile all the time. Aïwa's stepmother was jealous of her beauty and sweet attitude. Not only did she deprive and insult her, she gave Aïwa difficult tasks to complete. Aïwa would complete every task perfectly. The harder she worked Aïwa, the more Aïwa's smile and beauty increased. One of the truths in this folktale is the power of a smile.

Smiling is a mood booster. When you smile, you activate chemicals inside your brain such as dopamine, endorphins, and serotonin that make you feel better. It is said that one smile can generate the same level of brain stimulation as up to two thousand bars of chocolate.

As for physical appearance, smiling makes you look younger and thinner. Some people spend thousands of dollars on a facelift, but you can get a mini facelift just by turning up the corners of your mouth which raises the face, cheeks, jowls and neck.

"Because of your smile, you make life more beautiful."
~Thich Nhat Hanh

July 29
A Daring Escape

"To be or not to be, that is the question."
~William Shakespeare

William and Ellen Craft were slaves in America. William was a cabinet maker and Ellen was a house slave on the same plantation where they met and fell in love. While their situations were not as gruesome as most slaves, they had an unquenchable thirst to be free human beings. Ellen looked white, taking on the appearance of her slave master father rather than her mother. Oftentimes, she was mistaken as one of the master's children. Her 'white look' became the way of escape.

After they married in 1848, the cunning creative couple started planning their escape to freedom. For the escape, Ellen dared to dress as a sickly young white gentleman suffering from rheumatism. William traveled as her companion. To document the rheumatism, she wore a shoulder sling that connected to a mass of cloth to cover her 'inflamed rheumatic' hand. They used this tactic to avoid signing any papers at hotels since neither could read or write.

They had several close calls along the way. Ellen used her disguise and powers of persuasion to pass through forbidden boundaries. The couple traveled to Savannah, Georgia; Charleston, South Carolina; Washington, DC; Baltimore, Maryland; and finally, to Pennsylvania. They had almost made it to the free state of Pennsylvania when things got really testy. Ellen Craft was challenged. She was told 'he' needed a gentleman to certify 'his' slave. Her response was convincing and courageous with a hint of indignation. She wondered why someone was needed to certify that 'he' was the master of 'his' own slave. The attendant became flustered and let them get on the train.

Upon arrival in Pennsylvania, they were greeted by an abolitionist network. There, they learned to read and write. After the Fugitive-Slave Law was passed, life became more troubling. Abolitionist and others helped move them around to protect them from bounty hunters. Initially, they moved to Boston but to fully resist their captors, they had to leave America. They boarded a British vessel for England where they stayed for twenty years and raised five children.

William and Ellen Craft had a wealth of knowledge to share. God delivered them from the hands of their oppressor, through seen and unseen dangers. They returned to the United States in the 1870's and established a school in Georgia for newly freed blacks.

"Teach them [history]to your children, talking about them when you sit at home and when you walk along the road, when you lie down and when you get up" (Deuteronomy 11:19, NIV).

A Psalm of Divine Guidance and Worship (Psalm 95)

It is a blessing to our hearts, minds, and bodies when we take time to meditate. Not only is it invigorating, but it reminds us who reigns overall. Psalm 95 refreshes my soul and answers questions about God's sovereignty. Who do we worship? Why do we worship? How do we worship? When do we worship? Why would we not worship?

Who do we worship?

The Almighty Sovereign God—the rock of our salvation

The Great God—a great King above all God's

Why do we worship?

God reigns—God controls all—the deep places of the earth—the sea—the dry lands

The whole world is in the hands of God

We belong to God—we are people of God's pasture—we are God's sheep

How do we worship?

Bow down in worship—kneel before the Lord our maker

Come with singing—with joyful noise—with thankful hearts

With body, mind, and spirit—a soft heart—my whole being

When do we worship?

Today, if you would listen to God's invitation

Why would we not worship?

Why not try turning away from God? God has given you a free will—God is not an enforcer—The decision is yours

"Enter God's gates with thanksgiving and God's courts with praise" (Psalm 100:4, NIV).

July 31
An Instrument of God

As a part of my daily meditation, I include the Prayer of St. Francis of Assisi. It's about desiring to be an instrument for God. Webster defines an instrument as a device to produce music; a means whereby something is achieved, performed, or furthered; one designed for precision work. Each of these definitions helps to describe our purpose as an instrument of God. The prayer calls one to a higher level of being, thinking, and understanding about God.

Anyone who plays an instrument knows that it is not an easy task. It takes desire, practice, and patience. Those who are highly successful at playing an instrument can elicit emotions of joy, peace, hope, and love from its listeners. A brilliantly played instrument can shine light into a soul.

Similarly, to be an instrument of God's peace requires desire, practice, and patience. Desire is a strong feeling of wanting something. Is your desire to be an instrument for God? God will give you the desires of your heart" (*Psalms 37:4, NLT*). Practice will turn desire into a superior product. You become what you practice. The hardest part is patience. A musician who has mastered an instrument has learned the art of patience. She or he chooses to never give up. Likewise, the Christian must not give up. Christ gives us the strength to be used by God. The key is self-love.

The more we love ourselves, the more love others. The more we forgive ourselves, the more we forgive others. The more we are patient with ourselves, the more we are patient with others. As instruments of god, we play music that heals and harmonizes with others.

"Lord, make me an instrument of Your peace. Where there is hatred, let me sow love; Where there is injury, pardon; Where there is doubt, faith; Where there is despair, hope; Where there is darkness, light; And where there is sadness, joy. O Divine Master, grant that I may not so much seek to be consoled as to console; To be understood as to understand; To be loved as to love. For it is giving that we receive, It is in pardoning that we are pardoned, and it is in dying that we are born to eternal life."
~ *St. Francis of Assisi*

August 1
Check Your Rings!

"It's time to stand."
"You're way ahead of your goals. Keep crushing it!"
"You're usually ahead of goals by this time of the day.
Close your rings. A 15-minute walk will do it."

The above messages are programmed into my watch to support physical movement. Using the watch as a personal coach is a motivator for staying on track to reach fitness goals. The goals on the watch are called rings. I program the watch with caloric and exercise goals. For example, my goal is to burn at least four hundred calories a day and exercise at least thirty minutes a day. Congratulatory messages pop up when a ring (goal) is achieved.

If I'm behind on my daily goals, my watch sends me a message to get moving. When all three rings are closed, I receive a burst of colorful rings. The watch is programmed to share data with others. Motivational messages are cued in the watch to encourage friends who meet their goals. Are these bells and whistles needed to motivate me to exercise? It helps me and it's fun.

In addition to physical fitness goals, we need spiritual fitness goals. How do we close our spiritual rings in this fast-paced society when there is no creative watch that you place on your arm? Actually, what we have is much better. We have an internal divine-driven watch that is free, cannot wear out, break, or be stolen. Of course, I reference the Holy Spirit.

The Holy Spirit is a free gift that comes with salvation. The Spirit prompts, guides, and directs us to what is best for our lives. The more we use our gift, the stronger we become spiritually. The spirit encourages us to pray, study the Bible, and meditate. If you're feeling down, that's a prompt to pray more. If you're seeking direction, that's a nudge to read God's word or to be still and listen.

Are there congratulatory messages like the watch displays? Well, there's no burst of colorful rings. It's much better. You spring forth with vibrancy. You are more likely to exercise. Your countenance is radiant. You do more for others. Your physical health is improved. And, whatever you are going through, you definitely don't look like it. You feel joy and an abiding presence of the Spirit within. When we seek to strengthen our spiritual bodies, life becomes more meaningful, peaceful, and rich internally.

"All athletes are disciplined in their training. They do it to win a prize that will fade away, but we do it for an eternal prize. So I run with purpose in every step. I am not just shadowboxing. I discipline my body like an athlete, training it to do what it should. Otherwise, I fear that after preaching to others I myself might be disqualified" (1 Corinthians 9:25-27, NLT).

August 2
Forgiveness

I am fortunate to have a library filled with a collection of books, most of which belonged to my late husband. A few years ago, I catalogued our books to make them easy to locate. While looking through the novel section recently, I found *The Brothers Karamazov* published in 1879 by Dostoyevsky four months before he died. *The Brothers Karamazov* is considered Dostoyevsky's masterpiece, so I decided to tackle Russian literature.

I was amazed to see the deep focus the author placed on religion. This made the book much more interesting. The author's depth of understanding about forgiveness and the love of God was masterful. In one storyline, a lady feared death because she had never been able to feel forgiveness from a personal situation. How often does this happen to human beings? The author writes like one who knows the Creator and has experienced forgiveness. His ability to write at this depth is healing, amazing, and worth quoting:

"So long as you remain penitent, God will forgive you everything. There's no sin, and there can be no sin in the whole world which God will not forgive to those who are truly repentant." He goes on to say, "Why, man cannot commit so great a sin as to exhaust the infinite love of God. Or can there be a sin that would exceed the love of God? Believe that God loves you in a way you cannot even conceive of. Everything can be atoned for; everything can be saved by love."

The two keys to self-forgiveness are feeling genuine sorrow and accepting God's all-embracing love. The measure of forgiveness and love you give to those who offend you is a measure of your trust in God to forgive you and a measure of trust in God to forgive yourself.

"If God forgives me, I can trust God and forgive myself. If I can forgive myself, I can trust God and forgive others."
~Juanita Fletcher Cone

August 3
Pride and Vanity

"Woe to those who are wise in their own eyes and clever in their own sight"
(Isaiah 5:21, NIV).

As an adolescent, I would ask my mother for permission to go somewhere or do something that didn't meet her approval, and she always said no. I would respond that everyone else is going or doing it. And while I don't remember her full explanation (sixty plus years later), I remember the part that became a refrain: "If everyone else is jumping in the St. John's River, will you jump in with them?" Or she would say, "Use your head for something other than a hat rack." She was teaching her children to think critically and to not go along to get along.

Those parental sayings popped into my mind when my pastor used Hans Christian Andersen's fairy tale, *The Emperor's New Clothes* to make a point about the danger of pride and vanity. This tale was written almost two-hundred years ago, but the message rings true today.

The story is about an emperor who loved clothes more than he loved or respected himself. His self-worth was tied to clothes. All his time was spent in his dressing room fixated with clothing apparel rather than attending to the affairs of the nation. When you are a slave to something, you can easily be fooled. Two swindlers effortlessly convince the emperor they can weave him a suit that was not only elegant but supernatural. The suit would be invisible to those who were either unfit or too stupid for their jobs. He fell for their scheme and paid them an enormous amount of money to make this magical suit.

Even though the emperor and his officials observed the swindlers at work with nothing on the looms, they dared not question their work since they didn't want to be considered stupid. Once the swindlers decided the suit was finished, they had the emperor undress and put the new invisible clothes on. Everyone marveled at the beauty and perfection of the clothes that were not actually there. It was only when he went on parade and a little boy proclaimed that he didn't have clothes on that the crowd agreed. At this point, the emperor shivered and thought to himself that maybe this is true, but "the show must go on!"

How often do you make decisions based on what others think of you rather than truthfulness? Appearance and wealth are utmost importance in today's culture. That is not where God is. "The LORD does not look at the things people look at. People look at the outward appearance, but the LORD looks at the heart" (*1 Samuel 16: 7, NIV*).

Be aware of people who use haughty language to make you feel important for the purpose of getting you to do something that is beyond your abilities, unjust, or even illegal. "God desires honesty from the heart, so you can teach me to be wise in my inmost being" (*Psalm 51:6, NLT*).

"Be not wise in thine own eyes; fear the LORD and depart from evil" (Proverbs 3:7 KJV).

August 4
Fasting for Physical Health: Learning to eat to live

The summer before entering medical school at age twenty-two, I made a conscious decision to lose weight. My rationale for doing so was how could I counsel patients about weight management when I was overweight?

So, without the help of physicians, exercise, or appetite suppressants, I started a 1,000 calorie-a day diet for three months. Back then, there were no Paleo, Vegan, or Atkin diets. My summer job helped because I couldn't frequent the refrigerator in search of food. Plus, in the early 70's, there were only a few fast food places and our family rarely visited. It was still difficult. Three hundred calories for breakfast and lunch left me starving between these two meals. Snacking after dinner was more challenging because the next meal was nine hours away, but I persevered.

After about three weeks, my father noticed the physical changes taking place and spoke encouraging words. By the time I entered medical school, I was twenty-five pounds lighter.

As I reflect, this was my first encounter with fasting. While my pursuit was not for religious reasons, it was a conscious undertaking. And, while the reason I used to generate self-motivation was a good one, the best reason was simply because I chose to eat healthy. Still, without realizing it, I had moved to a higher level of thinking about food and its relationship to health.

My passion for prevention started before I entered medical school. Fasting is an activity that can break the bond to a poor diet and improve one's total health.

"The three most common preventable causes of death in the population of the United States are smoking, high blood pressure, and being overweight."
˜Centers for Disease Control and Prevention (CDC)

August 5
God's Natural Order

Years ago, I wrote an article entitled "Triumphant Faith" that focused on the interrelatedness and interdependence of all facets of society. When we fail to understand this divine connection, we end up frustrated, finding fault with each other, and living out of harmony with what I refer to as God's natural order.

God's natural order is that the universe operate holistically, balanced, blended—each part feeding on the other parts—all parts growing with seeds of love. God's natural order is that we all have life (good health) and that we have it more abundantly. God's natural order is that we love the Lord with all our hearts, minds, bodies, and souls—this means that we love God holistically.

God's natural order is that we cherish and respect relationships—marriages, families, church bodies, communities, our nation as well as other nations. God's natural order is that we care for babies, children as well as the elderly and the sick. God's natural order is that we respect and protect the animals, plants, and total environment.

"The earth is the Lord's, and everything in it, the world, and all who live in it"
(Psalm 24:1, NIV).

Juanita Fletcher Cone

August 6
Rays of Hope

"Those who bring sunshine into the lives of others cannot keep it from themselves"
~James M. Barrie

Barrie's quote resonates deep within me. Kindness rewards the giver and the receiver. During one of my meditations, I added a different ending. His quote seemed to also say, those who bring sunshine into the lives of others are God's rays of hope for the world.

In this topsy-turvy society, there is a need for a lot of hope. And people who give hope and sunshine are downright special. What are these people like?

When you are in the presence of one of God's rays, you know it. Like the sun, they brighten your life, and before you know it, your clouds have dispersed. God's rays are easy to love because their spirits are so generous. They don't hold back when it comes to giving out light. Without saying a word, they encourage you to be a bright spot in other people's lives.

You would never know what their life situation looks like because they don't complain. They are like the apostle Paul who wrote a letter from jail. His letter was so inspiring it sounded like he was writing to someone in jail and not the other way around. His words were filled with rays of hope – joy, strength, godly instruction, love, and concern.

People who beam rays of hope are able to rise above difficult situations. Like Paul, their thoughts are filled with gratitude and praise to God. They are always ready to speak healing words, give a warm hug, or a material blessing effortlessly and not want anything in return. Their actions say, "I can do all things through Christ who strengthens me" (*Philippians 4:13, NKJV*).

"Be the light that helps others see."
~Anonymous

August 7
Investing in Life (Matthew 25:14-30)

The above scripture refers to a parable about a man who gave three servants money to invest for him while he was away. Each received a sum based on their abilities. The first two servants strategized wisely and doubled their investment. However, the third servant lived in fear. Instead of investing the money, he buried it for 'safekeeping.'

When the master returned, he was overjoyed with the first two servants who invested their money and rewarded them by giving them more. The one who did nothing justified his actions: He was afraid that he might lose the money. He also didn't know how the master would respond since he was known to be unkind and a hard taskmaster. The master did not like his responses and called him unfaithful and useless. He took the money away from the one who did nothing and gave it to the one who earned the most. Why was the master so angry with the one who did nothing? Was the punishment too harsh?

We are not here on this earth to mope around and do nothing. The third servant had abilities, but he failed to apply them. Fear and mistrust blocked his ability to take action. He was miserly and grumpy. Investing money is similar to investing in life. The Almighty Sovereign God used Jesus to invest in us. Our value to God is priceless. God expects us to actively use the abilities we are given with gratitude and joy.

"For we are his workmanship, created in Christ Jesus unto good works, which God hath before ordained that we should walk in them" (Ephesians 2:10, KJV).

August 8
Love, Faith, and Humility:
The Syrophoenician Woman (Matthew 15:21-28)

The Syrophoenician woman was extraordinary. She was a Gentile (a heathen), a descendant of those who worshipped Baal. Yet, she came to Jesus pleading on behalf of her daughter whom she loved with every fiber of her being. Her daughter was controlled by an evil spirit. The mother had heard about the healing power of Jesus, so she came with resolve to be blessed. It did not concern her that they had different ethnic backgrounds. Neither did it concern her that Jesus and his disciples gave her the cold shoulder. She kept pleading. The desire for her daughter to be released from this evil spirit was a powerful driving force.

Initially, Jesus turned away from her. Perhaps, he was weary. We don't know why but this didn't discourage her. She exhibited another powerful act of faith. She kneeled before the Lord and asked for help. Jesus started to question her: Do you really know who I am? Do you know why I came?

The Syrophoenician woman never wavered in faith or humility. Though she doesn't say, her actions suggested: I am here because I know who you are. I may not understand all about your mission, but this I know. Your mission is big enough to include me and my daughter. A few crumbs are enough for us. At that point, Jesus marveled at her faith, told her to go home where she would find her daughter healthy and whole.

Sometimes, when our prayers are not answered to our hearts' desire, we give up. Stay encouraged and remain persistent and fervent. A rich prayer life nurtures our relationship with God and nourishes our spirits, emotions, and bodies.

"The effectual fervent prayer of a righteous man (woman) availeth much" (James 5:16, KJV).

August 9
Beauty and Brains: Courage and Calm in the Storm (1 Samuel 25:1-44)

In the book of Samuel, we find a story about a woman named Abigail. She was beautiful, wise, intelligent, and righteous. Abigail was married to Nabal, a very wealthy man who was mean spirited, selfish, boorish, and spent most of his days intoxicated. I suspect her homelife was unhappy. In spite of this, Abigail held to her marriage vows and remained with Nabal. If you read her story in its entirety, you would see God's hand in the midst of her life.

A vengeful murderous spirit overtook David because Nabal had refused to provide sustenance to David and his men as they roamed the desert running from Saul. David vowed to kill Nabal and his entire household because of his selfishness.

Abigail learned that a violent attack was about to take place and used her intellect and fast thinking to avert a disaster. She acted quickly, loading food, wine, sheep, and grain to meet David. As David headed out to kill Nabal and his men, they met Abigail who bowed low before him. Without hesitating, she accepted responsibility for the entire situation, placing her life on the line. She presented gifts to David in exchange for their lives, and the Almighty Sovereign God used her to intervene and save her household and calm David's ferocious temper.

David's turbulent passion dissipated at her courageous and humble appeal. He expressed gratitude to Abigail for acknowledging that it was God who sent her to keep him from being tainted by Nabal's blood and taking vengeance into his own hands.

Nabal weakened and died from a heart attack after Abigail told him what had taken place. After learning about his death, David asked Abigail for her hand in marriage, which she accepted.

"Do not take revenge, my dear friends, but leave room for God's wrath, for it is written: "It is mine to avenge; I will repay, says the Lord"
(Romans 12:19, NIV).

August 10
Fear and Flying

A recent airplane flight reminded me how much I dislike flying. The plane's take-off was delayed by an hour because of a severe thunderstorm. We sat on the tarmac until the storm lessened. When the plane finally started to ascend, things got shaky. I was holding on to the armrest for dear life. There were spells of turbulence that sunk my stomach. When my husband was alive, I would cuddle up next to him, and he would tease me, saying, "O ye of little faith." It was embarrassing to see my faith fall by the wayside during extreme turbulence.

As we moved above the storm, the plane ride smoothed out. I thought about the raging thunderstorms that occur in our lives, but God is always there to help us rise above or bring us through them. I shared the flight incident with my sister who told me of a similar plane experience. She, her husband (Alan), and two-year-old daughter (Ayanna) were flying through rough weather. Everyone on the plane was quiet, barely breathing, and holding on to their armrests. A forceful turbulence dropped the plane, and Ayanna burst out excitedly—Wheeee! Everyone on the plane laughed heartily as Ayanna changed the mood of the flight from fear to fun.

There is a similar story of a young girl on a turbulent flight who also showed no signs of fear or anxiety. A passenger asked her how she was able to remain calm. She told him, "My dad is the pilot, and he is taking me home." Children can teach us so much. Ayanna was happy as she sat with her mother and father, people she trusted beyond measure. She had nothing to fear. The young girl was calm because her dad was the pilot. We need to trust God the way children trust their loving parents.

"God is my refuge and strength, a very present help in times of trouble. Therefore, will not we fear, though the earth be removed and though the mountains be carried into the midst of the sea"(Psalm 46:1-2, NKJV).

August 11
Dropsy: A Failing Heart (Luke 14:1-4)

Dropsy is an ancient term used in the past to describe congestive heart failure (CHF). A person with CHF has an overabundance of fluids in the body because the heart is not able to adequately pump fluids out. The fluid build-up starts in the feet and legs and progresses to other parts of the body. If left untreated, CHF can cause difficulty breathing when the fluid fills up the lungs and can even lead to death.

Luke who was a physician and author of the Gospel of Luke writes about a person with dropsy. He is a guest in the home of a religious leader where Jesus is also in attendance. There is no mention that the man is having difficulty breathing. However, as any internal medicine physician knows, the accumulation of fluid in the lungs can sometimes occur suddenly without warning. Addressing the problem when first observed is paramount. This is what Jesus did by immediately healing him. Because it was the Sabbath, this posed a problem for the religious men who kept the law to the letter.

In today's society, people need proactive health care. However, because of the lack of health insurance, some are not able to see a physician in a timely manner. Instead, they present to the emergency room in imminent danger, and sometimes it is too late. Other times, they end up in a prolonged debilitated state with little hope of recovery while placing a huge burden on their families and the health care system.

The sabbath was a special gift from God and was to be honored. The religious men used the sabbath as an excuse for not providing health care to one in need. Jesus broke with tradition whenever there was a human need whether it was an emergency or not. How would you respond?

"If I had my way, I'd make health catching instead of disease."
~ *Robert Ingersoll*

August 12
The Light of the World

Some years ago, my husband, Cecil and I were attending an elegant Saturday night dinner party. I decided to wear my 1908 twenty-dollar gold coin studded with diamonds. The pendant was special because it was a gift from Cecil twenty years earlier. As we stepped onto the elevator, the pendant and chain slipped from around my neck into the elevator shaft. I had failed to secure the lock on the chain. What a blunder. We were informed that an elevator technician wouldn't be able to assist us until the next business day. To my surprise, after about thirty minutes, an attendant brought the pendant to us. We were thrilled, appreciative, and able to enjoy the evening.

This story came to mind while reflecting on the parable of the lost coin in Luke chapter 15. In the biblical story, a woman loses a valuable coin and searches high and low for it. She takes a searchlight, sweeps in every corner of the house and finally finds her coin. She is thrilled and so are her friends who celebrate with her.

Indeed, my coin and the woman's coin are valuable and deserve a painstaking search. However, Jesus' message is about the value of a human life. The coin is a metaphor for a lost soul. Sometimes in life we blunder. Human beings veer off track and sometimes can't figure their way back to normalcy. Our predicament can sometimes be like a coin—a coin doesn't know it's lost. The woman is a metaphor for a Christian. She appreciates the value of every human being. Not one soul should be lost. With her light shining bright, she searches in the hedges and highways of life until she finds a lost soul. With her light she speaks words of faith, consolation, understanding, forgiveness, and love. Her light finds one who has been lost and there is cause for joyful celebration.

As John Newton wrote, "I once was lost but now, I'm found." This is the heart of the gospel of Jesus Christ. "For the Son of Man is come to seek and to save the lost" (*Luke 19:10, KJV*).

"Let your light so shine before men, that they may see your good works, and glorify your Father which is in heaven" (Matthew 5:16, KJV).

August 13
Beauty is Only Skin Deep (Genesis 30)

In the book of Genesis, you'll find the story of two sisters. Rachel was the youngest sister who Jacob loved and wanted to marry. Jacob was enamored by her beauty. Leah was the oldest sister and not as fair as Rachel. Leah's blessing was her relationship with the Lord. Jacob had been promised Rachel's hand in marriage by her father. Instead, the father used trickery to deceive Jacob into marrying Leah instead.

Jacob ended up marrying both sisters though he loved only Rachel. The result was a home filled with animosity and bad blood. Although Jacob chose Rachel because of her external beauty, God chose Leah to give birth to Judah, through which Jesus Christ descended. While Jacob chose Rachel because of her physical beauty, God was attracted to Leah because of her inner beauty.

When sisters are close in age, there is natural rivalry. There was only one year between me and my only sister, Cassandra. We are best friends now, but during adolescence, there was sibling friction. I can't even imagine the challenges Rachel and Leah faced being married to the same man. In my opinion, regardless of belief systems and world-views, polygamy sets up a hostile, unhealthy environment.

This story is similar to life today. It has a lot of complicating factors. This particular storyline tells us that Jacob chose Rachel only because of her beauty. The best decision for you is to rely on God's faithfulness and direction as you search for a life partner. "In everything you do, put God first, and he will direct you and crown your efforts with success" (*Proverbs 3:6, TLB*).

"There are two kinds of beauty; there is a beauty which God gives at birth, and which withers as a flower. And there is a beauty which God grants when by His grace men are born again. That kind of beauty never vanishes but blooms eternally."
~ Abraham Kuyper

August 14
Gratitude

There is never enough space or time to write about gratitude. Gratitude makes moments meaningful regardless of life conditions. Gratitude adds to life. Think about the hymn, "This little light of mine, I'm gonna let it shine." This song is about gratitude, a melody of thanksgiving for the transformation that has taken place in one's life. "This little light of mine" sings of obedience to Jesus' instructions, "Don't hide your light under a basket! Instead, put it on a stand and let it shine for all" (*Matthew 5:15, NLT*).

The beat of the music is bubbly and mood boosting for every age group. Gwendolyn Sims Warren writes in her book, *Ev'ry time I feel the Spirit*, how her four-year-old daughter and three-year-old son couldn't stop singing "This little light of mine" after receiving their first record player. Such a beautiful display of gratitude.

When Christians sing about letting their light shine, the subliminal message says you made a way; you healed my body; I am forgiven; you saved my soul; I am lost without you. And a thousand other reasons too numerous to name.

There are reasons and ways to express gratitude and that's why keeping a gratitude journal is helpful. All the reasons and ways for the Christian to be grateful lead to God's unconditional love for us best demonstrated through Jesus Christ whose life was sacrificed that we might have eternal life. That's the number one reason to let your light shine and be grateful.

"But God showed great love for us by sending Christ to die for us while we were still sinners" (Romans 5:8, NLT).

August 15
The Symbol of the Cross

In my opinion, more than any other religious symbol, the cross is the primary icon of Christianity. However, the crosses we see today do not depict the reality of the cross where Jesus was executed. We decorate it like jewelry and hang it around our necks. My husband presented me with a beautiful cross necklace when I was ordained an elder in our church. The cross symbol is the tallest steeple atop churches. It beautifies the architecture of walls of our sanctuaries and is seen on most Christian literature. Still, it is important to be reminded that what happened on Good Friday was not pretty.

Jesus was accused of treason by the Roman government. He underwent a public execution of humiliation, shame, and suffering. And, like countless other criminals of his day, he was nailed hands and feet to the cross. A crown of thorns was driven into his scalp causing a lot of bleeding. Before the actual placement on the cross, he is beaten with leather lashes which also caused a large amount of blood loss. Criminals are usually required to carry the upper crossbeam to the site of the crucifixion where the central stake has already been set up, but Jesus was so weak from blood loss that Simon of Cyrene was compelled to carry the cross for him.

After being firmly fixed to the crossbeam, Jesus, our Lord, was lifted against the standing vertical stake. His body was tormented with pain as it stretched from the weight of the nails in his hands and feet. As his body started to slump from the outstretched arms and shoulders, breathing became more and more difficult. Eventually, he succumbed from the lack of oxygen throughout his entire body.

Pain can be excruciating in patients nearing the end of their life. Physicians try to provide the most compassionate care possible to those who are suffering. Jesus received no such care. They were sadistic and wanted him to suffer. But this was the Almighty Sovereign God's providential plan, "Yet it pleased the LORD to bruise him; God put him to grief: when thou shalt make his soul an offering for sin, he shall see his seed, he shall prolong his days, and the pleasure of the LORD shall prosper in his hand" (*Isaiah 53:10, KJV*).

I encourage you to remember the cross, not just at Easter time. When you see crosses around necks, on steeples, or in church windows, think about Jesus suffering on the cross. The next time doubt and fear cloud your view of Jesus, hold your arms out and act out nailing doubt and fear to the cross. Then, thank God and move forward. Your whole perspective will change.

"He was wounded for our transgressions. He was bruised for our iniquities. The chastisement of our peace was upon him and with his stripes, we are healed" *(Isaiah 53:5, KJV).*

Encouraging Excellence in Young People

My husband was a strong believer in education. He wanted every young person to succeed and strongly believed that a solid education was key. When we were at church or in the grocery store, he would stop young people and ask, "Are you in school?" If they said yes, he'd ask, "What kind of grades do you make?" Some would say A's and B's. Others might say B's and C's. Then, he would ask them all the same question, "Can you make all A's?" Invariably, they would say, "Yes, sir!" And his next response was, "Then do it!" And they would answer in the affirmative. Their parents would thank him for taking the time to talk with their child. If the young person was not in school, he would encourage them to get back in school right away.

Below is a standard message for young people that he often delivered from the pulpit:

"If you are not in school, you go to school. If you are in school, study hard. Study as if your life depended on it. Study, study, study! Study geology and learn to differentiate the strata of the rock. But don't stop there. Keep on studying and searching until you can discern the Rock of Ages. Then you can sing, 'Rock of Ages, cleft for me. Let me hide myself in thee.'"

Study botany and learn about the classification and distribution of the rose, but don't stop there. Keep on studying; keep searching until you can see the Rose of Sharon.

Study astronomy. Learn about the movement of the heavenly bodies and the orbits of the stars, but don't stop there. Keep on searching until you discover the Star of Bethlehem, the bright and morning star; the star that leads to the message of brotherhood and sisterhood; the star that leads to hope, and the star that leads to peace. Yes, that star is Jesus. Jesus is the answer above all.

"Study to shew thyself approved unto God, a workman that needeth not to be ashamed, rightly dividing the word of truth" (2 Timothy 2:15 KJV).

August 17

The Design on the Dime

The thirty-second President of the United States, Franklin D. Roosevelt is depicted on the front side of a dime or ten-cent piece. The history behind the design is also most notable.

In 1900, Selma Burke, a renowned sculptor was born in Mooresville, North Carolina. As a young child, she became fascinated by the artifacts her father collected and would mold the soft clay of the riverbanks into similar small figures.

I suspect that her parents encouraged her to seek a sound education as opposed to sculpturing. She graduated from Winston-Salem University and completed nurse training at St. Agnes Hospital Nursing School in Raleigh, North Carolina. She then moved to New York City to work as a private nurse. In New York, she became inspired by the Harlem Renaissance movement. There, her natural artistic abilities were noticed. In 1938, she was awarded fellowships to study with Aristide Maillol and Henri Matisse, two acclaimed French sculptors and painters.

In 1941, she earned a master's degree in fine arts at Columbia University. Burke founded two art schools where she taught art. She is most noted for her bronze plaque of President Franklin D. Roosevelt. She won a competition to sculpt the president and personally wrote the White House requesting a sitting with Mr. Roosevelt, which she was granted. The plaque listed four freedoms above Roosevelt's face: freedom from want, freedom from fear, freedom of worship, and freedom of speech. It was then installed at the Recorder of Deeds Building in Washington, D.C.

John R. Sinnock, the chief engraver at the U.S. Mint has his initials on the profile. However, with the exception of a few changes in the arrangement of Roosevelt's hair, the dime's head is a mirror image of the plaque created by Selma Burke. Additionally, the National Archives and Records Administration of the Franklin D. Roosevelt Library stated that the dime portrait originated with the sculpture of Franklin Delano Roosevelt done by Selma Burke.

The next time you hold a dime in your hand, reflect on our thirty-second President, but also think about Selma Burke, the artist who is responsible for its design.

"The future belongs to those who believe in the beauty of their dreams."
~ *Eleanor Roosevelt*

August 18
Gideon's Character (Part 1)

Gideon was the son of a poor farmer. His father worshipped the idol, Baal, but Gideon was God-fearing. He was an Israelite who lived during the time when God chose judges to help the Israelites during times of distress. The Israelites were the people of God who centuries before had been delivered from the evil oppression of the Egyptians. But most had forgotten their history and failed to obey God's voice and keep God's covenant. As a result, God would allow other nations to oppress them until they cried out for help. Then, God would send a judge to deliver them. Gideon was chosen to be a deliverer and a religious leader. While we can never know why God chooses one over another, the Bible does tell us something about Gideon's character.

First of all, Gideon was resourceful and found ways to skillfully work through difficulties. Israel's oppressor destroyed their crops, stole their livestock, and caused many Israelites to run into mountain caves. To keep his family from hunger, Gideon used a winepress to thresh wheat and hide it from the enemy. Indeed, like the old spiritual says, "God makes a way out of no way."

Secondly, Gideon was not like most of the Israelites. He had a relationship with God. As with Mary and Zacharias in the New Testament, the angel appeared to Gideon and affirmed, "The Lord is with you, mighty warrior" (*Judges 6:12, NLT*). Gideon was comfortable entering into a dialogue with the angel, questioning why God had abandoned the Israelites. This is when the angel informed him that he was selected to be their deliverer. There are worlds of cares that impede our time with God, but life itself depends on spending time with God. Gideon discovered his purpose through prayer time.

Thirdly, Gideon knew his history. He remembered that God had brought his people out of Egypt and miraculously delivered them from their oppressor. It was his great expectation that God would do the same once more.

It should not matter that eons of generations have passed. It is important to know history and the lessons learned along the way. It is through history that we can appreciate God's sovereignty and see the hand of God as a deliverer and liberator. Just as God was disclosed in historical events of the Israelites, we too can encounter God in the everyday affairs of our lives.

"Remember the former things, those of long ago; I am God, and there is no other; I am God, and there is none like me. I make known the end from the beginning, from ancient times, what is still to come. I say, 'My purpose will stand, and I will do all that I please'" (Isaiah 46:9-10, NIV).

August 19
Gideon's Doubt (Part 2)

When the angel of the Lord informed Gideon that God had chosen him to deliver the Israelites from bondage, he was filled with doubt. He had no self-confidence for such a monumental task.

Gideon was looking at himself and not at an omnipotent God and begins to doubt. Gideon asked for a sign three different times, and each time God obliged his request.

There are many stories of our heroes expressing doubt in the scripture. Later in the Bible, we find Peter doubting Jesus when he was instructed to walk on water. Human beings are doubting creatures and need a lot of reassurance.

How often have you asked the Lord for a sign? Or, hesitate to move forward—think of a hundred reasons why you'll fail—the world has changed—I am too shy. The list goes on and on. Even when God gives a sign, human doubt remains.

Like Gideon, we want to put everything into a category so that it makes total sense. If we can't see, smell, touch, hear, or taste it, then we don't move forward.

To be sure, this is a faith journey that requires trust, courage, obedience, humility, and servanthood. Like the Lord told Gideon, "I will be with you" (*Judges* 6:16, *NLT*). We have to believe God's Word and act on it.

"And without faith it is impossible to please God, because anyone who comes to him must believe that he exists and that he rewards those who earnestly seek him" (Hebrews 11:6, NIV).

August 20
Gideon's Change of Character (Part 3)

Gideon's confidence soared when he followed God's direction. With God's help, he and his troops successfully defeated their enemy.

Unfortunately, Gideon's success changed his behavior. He stopped listening to God and became heartless and vengeful. He started to take advantage of people, killed for spite, stole from those he murdered, and constructed an idol to worship. The people started to claim that it was Gideon and not the Lord who delivered them from their enemy.

Gideon's behavior is an example of how power can corrupt even religious leaders. Because he turned away from God, Gideon stopped growing spiritually. As a result, he became absorbed in himself. When one is self-possessed, it is impossible for them to see their human shortcomings. They surround themselves with people who nourish their ego.

Jesus showed us that the temptation to fall for idolatry is ever before us (*Luke 4:1-13*). In the twenty-first century, the visual temptation to maintain a dream job, have more money, a fabulous house, big car, and/or power at any cost can easily move our hearts and minds away from God as we attempt to find our worth in material things.

Thank you, God, for the gift of having a relationship with you. Thank you for the spiritual and material blessings that you provide. May I always remember that my true worth is linked to you. And that this divine link connects me to my fellow human beings and with this magnificent abundant universe. AMEN

August 21
Moving Down the Seasons of Life

The writing below has been around for years. The author is unknown although many people seem to claim it. The writing uses humor to describe the changes that take place in our bodies during the golden years. See what you think:

Remember, old folks are worth a fortune with silver in their hair, gold in their teeth, stones in their kidneys, lead in their feet, and gas in their stomach. I have become a little older since I saw you last, and a few changes have come into my life since then. Frankly, I have become quite a frivolous old gal. I am seeing five gentlemen every day. As soon as I wake up, Will Power helps me get out of bed. Then, Charlie Horse comes along, and when he is here, he takes a lot of my time and attention. When he leaves, Arthur Ritis shows up and stays the rest of the day. He doesn't like to stay in one place very long, so he takes me from joint to joint. After such a busy day, I'm really tired and glad to go to bed with Ben Gay. What a life!

(Note: If you are not familiar with Ben-Gay, years ago it was a salve used for joint aches and pains).

The first time I read this, I laughed heartily. My perspective is different since I'm now included in this population. While we laugh at this say-so, we must remain respectfully mindful about our senior population and our value to one another.

Our spirit is a part of us that does not age. Some call it our soul. It is just as alive at age ninety as it was the day of our birth. The spirit is our connection to God, to each other, and to this magnificent beautiful universe. It is where love, grace, kindness, and beauty abounds. Try reaching out from the depths of your soul to the soul of a senior with Alzheimer's, a person dying, or one who is unconscious. They hear and receive the generosity of your soul and appreciate it deeply.

"That is why we never give up. Though our bodies are dying, our spirits are being renewed every day" (2 Corinthians 4:16, NLT).

August 22
A Woman's Viewpoint

I'm fond of the movie *Fences*. It's so true to life. During the March 5th reflection, I introduced the theme of bitterness demonstrated by the main character Troy. His bitterness stems from racism and classism that prevents him from achieving his dreams. However, Troy's wife has three strikes against her: racism, classism, and sexism. Troy is unaware that he has a superior attitude toward women. He does not realize they are interrelated. Therefore, he is an unconscious active participant in the same system that oppresses him.

In one scene, Troy and his best friend use sexist language to belittle a woman Troy is having a relationship with—"*men who frequent Alberta's house—hips wide as the Mississippi River—legs don't mean nothing, all you do is push them out the way.*" Troy's oppressive ways get worse. He impregnates the same woman he belittles and then ask his wife to mother the baby when Alberta dies in childbirth.

Sexism is deeply rooted in the cultures of the world. The oppressed and the oppressor—men and women (unknowingly) say or do things that promote sexism. Until there is a better understanding of the pervasiveness of sexism in our country and throughout the world, racism, sexism, and classism will continue to be prevalent and create divisiveness and disunity.

"Of all the evils for which man has made himself responsible, none is so degrading, so shocking or so brutal as his abuse of the better half of humanity; the female sex."
~*Mahatma Gandhi*

August 23
God Always Has a Powerful Antidote to Our Doubts

If I say, there's no way this can be done. God says, "What is impossible with man is possible with God." -*Luke 18:27, NIV*

God's answer to my complaint of being too tired: "Take my yoke upon you and learn of me; for I am gentle and humble in heart; and you shall find rest unto your souls. For my yoke is easy and my burden is light" -*Matthew 11:29-30, NIV*

If I dare say, love seems to escape me. God says, "I have loved you with an everlasting love. I have drawn you with unfailing kindness." -*Jeremiah 31:3, NIV*

Times when I don't feel like going on, God says, "They who hope in the Lord will renew their strength. They will soar on wings like eagles; they will run and not grow weary; they will walk and not be faint." -*Isaiah 40:31, NIV*

When I can't figure things out, God says, "Trust in the Lord with all your heart and lean not on your own understanding." -*Proverbs 3:5, NIV*

I mumble, I don't think I can do it; God says, "So do not fear, for I am with you; do not be dismayed, for I am your God. I will strengthen you and help you; I will uphold you with my righteous right hand." -*Isaiah 41:10, NIV*

"Your word is a lamp for my feet, a light on my path" (Psalm 119:105, NIV).

Attention and Intention for Life and Health

"My son, pay attention to what I say; listen closely to my words. Do not let them out of your sight, keep them within your heart; for they are life to those who find them and health to a man's whole body" (Proverbs 4:20-22, NIV).

Attention means to direct the mind to an object; to concentrate. Intention means having a goal or determination to achieve something. This is what Proverbs 4:20-22 is all about.

Attention is needed to read God's word. With intention, I reap the benefits from reading God's word. Attention says I will make time to read the Bible or listen to God's word. Intention says with regular Bible reading, I expect to gain wisdom, understanding, and direction for living the best possible life in the midst of my circumstances.

In Proverbs 4:22, an added benefit is listed. It says that the word is life to those who find them and health to one's body. Now, it makes sense that the Bible gives life to those who read it, but the reward of health is an added benefit. How does this happen? Is there science to back this up?

I can't provide any specific scientific evidence for how reading the Bible improves our health. But after practicing medicine for more than thirty-seven years, I have learned that health is more than the result of taking a handful of pills. Health is more than the absence of disease.

The physical body makes up only one part of who we are. The physical body works with our emotions, intellect, and spirit to create health and wholeness with God, with ourselves, with each other, and with this magnificent universe. A good starting place to heal our emotions, strengthen our minds, and empower our spirits is God's word. When we heal these three, there is less stress on the physical body and improved health.

Now, reading the Bible is not easy. To find pearls of wisdom requires one to dig deep into the scriptures. Most are not on the surface. Jesus compares it to a man in search of pearls. When he discovers one of great value, he sells all he has to purchase the pearl of great price.

If this is your goal, then it requires your attention. If you believe it is worth your time, then you will apply intention.

"The word of God is living and active. Sharper than any double-edged sword, it penetrates even to dividing soul and spirit, joints and marrow; it judges the thoughts and attitudes of the heart" (Hebrews 4:12, NLT).

August 25
The Prime of Her Life

In 1967, Philippa Schuyler died in a helicopter accident while helping to evacuate children from a Catholic school in Vietnam. At the time of her death, she was thirty-six years old and in the prime of her life. Reading her life story makes me think she had already passed her prime for it is reported that she crawled at four weeks, walked at eight months, read at the age of two, and played the piano at age three. She became a talented composer, and by the age of thirteen completed her first symphony that was performed at Carnegie Hall by the New York Philharmonic Orchestra. Additionally, she was fluent in French, Spanish, and Italian and toured more than fifty countries as a goodwill ambassador for the United States.

This young lady accomplished more in her brief life than most in two or three lifetimes. According to God's word, this was God's plan. "Your eyes saw my unformed body; all the days ordained for me were written in your book before one of them came to be" (*Psalm 139:16, NIV*). At the age of thirty-six, she died helping children. There is no eternal value in the things of this world. One additional note: there were several other well-known helpers who also died in their thirties: Dr. Martin Luther King, Jr., at the age of thirty-nine, Malcolm X at age thirty-nine, and Jesus Christ, at age thirty-three.

"So we make it our goal to please him, whether we are at home in the body or away from it. For we must all appear before the judgment seat of Christ, so that each of us may receive what is due us for the things done while in the body, whether good or bad" (1 Corinthians 5:9-10, NIV).

August 26
Pretense

"You try to look like upright people outwardly, but inside your hearts are filled with hypocrisy and lawlessness" (Matthew 23:28, NLT).

Jesus tells the story of a father and his two sons (*Matthew 21:28-32*). The father instructs his sons to work in his vineyard. The first son refuses but later regrets his actions and goes to work. The other son says with sincerity and respect, "Yes, sir, I will." However, he never goes.

The first son represents sinners who flat out refuse to accept Jesus. They do not fear God and have no intention of being obedient. They are honest with themselves, but somewhere along the way, they hear and receive God's message, repent, and are received into the body of Christ.

The second son represents those who live a life of pretense, pretending to be religious or as some say, 'holier than thou,' but are spiritually bankrupt. They are in church every Sunday. They criticize others who don't follow the law. Jesus had no sympathy for this population.

Pretending to be who you are not is self-deception. Pretend illness—pretend wealth—pretending to be a friend—pretending nothing is wrong—pretending to be religious and living a life of disobedience.

"God desires truth in the inward parts and in the hidden part thou shall make me know wisdom" (*paraphrased Psalms 51:6, KJV*). It is near impossible to gain wisdom without being honest with one's self.

"This above all: to thine own self be true. And it must follow, as the night the day; thou canst not then be fall to any man."
 ~Williams Shakespeare

August 27
Thank God!

"Devote yourselves to prayer, being watchful and thankful" (Colossians 4:2, NIV).

Whenever I consulted my mother for guidance on personal issues, the first words she spoke were, "Thank God!" She exhibited an attitude of gratitude to God regardless of life circumstances and wanted to remind me of its value. She didn't know anything about the science behind being grateful. She had not read that gratitude improves overall well-being, increases happiness, reduces depression, and strengthens resiliency; and, she didn't keep a gratitude journal.

Being grateful was a way of life for my mother. She signs her memoir *Waving from the Balcony*: "This book is my testimony of how good God has been to me. To God be the Glory." Inside her book, she writes, "From my perspective, God always moves according to what is best for us in the stream of human history." Nothing was outside of the boundary of God. In other words, she believed that, "All things work together for good to them who love God, to them who are called according to God's purpose" (*paraphrased Romans 8:28, KJV*).

There is an abundance of scientific knowledge about the benefits of having an attitude of gratitude. In this time of divisiveness in our nation, everyone could benefit from being more grateful. If we are really honest with ourselves, we would acknowledge that we don't need instructions on how to be grateful or how to express kindness and appreciation to others. God placed these characteristics in our spiritual, physical, and emotional make-up. As my mother would say, "Thank God!"

"Let gratitude be the pillow upon which you kneel to say your nightly prayer. And let faith be the bridge you build to overcome evil and welcome good."
~ Maya Angelou

August 28
Godly Nutrition

In the twenty-first century, everything is based on scientific evidence. This includes food, and that is good because when people know the science behind a recommendation, they are more likely to change their behavior. Long before evidenced-based studies, Hippocrates, who was born 460 BCE and known as the father of medicine said, "Let food be thy medicine and medicine be thy food." And, long before Hippocrates, God said, "I have given you the seed-bearing plants on the face of the earth, and every tree that has fruit with seed in it. They will be yours for food" (*Genesis 1:29, NIV*).

Scientific studies have shown that eating more fruits and vegetables improves mental well-being as well as increases energy and manages weight.

Raspberries improve blood sugar in persons at risk for diabetes.

High-fat diets lower the "good" bacteria in the gut and increase the risk for development of chronic diseases.

Red meats in diet increases the amount of a chemical in the blood that is linked to heart disease.

It's amazing that Hippocrates knew the health benefits of vegetables and fruits. It is even more amazing that this is found in the first chapter of Genesis.

"So whether you eat or drink or whatever you do, do it all for the glory of God"
(1 Corinthians 10:31 NIV).

August 29
Readiness: Staying Woke (Matthew 25:1-13)

One of my favorite contemporary gospel songs is titled *Will you be ready when Jesus comes?* It was popular in the late 70's and early 80's. Each time I heard it sung by our choir, I could feel the prospect of Jesus' return with great expectations. Throughout the New Testament, there are many reminders about the second coming of Christ. "Therefore, keep watch, because you do not know on what day your Lord will come" (*Matthew 24:42, NIV*).

Jesus shared the parable about the ten bridesmaids and the bridegroom to emphasize this point. The bridesmaids are metaphors for ten Christians. The bridegroom is a metaphor for Jesus. From a glance, all the women were typical church attendees. They had bright smiling faces, groomed hair, polished nails, and stylish apparel. The difference was their inner beauty. Jesus says that five were foolish and five were wise.

The foolish Christians were like those whose faith had no depth. They enjoyed listening to sermons. They moved their bodies and waved their hands to the gospel music every Sunday, but the message never took root inside their souls. When the bridegroom (Jesus) makes his appearance, the foolish Christians miss out because they were not ready to enter the wedding feast.

The wise Christians also enjoyed the sermons and gospel music. However, they made preparations internally by burning the midnight oil for Christ. They spent time praying, reading and meditating on God's Word. Their lives shined with faith, patience, love for God, love for self, and love for others. The wise Christians are welcomed into the wedding feast. They knew that the Christian life is not just for Sunday mornings, but a life lived in a state of readiness to serve.

"When Christ, who is your life, appears, then you also will appear with him in glory" (Colossians 3:4, NIV).

August 30
Forgiveness

In the book of Acts, there was a man named Stephen, a devout follower of Jesus Christ. The Holy Spirit empowered Stephen with boldness, wisdom, and love. He was despised because he spoke truth to power. What was most unusual about Stephen was his response to the violent attacks on his life. Eventually, he was stoned to death because of this. As he succumbed to the religious leader's savagery, he prayed, asking that God would not hold it against them. In other words, instead of focusing on his predicament and being bitter, angry, or upset, he prayed for his perpetrators well-being.

At one time or another, each of us have experienced hurt, agony, and anger at being mistreated. When we get angry, there is a tendency to strike back, retaliate, or get even. Sometimes, we allow the experience to linger in our thoughts for years. Either way, the focus is on self, what has been done to me. Neither way is helpful or healthy.

Our challenge is to overcome these feelings by rising to a higher level of spirituality in Jesus Christ, through the act of forgiveness. Similar to Jesus, Stephen showed us a better way. He prayed for the forgiveness of his enemies even as they were about to triumph over him. How was he able to do this? It was through the gift of the Holy Spirit which every believer has.

The Holy Spirit is God inside us. The Holy Spirit empowers us to love and forgive. We are born with free will, and it will always remain. But if we choose, we can resist and forgive.

"But the fruit of the Spirit is love, joy, peace, forbearance, kindness, goodness, faithfulness, gentleness and self-control. Against such things there is no law" (Galatians 5:22-23, NIV).

August 31
Remembering My Mother

"Love thy neighbor as thyself; put all hatred on the shelf and don't give way to hating. Wait on the Lord and do good and don't get tired of waiting. Lose no time in judging one another, for with the judgment you judge, so shall you be judged my brother."
~Nan Campbell Fletcher

Born in 1921, my mother grew up in abject poverty in a small country village on the outskirts of Bainbridge, Georgia. Although poor, her family never went hungry because they planted fruits and vegetables every year and raised chickens, cows, and hogs on their farm. A college education was not possible.

In her memoir, *Waving from the Balcony*, she writes about the time when the president of Albany State College came to their home and offered her a partial scholarship. She declined the scholarship to avoid placing strain on her parents. In her heart, she knew her future would be fine. After high school, she was able to obtain a job in the Franklin D. Roosevelt's Work Progress Administration (WPA) program and save enough money to attend nursing school in Jacksonville, Florida.

Her life was transformational from start to finish. Not only did she receive her nursing diploma, she earned a BS and an MA degree. Her work history included serving as nursing supervisor of obstetrics and gynecology, public health nursing, and she designed and taught a health occupations course in the Duval County school system. After her retirement, she came to work in my medical practice as a staff RN. To top it all off, at the age of eighty-five, she was finally able to complete her book. Now, she too is waving from God's balcony, cheering us on toward the finish line.

"Wherefore seeing we also are compassed about with so great a cloud of witnesses, let us lay aside every weight, and the sin which doth so easily beset us, and let us run with patience the race that is set before us" (Hebrews 12:1, KJV).

September 1
Friendship: The Blessing of Belonging

"Entreat me not to leave you, or to turn back from following you. For where you go, I will go. Where you stay, I will stay. Your people will be my people and your God will be my God. Where you die, I will die, and there I will be buried"
Ruth 1:16-18 (NIV).

One of the greatest blessings of all is the bond of friendship. The story of Ruth and Naomi is one of the most beautiful friendship stories in the Bible. Naomi had two sons who were married to Ruth and Orpah. After her husband and both sons died, Naomi decided to return to her homeland of Bethlehem in Judea. Although Naomi tenderly loved her daughters-in-law, she did not want to stand in the way of their future, so she encouraged them to stay in their homeland.

Orpah and Ruth had to decide. Should they remain in their country with their families and friends, or should they follow their mother-in-law to a foreign country? Orpah kissed Naomi goodbye, but Ruth clung to her. Naomi tried multiple times to get Ruth to leave, but she refused. She was bonded to Naomi. She wanted to share her joy, be a part of her family, comfort her in sorrow, and most importantly worship her God.

I believe Ruth felt nothing was greater than the blessing of being with Naomi. Naomi finally realized Ruth's mind was made up. Their relationship led to Ruth marrying Naomi's brother-in-law. From that line of descendants King David is born and ultimately from that same line comes our Lord and Savior Jesus Christ. There are blessings more precious than gold that result from God-filled relationships.

"I believe in angels,
The kind that heaven sends,
I am surrounded by angels,
But I call them friends"
˜Aizabel Parinas

September 2
A Pedigree Like No Other

This reflection is an extension of the one shared on September 1 where I wrote about Ruth's love for her mother-in-law, Naomi. Ruth left her country of Moab and immigrated with Naomi to Bethlehem in Judea. Ruth and Naomi's special relationship is only one of the beautiful stories in the Book of Ruth. Another is to see how God's plan of salvation included people from a variety of ethnic and cultural groups.

Ruth, an immigrant from Moab, marries an Israelite named Boaz. Boaz is the son of a prostitute named Rahab, who sacrificed her life for two Jewish spies. Ruth married into a leading Israelite family. Ruth and Boaz have a son named Obed. Obed's son is Jesse. Jesse's son is King David. David and Bathsheba's ancestral line leads directly to Jesus Christ. The genealogy of Jesus Christ can be traced from a lineage that is inclusive of an immigrant, a prostitute, and one convicted of sexual exploitation and murder.

It appears to me that pedigree was not of high importance in God's plan. Immigration status did not keep one from being in God's divine lineage. Negative societal practices were not excluded. And in today's society who would have kind words for David? Yet, each one of these people were used by God. He did not snub them. In a similar way, every human being has a purpose on this earth. Perhaps the lesson to learn is to follow God's ways of divine inclusiveness. Show love to every human being you meet. They are special in God's eyesight just as much as you are.

"Oh, how great are God's riches and wisdom and knowledge! How impossible it is for us to understand God's decisions and God's ways! For who can know the Lord's thoughts? Who knows enough to give God advice? And who has given God so much that God needs to pay it back? For everything comes from God and exists by God's power and is intended for God's glory. All glory to God forever! Amen" (Romans 11:33-36, TLB).

September 3
Room to Grow: A ZZ Plant

Twelve years ago, I received the gift of a ZZ plant. ZZ is short for Zanzibar. When I first received the plant, it was in a beautifully decorated stoneware pot that was small enough to sit on a table in my office. It didn't require much care, minimal water, a little laughter, and some small talk. It kept growing and expanding over the next few years.

Five years later, ZZ had grown significantly. To continue to expand, it would need more room to grow. Not having a green thumb, I took the plant to a nursery, selected a new pot, and let them work their magic which they did. It was at this same time that my work experience was changing, and the thought came to me that I too needed room to grow and that maybe ZZ was a metaphor for my life.

Three more years have passed, and my plant is due for another transplantation. It has outgrown the huge pot it now sits in. I'll need help getting it to a nursery this time because of its size. Once ZZ is removed from the pot, the gardener will prune the roots and soil to remove the moldy and tightly coiled areas. Pruning stimulates a plant's natural healing process and promotes healthy growth.

Like a plant, if we don't make adjustments, we stop growing. Our spiritual roots need to be pruned and stimulated in God's soil. Those things that are keeping us stuck need to be cut away. Then, we can breathe again. This new growth helps us to mature spiritually and grow in a new place or new position in life.

"For I know the plans I have for you," declares the Lord, "plans to prosper you and not to harm you, plans to give you hope and a future" (Jeremiah 29:11, NIV).

September 4
A Pity Party

Sojourner Truth was an abolitionist who spoke both against slavery and in support of women's rights. In Sojourner Truth's memoir, the story is told that she and Frederick Douglass were attending a conference in Akron, Ohio. The Fugitive Slave Law had become a major obstacle to freedom for the enslaved, and Mr. Douglass was feeling low. He expressed, "There is no longer any hope for justice other than bloody rebellion. Slavery must end in blood."

A woman of large stature, 6-foot-tall Sojourner Truth leapt to her feet and thunderously spoke out from the audience. "Frederick, is God dead," she poignantly asked. Douglass knew she was right and came to his senses. In other words, even with all we face, there is no time for pity parties. Sojourner refused to take this outlook on slavery.

Sometimes friends and family members want us to participate in their gloom and doom perspective. Have you ever been invited to a pity party? What was your response? Have you had a pity party? Dare I ask you to ponder how often you have pity parties.

Indeed, there are challenges we face every day, sometimes every hour. We have to move quickly to our best self and remember who is the lifter of our heads. We have to remember that the best is yet to come.

In spite of the bleakness of slavery, Sojourner Truth and many like her held on to their faith in God. We have to remember that God is with us even when we walk through valleys of darkness and death.

"Most of the important things in the world have been accomplished by people who have kept on trying when there seem to be no hope at all."
~ *Dale Carnegie*

September 5
Fig Tree Faith

One of the most thought-provoking stories in the Bible are five verses in the Gospel of Matthew 21:18-22. A fig tree covered with leaves is a sure sign that figs are on the tree. Jesus spots a fig tree that is filled with leaves but has no figs. Something is clearly wrong. Although it appears in fruit-bearing form, the tree is flawed and unable to grow figs. It looks good with all those beautiful leaves but will never produce fruit.

What does faith have to do with the flawed fig tree? The flawed fig tree is a metaphor for a flawed religion. Flawed religion is not productive or powerful. "They will act as if they are religious, but they will reject the power that could make them godly" (*2 Timothy 3:5, NLT*). To add to this, Jesus says: "A tree is identified by its fruit. Make a tree good, and its fruit will be good" (*Matthew 13:33, NIV*). The fruit of the spirit are love, joy, peace, patience, kindness, goodness, faithfulness, gentleness, and self-control (*Galatians 5:22-23, NIV*).

Faith in God and fruits of the spirit work hand-in-hand. The more your life produces fruit born of the spirit, the more your faith in God increases. The more your faith in God increases, the more God's power will become manifest through you. As Jesus told his disciples, "If you have faith and don't doubt, you can do things like this and much more. You can even say to this mountain, 'May God lift you up and throw you into the sea,' and it will happen. You can pray for anything and if you have faith, you will receive it" (*Matthew 21:21-22, NLT*).

"But you will receive power when the Holy Spirit comes on you; and you will be my witnesses in Jerusalem, and in all Judea and Samaria, and to the ends of the earth" (Acts 1:8, NIV).

September 6
Confidence

Today's society has a way of culturally conditioning us to feel we are better or less than others based on what behavioral scientist call our extrinsic worth. Extrinsic worth is when one's self-confidence is based on physical appearance, economic and social status, educational achievements, country of origin, or whether we have committed a scandalous act or broken the law or what others think about us. We find ourselves constantly trying to prove ourselves. Confidence goes up or down based on what we have, don't have, and what we have done, or didn't do.

On the other hand, when self-confidence comes from within, one does not need outside validation to boost self-worth. This is known as intrinsic worth. In my opinion, intrinsic worth is hard to maintain if you are trying to do it alone. You will still end up comparing yourself to others.

From a Christian perspective, intrinsic worth makes sense not because we boast with confidence, but because our worth comes from the Holy Spirit that abides in us and validates our being. We no longer seek validation from external circumstances or people. The Holy Spirit gives us wisdom, understanding, counsel, strength, knowledge, zeal, and fear of the Lord. These are the drivers of our self-confidence and why we can say, "I can do all things through him who gives me strength" (*Philippians 4:13, NIV*).

Thank you, God for the divine confidence you give me to live out your vision for my life. You believe wholeheartedly in me. Thank you for the blessed gift of life of which there is nothing greater. That is what you demonstrated through Jesus Christ. You are my confidence. You are my light and my salvation. Your faith in me gives me divine confidence that can never be taken away. AMEN

September 7
The Emotion of Fear

Fear is an emotion that controls our actions and reactions more than any other. Fear of what others think about us, fear of being rejected, fear of failing, fear of being attacked, fear of speaking, fear of getting caught, fear of stepping out and witnessing of God's saving power, fear of asking someone to come to church or Sunday school, fear of job loss, fear of losing financial investments.

God understands the emotion of fear. The word of God says a lot about fear: "Do not be afraid. I have ransomed you. I have called you by name. You are mine. When you go through rivers of difficulty you will not drown. When you walk through fires of oppression, you will not be burned up. The flames will not consume you" (*Isaiah 43:1-2, NLT*). Even so, fear dominates our being, whether we admit it or not.

The Almighty Sovereign God reminds us the safest fear is fear of Him. Fear of God is more of a reverence and respect for the Creator of the Universe. Fear of God does not eliminate problems. Rather, fear of God gives us courage to trust God, to expect God to prepare the way for us, to always remain prayerful, and to rest in God regardless of the external circumstances.

"The Lord is my light and my salvation, whom shall I fear. The Lord is the strength of my life. Of whom shall I be afraid" (Psalm 27:1, KJV).

September 8
Forgiveness

As long as we live, there will always be a need to ask God to forgive us for something. As long as we live, there will always be someone we need to forgive.

A story by an unknown author is told of a brother, Johnny and a sister, Sally who spent the summer with their grandmother on her beautiful farm. Their grandmother had a favorite duck. She instructed her grandchildren not to throw rocks because one might hit her pet duck. One day, Johnny was all excited and felt a little mischievous. He spied Grandma's pet duck and threw a rock, hitting the duck in the head and killing him instantly. When he went to hide the dead duck in a wood pile, there was his sister giving him a sly look.

Sally told Johnny this would be their secret forever as long as he did what she said, and he agreed. Every time there were chores to do, Sally would give her brother that sly look. For days, he did both of their chores while Sally had all the fun. One day, he got tired of being black-mailed and went to his grandmother and confessed, asking for her forgiveness. She responded that she saw him when he hit her duck and that because she loved him, she had already forgiven him. She wanted to see how long he would put up with his sister's antics.

In this beautiful story, the grandmother symbolizes God, the one who sees everything we do. Johnny's sister symbolizes his conscious, never letting him forget what he had done.

Our loving God forgives us for those sins we don't confess, re-member, or even recognize as sins. We must trust God's words about forgiveness. "As far as the east is from the west, so far has he removed our transgressions from us" (*Psalm 103:12, NIV*).

"*If we confess our sins, He is faithful and just to forgive us our sins and to purify us from all unrighteousness*" (*1 John 1:9, NIV*).

September 9
True Love (1 Kings 3:16-28)

Two women lived in the same residence, and both had recently given birth. One woman fell asleep and rolled over on her child suffocating him to death. While the other mother was sleeping, the one woman took the other mother's baby and placed her dead child alongside the sleeping mother. Upon awakening, the mother immediately knew the dead baby was not hers. The women argued back and forth about who the living baby belonged to.

Finally, they consulted King Solomon, known to be the wisest man on the earth. King Solomon ordered a sword to cut the baby in half. The baby's real mother begged that he not cut her son and quickly gave up ownership to save her son. As for the other mother, it was okay for Solomon to cut the baby in two. At that point, the King knew the infant's mother and gave him to her.

The true love of a mother extends beyond the female gender. Motherhood takes full responsibility for the child's life. Motherhood love is loyal, trustworthy, and unconditional. She will sacrifice motherhood for her baby: "Please, my lord, give her the living baby! Don't kill him" (*1 Kings 3: 26, NIV*).

"Love is patient and kind. Love is not jealous or boastful or proud or rude. Love does not demand its own way. Love is not irritable, and it keeps no record of when it has been wronged. It is never glad about injustice but rejoices whenever the truth wins out. Love never gives up, never loses faith, is always hopeful, and endures through every circumstance (1 Corinthians 13:4-7, NLT).

September 10
Funeral Procession: The Terminator
(Luke 7:11-17)

This story found in Luke is about death. If anyone needed to live, it is this young man. For he was the only son of a poor widow. He is dead, and the mother walks this lonely road to the gravesite to bury him. On her way there, the funeral procession gets interrupted by Jesus and his followers coming from the opposite direction. Jesus is filled with compassion and says to the weeping widow, "Don't cry."

A person who tells someone on the day of their loved one's funeral not to cry must have something better to offer. Sure enough, Jesus walks over to the coffin touches it and says to the young man, "Rise!" A miracle takes place. The son sits up, starts talking, and Jesus gives him back to his mother. Jesus shows unmerited grace to the young man. He gets to live again.

The resurrection of this young man's life is a sign of what is to come to those who believe in Jesus. Yes, we all will die. A human body cannot live forever. When Jesus says, "Don't cry," he is talking about eternal life: "I am the resurrection and the life. Whoever believes in me, though he die, yet he shall live, and everyone who lives and believes in me shall never die" (*John 11:25-26, NLT*).

Those who believe in Jesus receive unmerited grace. Because of grace, at the appointed time, those who have died will rise up and live again. For those who do not believe, there will be a second funeral procession that will not be terminated by Jesus.

"Jesus said to her, 'I am the resurrection and the life. The one who believes in me will live, even though they die; and whoever lives by believing in me will never die. Do you believe this'" (John 11:25, NIV)?

September 11
2001

On this day in 2001, a catastrophic event happened in our country. Two thousand nine-hundred seventy-seven people lost their lives. If you were alive and old enough like me, you'll probably always remember September 11th for the rest of your life. I remember where I was and what I was doing. Fear gripped my soul. During that time, people talked about the depravity of the minds of people that would fly passenger planes into buildings. September 11th was a day of terror that caused some to question the existence of God, or ask the question like Jeremiah, "Why, O God, does the righteous suffer?" Why is there so much misfortune?

My husband reminded me the Almighty Sovereign God speaks to us in the midst of crisis. In fact, God speaks to us all the time, but it is not easy for us to give God our undivided attention. Proverbs 16:1 says that the preparations of the heart belong to man, but the answer of the tongue is from the Lord. In other words, our hearts are filled with strong feelings of hurt and fear about what happened on that awful Tuesday, but only the Lord has the answer. We must somehow find a way to listen to what God is saying even when the presence of God comes to us in terror.

More than two thousand years ago, God used an act of terror to bring salvation to the world. There was nothing to suggest that an all-powerful God was on that cross, but God was, and it was the way God chose to redeem humanity. Throughout history, God has allowed man free reign to live however we choose. As a result, we have seen terror, oppressed nations, races, and families to the extent that evil transcends rational understanding. We have to learn to be still and listen to God's message. This is where faith comes in. The righteous live by faith and it is far better to live by faith and be patient in silence because God never forsakes the righteous.

"In the world you will have tribulation. But take heart; I have overcome the world" (John 16:33, NIV).

September 12
The Power of Divine Prophesy

There are certain experiences that are impossible to stop even when it seems that a simple action would change the course of events. Five hundred years before Jesus lived, Zechariah prophesied that Israel would see their king coming to them, "humble and riding on a donkey" (*Zechariah 9:9, NLT*). When Jesus told his disciples where to find the donkey and to tell the owner the Lord needs it, it would have been virtually impossible for the donkey's owner to say no. It is impossible to stop what had already been prophesied.

The Pharisee's wanted Jesus to not just quiet the crowd but to reprimand them. Jesus informed them that their request was impossible. Speaking from the Old Testament, Jesus said, "If they keep quiet the stones would cry out" (*Luke 19:40, NIV*). It is impossible to stop that which is ordained by God.

Another such event occurred long after the resurrection of Jesus. A wise man warned a group of religious leaders against killing Peter and several other apostles. He reasoned, "If they are teaching and doing these things merely on their own, it will soon be overthrown, but if it is of God, you will not be able to stop them. You may even find yourselves fighting against God" (*Acts 5:38-39, NLT*). You cannot stop what is God ordained.

James reminds believers to be mindful of the prophet's messages: "You must pay close attention to what they wrote, for their words are like a lamp shining in a dark place—until the Day dawns, and Christ the Morning Star shines in your hearts. Above all, you must realize that no prophecy in Scripture ever came from the prophet's own understanding" (*2 Peter 1:19-20, NLT*).

"I make known the end from the beginning, from ancient times, what is still to come. I say, 'My purpose will stand, and I will do all that I please'" (Isaiah 46:10, NIV).

September 13
Making a Bold Statement With Your Life

Do you know people who are bold witnesses for Christ? Regardless of their ethnic background, social status, job, education, expectations of family or friends, they dare to make a statement for Jesus with their life. While some people admire Jesus from the sidelines, play it safe, and go with the flow, there are others who make a statement for Jesus with their life.

In the Gospel of Luke, chapter 8:3, Joanna is a woman who made a bold statement with her life. Joanna was the wife of Chuza, who managed the monetary affairs of Herod, the governor of Galilee, the same one who had John the Baptist killed. Joanna was from the upper class and ordinarily had nothing to do with 'regular people.' But she moved beyond that character description. She had been healed by Jesus, but the type of healing was not known. She was very grateful for her healing and followed Jesus from that point on.

After her healing, Joanna used her life, time, talents, and wealth to support the ministry of Jesus. She could have received her healing and to avoid creating a stir with Herod chose not to become a disciple, but she felt compelled to follow Jesus.

Joanna was at the cross where she watched Jesus die in agony. She was among the women who gathered at the tomb to discover that it was empty and hear the angel say, "Why do look for the living among the dead" (Luke 24:5 NIV)?

What statement do you make with your life? Do you dare to be different? Women like Mother Teresa, Rosa Parks, Sojourner Truth, Harriet Tubman, Eleanor Roosevelt, Coretta Scott King, and Oprah Winfrey made a statement with their lives and helped change the course of history.

"Think like a queen. A queen is not afraid to fail. Failure is another steppingstone to greatness."
~ *Oprah Winfrey*

September 14
Eyes on the Poor (Luke 16:19-31)

In the above scripture reference, Jesus dramatizes the danger of clinging to money as if life depended on it. Wait a minute. It just might.

Jesus tells the story how a poor sickly beggar named Lazarus and an unnamed wealthy religious man end up changing places. The rich man regarded his wealth as a special blessing to do with as he pleased. He went to church every Sunday, lived in a majestic mansion with multiple servants, and dressed in designer clothes every day.

Lazarus lay peacefully at the home of the rich man's gate and begged for crumbs until starvation and illness overtook him. He died without a funeral or respectful burial. Jesus said he was carried away by angels to be with Abraham in paradise and live in eternal peace, joy, and heavenly communion.

The wealthy man died and had an unrivaled funeral. The church was filled to capacity. His gravestone was made from beautiful granite. Jesus says his spirit was dropped off in a place where he is stripped bare of any eternal inheritance, forever to experience continuous pain and suffering.

It appears that the two men exchanged positions in the afterlife. Is Jesus saying that wealth and social status are primary indicators of who goes to heaven and who goes to hell? I don't think so. I suspect that there are some poor people in hell and some rich people in heaven.

Here are questions this story asks: Who is Lord of your Life? What is most important to you in this life? Is it the love of money and what it does for you? Have you discovered the secret to contentment in life? What is your response to those in need?

"Looking at his disciples, he said: 'Blessed are you who are poor, for yours is the kingdom of God. Blessed are you who hunger now, for you will be satisfied. Blessed are you who weep now, for you will laugh'" (Luke 6:20-21, NIV).

September 15

Children Are Our Future

Eighteen days after the 1963 historic March on Washington, a bomb exploded in the 16th Street Baptist Church in Birmingham, Alabama. At 10:22 AM, on September 15, three fourteen-year-old girls: Addie Mae Collins, Cynthia Wesley, Carole Robertson, and eleven-year-old Carol Denise McNair were killed. The Ku Klux Klan planted fourteen sticks of dynamite beneath the church steps and destroyed the future of these young girls. Their deaths became a major catalyst for the Civil Rights Movement.

These young girls were sweet adolescents, typical fun loving, artistic, quiet, soul mates. The one survivor says that just before the explosion, the girls were doing girl stuff in the bathroom: primping, talking, and laughing together. Their future was stolen from them, but they will always be remembered.

At that time, Condoleezza Rice, former Secretary of State and a native of Birmingham, was just a few blocks away at her father's church when the attack happened. Her memory of the event is worth sharing. "It is a sound that I will never forget, that will forever reverberate in my ears. It was meant to suck the hope out of young lives, bury their aspirations, and ensure that old fears would be propelled forward into the next generation." Ms. Rice was among many who refused to let this evil act destroy their hope for a successful future.

On May 24, 2013, President Barack Obama posthumously awarded a Congressional Gold Medal to these four girls. The tragic bombing was a significant milestone in the civil rights movement leading to the passage of the Civil Rights Act of 1964.

"Truth forever on the scaffold, wrong forever on the throne, yet that scaffold sways the future, and behind the dim unknown, standeth God within the shadow, keeping watch above His own."
~*James Russell Lowell*

September 16
The Divine Cling

Sometimes, when I look back through my daily journaling, I am amazed at some of the things I have written. On one particular entry, the contrast found in my writing was quite revealing:

Thank you, God for this new morning. There is beauty, sunshine, peace all around me. The grip of loneliness is trying to cling this morning. Cling loneliness. But, rest assured. God's cling is much, much tighter. God bless this day.

It is amazing how our faith walk is filled with struggle against evil, but what is more important is the fact that God always has an answer. In Mary Fishback Powers' poem, "Footprints in the Sand," her faith is strengthened when she acknowledges that regardless of life situations, God's hands are holding her and will never let her go. We have to keep on pushing and not give in until God speaks.

In the spiritual, "Nobody knows the trouble I see. Nobody knows but Jesus. Nobody knows the trouble I see, glory hallelujah," the contrast is beyond rational thinking. The song has been associated with a mother witnessing her daughter being sold away in slavery. It depicts not only the separation, but the anguish and grief heard in the cries of her child, which is more than she can bear. In the midst of horrific suffering and sorrow, she shouts, glory hallelujah! Giving God praise in the midst of her pain is a demonstration of her faith walk.

As you read through the Psalms, try to appreciate the peaks and valleys the Psalmist experiences repeatedly:

"I had fainted unless I had believed to see the goodness of the Lord in the land of the living" (*Psalm 27:13, KJV*).

"O Lord, how long will you forget me? Forever? How long will you look the other way? How long must I struggle with anguish in my soul with sorrow in my heart every day? But I trust in your unfailing love. I will rejoice because you have rescued me. I will sing to the Lord because God has been so good to me" (*Psalm 13: 1-2, 5-6, NIV*).

Thank you, God, for your love that covers us like a baby floating around in her mother's placental fluid. Your love is deep and keeps us from drowning. May we always be reminded that this is a walk by faith, and it is far better to live by faith and patiently wait because God never forsakes the righteous. AMEN

"Yet, I will rejoice in the Lord. I will joy in the God of my salvation. God makes my feet like hinds feet. God makes me tread upon high places" (paraphrased Habakkuk 3:18-19, KJV).

September 17
Live for Me

A father wrote an article to express the grief he still felt after his four-year-old son died following a long and complicated illness. Fifteen months had passed and the wound in his heart was still fresh. The young son's illness kept him in the hospital for seven months. His recovery took another seven months after being released from the hospital, and then he had a relapse and passed away. The father and his wife had been given a precious gift that gradually and agonizingly slipped out of their hands. As I read his story, I ached for him and felt his broken heart.

This family's story is the story of all of our lives. As sure as we make our miraculous entry into life, we will eventually transition out. We can't look into a crystal ball and see the age or circumstances leading up to death. Yet, the loss of a young child is still most disturbing.

In the Bible, there is the story of Job. All of Job's children died. Although he was blessed with more children, I believe his heart still ached for his children who died. As Christians, we earnestly say to be absent from the body is to be present with the Lord. But that does not stop the heart from breaking. Grieving is normal and healthy.

In Dostoyevsky, *The Brothers Karamazov, Volume 1*, a priest tells the story of his first experience with death. He was eight years old when his seventeen-year-old brother died after living with an extended illness. During the time he was ill, he gained wisdom and insight. Some days before he passed, he tenderly and lovingly told his young brother, "Live for me."

Children always seem to get it. The message "live for me" is like 'golden apples in a silver basket' (*Proverbs 25:11, NLT*). In my opinion, this request demonstrates his faith in his brother and his desire for him to be happy after his earthly departure. He was saying, while my earthly life is ending, enjoy life for me. Have fun for me. Live like it is your second time around. Live each day like it is your last day on earth. We all can use this wholesome advice.

"*The reality is that you will grieve forever. You will not 'get over' the loss of a loved one; you will learn to live with it. You will heal and you will rebuild yourself around the loss you have suffered. You will be whole again, but you will never be the same. Nor should you be the same nor would you want to.*"
~ *Elizabeth Kübler-Ross and David Kessler*

September 18
A Poem About Love

Here's my hand at poem writing based on (1 Corinthians 13, TLB)

You may have a voice to sing like an angel
Or preach with power and fire,
But without love your words and your voice
Will merely sound like noise

You may have faith to move a mountain and cast it into the sea;
You may have wealth to give all you want, still miss eternity—
Money is no guarantee

If you see someone whose head is hanging low,
Put your arms around their heart and watch them glow

Love is gentle and love is strong
Love keeps no record of when it's been wronged;
Love is patient and love is kind
Love is giving and forgiving all the time

Faith keeps holding to God's unchanging hand
Hope sees that the best is yet to come
Love matures, endures, and withstands the test of time

"Love must be sincere. Hate what is evil; cling to what is good. Be devoted to one another in love. Honor one another above yourselves" (Romans 12: 9-10, NIV).

September 19
A Healthy Relationship with God—
Mind, Body, and Spirit

There are no boundaries between the physical body, mind, and the spirit. The physical body works in harmony with our emotions, intellect, and spirit to create health and wholeness. Proverbs: 3:7-8 (KJV) is a wise saying about holistic health: *"Be not wise in your own eyes; fear the Lord and depart from evil. It shall be health to thy navel and marrow to thy bones."* Let's look closer.

Mind—Be not wise in your own eyes. In other words, don't be a know it all. This can be a challenge for most of us. We like to think we know the right answer and are quick to tell another in a condescending tone, "You're wrong." With respect to health and depending on who you ask, there are a variety of answers on what it takes to be healthy. There is much we don't know. There's even more we don't know that we don't know. The Almighty Sovereign God is the only omniscient one.

Spirit—Fear the Lord and depart from evil. How many people hide unacceptable behavior when the pastor comes around? It's nice to be respectful of the minister, but God sees everything we do. To fear the Lord is a blessing. The angel of the Lord guards all who fear God. Psalm 103:17 (KJV) says, "The mercy of the Lord is from everlasting to everlasting upon them that fear Him." To fear God means to have faith in God.

(Body)—It shall be health to your navel and marrow to your bones. This is a wonderful promise. What does this mean? Here's what I believe. The divine peace that comes from a close relationship with God takes a lot of stress off of the entire body. It is well documented that stress leads to many health problems. The peace of God is a path to a healthy body, mind, and spirit.

"Be not wise in your own eyes; fear the Lord and depart from evil. It shall be health to thy navel and marrow to thy bones" (Proverb 3:7-8 KJV).

September 20
Patience and Courage

"I must be patient. When I am patient, I can accomplish twice as much."
~ Juanita Fletcher Cone

Lauren Martin shares a story about a taxi-driver who had one more customer to pick up before his long day would end. He was parked at a house. After waiting several minutes, he started to leave. Then, on instinct he went and knocked on the door where he found an elderly lady placing the last of her personal items into a small suitcase. He assisted with the belongings and held her arm to support her down the stairs and into his cab. He thought to himself how glad he was that he had knocked on her door.

She gave him the address to her destination and then asked if he would drive through downtown. This way would take much longer, but she explained, "I'm in no hurry. I'm on my way to hospice." She was ninety-years old, with no family left, and was on her way to spend her final days on earth in a hospice home. At that point, he turned off the cab meter and followed her directions. Over a span of two hours, he became her guardian angel, following her lead. She went to her former workplace, to the neighborhood where she and her husband had lived, and to a ballroom where she used to go dancing, sharing with him quaint stories about those special places as they went. It warmed the taxi driver's heart, and he felt grateful to share these moments with her.

After a while she asked to be taken to her destination. She thanked him for giving an old woman a little moment of joy. In the moment she needed help, God worked through a tired taxi-driver whose heart was kind and patient enough to be her angel. The blessings were both hers and his. The experience changed his life forever, and he was grateful to be an instrument in God's hands.

"The end of something is better than its beginning. Patience is better than pride"
(Ecclesiastes 7:8, GNT).

September 21
Florence Griffith Joyner (Flo Jo)

"Like an athlete I punish my body, treating it roughly, training it to do what it should, not what it wants to" (1 Corinthians 9:27, TLB).

On this day, twenty-two years ago at the young age of thirty-eight, Olympic track star Florence Griffith Joyner was eulogized. I used to enjoy watching her perform at track and field events where she exemplified strength, beauty, and self-confidence.

She was a class act who never let her supporters or her country down. And, to date, she is still the fastest woman of all time because no one has broken her 1988 100-meter and 200-meter records. What was most inspiring to learn about Joyner was her faith in God.

"Florence read her Bible every day. She walked the walk and talked the talk," her husband, Al Joyner said. Bob Kersee, her former coach said, "What was in her heart every time she laced up her spikes was Jesus."

No human being knows the moment, time, or hour of their earthly transition. Whatever one does for the Lord, should be done like it is the last thing we are going to do on this planet. If you are not doing it for the Lord, it won't matter anyway because only what you do for Christ will last.

"...Whatever you do, do it all for the glory of God" (1 Corinthians 10:31, NLT).

September 22
"Ain't Got Time To Die"

Don't let the title of the above Negro spiritual mislead you. The words and music written by Hall Johnson (1880-1970) was meant to describe one of the ways the enslaved took care of their spiritual, emotional, and physical needs. In spite of consequences from the overseer or slave master, some of the enslaved became ministers and evangelists to help heal the ill, feed the hungry, and encourage those in despair.

Because there were so many who needed help, these ministers and evangelists had to move courageously and with deliberate haste. Time was of the essence as they moved. Their work was directed by the Lord and reiterated in their singing, "Keep so busy praising my Jesus, working for the kingdom, healing de sick, giving my all, I ain't got time to die."

"Ain't got time to die" was the way these ministers and evangelists expressed the critical importance of their work. As I listened closely to the words, I could hear Jesus saying, "I must work the works of him that sent me, while it is day: the night cometh, when no man can work" (*John 9:4, KJV*). They were doing the Lord's work and as such, there were inordinate risks.

"Ain't got time to die" speaks to the courage, resolve, and patience of the enslaved. They were saying, if we are to live, we must find ingenious ways to heal our bodies, keep our minds strong, and keep our spirits above the absurdity of slavery. Because they lived their life with spiritual power and their eyes on the future, their descendants are alive today. Many are teachers, authors, research scientists, college presidents, supreme court justices, astronauts, CEO's of major corporations, world renown neuro-radiologists, endocrinologists, and presidents of national medical societies, and medical colleges.

"And he said unto them, How is it that ye sought me? wist ye not that I must be about my Father's business" (Luke 2:49, KJV)?

September 23
Illegitimate

When you read about Saint Martin de Porres, the first thing you learn is that he was the illegitimate child of a Spanish man and a freed slave. It is unfortunate that society stigmatizes children with words that have negative connotations. There is nothing illegitimate about a child. And certainly not Saint Martin de Porres who lived in Peru from December 9, 1579, to November 3, 1639.

What is even more astonishing is that he never denied his identity. He just went about doing good. He grew up in poverty and was blessed to be taken in by the Dominican Monastery. He worked as a servant or "lay helper." De Porres was obsessed with goodness and generosity in a world of oppression and obstacles. Even though the rule was that a mulatto could never become a monk, over a nine-year period of observing his charity, care for the sick, humility, penance and intense prayer life, the rules were suspended, and he was made an "unofficial priest."

In addition to his love and care of people and animals, he had unusual spiritual gifts. Light filled the room when he prayed. It was said he could teleport himself. De Porres was spotted in faraway countries though he never left his monastery. He was able to levitate, pass through locked doors, and share miraculous knowledge.

He established an orphanage and hospital in Peru for the impoverished population. It was this tireless work that gained him national and international recognition.

Saint Martin of Porres was beatified in 1837, by Pope Gregory XVI and canonized on May 6, 1962, by Pope John XXIII. Indeed, there was nothing illegitimate about St. Martin de Porres.

"For he chose us in him before the creation of the world to be holy and blameless in his sight. In love" (Ephesians 1:4, NIV).

September 24
When the Vision becomes Clear

"How long must I call for help before you will listen? I shout to you in vain, there is no answer" (Habakkuk 1:2, TLB).

The prophet Habakkuk begins to question and complain to God on behalf of his people. Habakkuk whose name means 'strong embrace of God' had a great love for his people. He fulfilled the role of watchman over them. He just wanted to know, how long?

Habakkuk lived at a time when Judah was constantly being oppressed by great empires. He prayed to God and asked: why do you allow 'wicked' men to continuously oppress your people? He argued that although God's people were not perfect, their sins did not compare with those who oppressed them. Then, he waited, and God's answers came. The response was similar to the answer God gives us when we feel taken advantage of, helpless, or over-burdened.

The answers may or may not be what we expect to hear but it is through our divine encounter with God that we are able to rise above the situation. When we enter into God's gates with thankfulness, humility, and an openness, like Habakkuk, God's larger vision for justice and righteousness becomes crystal clear. The vision is more trustworthy than the present circumstances.

A few days before Dr. Martin Luther King, Jr. was assassinated, I believe God's vision of justice was made perfectly clear to him: "I've been to the mountaintop...I've seen the promised land. I may not get there with you. But I want you to know tonight, that we, as a people, will get to the promised land."

Pay no attention to those who trust in themselves and their might. "The just shall live by faith" (Habakkuk 2:4, KJV). Not by sight—not by rationality.

Habakkuk's encounter with God gave him strength and faith to rise above the situation which contradicts that God reigns. He could express with power and blessed assurance:

"Though the fig tree do not blossom and there be no fruit on the vine. The produce of the olive fail, and the field yield no food. The flock be cut off from the fold and there be no herd in the stall. YET, I will rejoice in the Lord, I will joy in the God of my salvation. For God the Lord is my strength. God makes my feet like hinds feet. God makes me tread on the high places" (Habakkuk 3:17-19, KJV)

September 25
The Power of Sharing:
The Widow of Zarephath (1 Kings 17)

It is easy to share out of your abundance, but it takes faith to share with limited income. It is easy sharing with believers in your church, but it takes unconditional love to share with people you know nothing about. This is what the widow of Zarephath faced. She lived in abject poverty and in a city that worshipped the idol god Baal. Baal was the lord of rain and fertility, but everything was dry. The widow's barley field had dried up, and she only had a tiny amount of oil left. Just as she was expecting death from starvation, something happened.

Elijah, God's prophet needed housing and sustenance, and although she was poor and of a different religion, God sent him to her. When he arrived, she was about to cook the last of her food. She was puzzled when he requested a cake be made for him before she or her son ate. Elijah assured her from now on, she and her son would have plenty. The widow followed his request and her cupboards started to fill and remain full of flour and oil.

The Almighty Sovereign God uses a worshiper of Baal to feed and house the prophet Elijah. In return, she is blessed in a land with drought. The widow came to realize that God sent Elijah and she believed.

This Old Testament story is similar to the New Testament stories about the poor widow who placed all she had in the offering and the little boy who shared his meal that ended up feeding five thousand. Don't be afraid to share! Share a smile. Take time to be present with someone and listen to them. Share a meal. Share a financial gift, regardless of the amount. Always remember the five loaves of bread that fed five-thousand people (*John 6:14, NIV*).

"The generous will prosper; those who refresh others will themselves be refreshed" (*Proverbs 11:25, NIV*).

September 26
A Miracle From Grief

Thomas A. Dorsey is known as the father of gospel music. He was a songwriter, pianist, and singer. He wrote the classic gospel hymn, "Precious Lord, take my Hand." The circumstances surrounding the development of the song are most notable.

Mr. Dorsey and another musician were about to leave town to participate in a revival. Mr. Dorsey wavered about taking the trip because his wife was pregnant and close to delivery. He made the decision to go but after about thirty miles, he returned home to retrieve music papers he had left. He observed his wife resting, so he left again. At this point, his musical companion decided not to make the trip, so he drove alone. The following night he received a telegram that his wife had died in childbirth, and the baby died shortly thereafter.

Dorsey was shattered by the death of his wife and baby. He blamed himself and multiple 'ifs' started to press on his mind: If I had canceled the revival. If I had stayed with her after I returned home to get the music, things may have turned out differently. Initially he lost his heart for writing gospel music but with renewed strength and faith in God, he says, "the words 'Take my hand, Precious Lord' came twisting out of my heart."

Heavenly Father, thank you for Mr. Thomas Dorsey, a great lyricist and musician. He showed us how to use the painful circumstances of life to create hope, not just for himself but for people around the world who sing his beautiful hymn. "Precious Lord, take my hand." AMEN

September 27
Voices, Writings, and Pictures of Love

Memories are especially important after the death of someone special. After my husband died, I wished I had kept his voicemail recording as a keepsake before turning off his phone.

Here's a thought. Take some time to write a letter or two to special people in your life. Let them know their value to you and how they make you happy. Give it to them as a keepsake. After my husband died, while sorting through old papers, I found a letter Cecil wrote to me eleven years before he passed. It was like I had found a million dollars. I was overjoyed to see his handwriting and reading the letter was comforting, healing, and inspiring.

Hearing a loved one's voice is also cheering. My husband was a preacher, so I have tapes of his sermons. But to have a voicemail left specifically by him on my phone that I could listen to periodically would be heartwarming.

Pictures are wonderful, and I have hundreds of them. But if you're really good with technology, consider making a video of you and the family being active together.

Grief is not easy; though it is something most people will eventually experience. As the grief starts to wane, having unique mementoes of personal writings, voice recordings, and videos bring joy, while keeping your loved one's spirit alive.

"...Use each precious moment with all the precious seconds in it to love each other for Christ's sake for the next precious moment may very well be too late..."
~Nan Campbell Fletcher

September 28
Aging Well from an Elderly Prophetess Perspective

During my childhood, I used to wonder what being old would be like. Now at seventy-one, I'm learning fast. My hair is thinner with lots of gray strands. My teeth are starting to shift. I have my share of word-finding difficulties and a mean case of arthritis in both knees. As well as a few lady issues that I'll leave to your imagination. In spite of these challenges, I believe I am aging well. I was able to retire from the practice of internal medicine. I only take three pills a day (blood pressure, cholesterol, and thyroid). I exercise every day and three of those days are at a supervised wellness center. And six months after retiring, I published my first book.

In the Gospel of Luke 2:36, there is a story about an elderly prophetess named Anna, a widow most of her adult life. She was devoted to God and spent most of her time praying and fasting at the temple. On the special day when Anna's prophetic abilities became evident, Mary and Joseph had come to the temple to present baby Jesus for circumcision and purification. Anna began to "prophesy about the child all were looking forward to for the redemption of Jerusalem."

Anna was aging well. Her relationship with God continued to mature down through the years. Anna embraced aging with dignity and humility and, as such, is filled with gratitude. To have a place in the Bible is indicative of how well-regarded she was. Most of all, she had faith that one day the savior would come and bring redemption to the world.

"The preacher came to call the other day. He said at my age I should be thinking of the hereafter. I told him, oh, I do that all of the time. No matter where I am, in the parlor, upstairs, in the kitchen or down in the basement, I ask myself, what am I hereafter?"
~Author Unknown

September 29
Anxiety

During my senior year in high school I was invited to participate in an oratorical contest sponsored by the Elks organization. Three college scholarships would be awarded to the top three contestants.

I was afraid of embarrassing myself, so I tried to wiggle out of participating, but my mother wouldn't let me. My sister who had excellent writing skills wrote this magnificent speech for me, which I memorized and practiced until I knew it by heart. But I was still anxious and afraid until I learned that on this particular year, only one other individual had entered the contest.

The event was being held about two hours from our hometown of Jacksonville, Florida, and on the day of the contest, we encountered a severe thunderstorm, but our family made it safely to the site. Upon arrival, we learned that the weather prevented the only other contestant from coming, and I was one happy camper.

To this day, I remember the speech entitled, "Education, our greatest challenge" and because of unforeseen circumstances, I was able to speak with power and confidence and won the first-place scholarship by default.

It was amazing how my mother, sister, and stormy weather helped allay my anxiety, making it easy for me to demonstrate a speaking skillset that I never knew was in me.

"Therefore, do not worry about tomorrow, for tomorrow will worry about itself. Each day has enough trouble of its own" (Matthew 6:34, NIV).

September 30
A Contribution of a Lifetime:
William Augustus Hinton, MD

Untreated syphilis was one of the first diseases that alarmed me as a first and second-year medical student in the 1970's. From infancy to the elderly, no age group was spared. Syphilis is a disease that can affect almost every part of the body if left untreated, from the eyes to the brain. It can be confused with a variety of diseases. In fact, syphilis is known as the great imitator. The good news is there is a test to diagnose the disease. Indeed, it is worth reflecting on the life of the man who set the standard for the development of accurate syphilis testing. He overcame a lot of obstacles.

Dr. Hinton was born in 1883. His parents had been slaves. His brilliance was recognized early when he earned a B.S. degree from Harvard in 1905. In 1909, after teaching for a while, he enrolled in Harvard Medical School, declining a scholarship reserved for African American students. Instead, he competed and won two prestigious scholarships two years in a row that was open to all students. Medical school is a four-year course of study, but he graduated with honors in three years.

In spite of this, he was denied a medical internship due to his race, so he worked as a 'voluntary assistant' in the pathology laboratory at Massachusetts General Hospital. This is where he became an expert in syphilis and in 1915, wrote a chapter in a leading medical textbook. In 1918, he returned to teach at Harvard Medical School and remained there for over thirty years.

In 1927, William Augustus Hinton, MD developed a test that reduced the number of false positive test for syphilis, lessening the need for unnecessary hazardous treatment. His test was endorsed by the U.S. Public Health Service. In 1936, he published the first medical textbook by an African American: *Syphilis and its Treatment*.

Dr. Hinton did groundbreaking research and work in the diagnosis and treatment of syphilis during the dark days of reconstruction and Jim

Crow. He was determined to not let mountains of obstacles stop him from achieving goals that would advance health care of all people.

"God has not called me to be successful. God called me to be faithful."
~Mother Teresa

October 1
Shedding the Leaves

"The earth is the Lord's, and the fulness thereof; the world, and they that dwell therein" (Psalm 24:1, KJV).

Except for evergreens, every October, leaves begin to fall until trees are bare. I was amazed to discover that leaf shedding is a God-designed built-in process that protects trees during cold weather. It's not just the October winds and hard rains that cause leaves to fall.

Scientist have discovered hormones that trigger the leaves to break off and shed. As this occurs, the trees reabsorb and store nutrients. At the end of this process, a protective layer of cells grows over the exposed areas. This process not only protects trees during the winter but prepares them for the growth of new leaves in the spring.

In a similar way, God's master creation, human beings, have multiple built-in mechanisms to protect and keep the body working in balance. Ever wonder how we breathe, talk, walk, or dance at the same time? And when we sleep, everything continues to function effortlessly. We, human beings have the ability to consciously decide what we want to do with our bodies. Sometimes these decisions work against natural survival mechanisms inside the body, but God never intended this. It's important for us to employ godly wisdom as we exist inside our awesomely crafted bodies.

From time to time, reflecting on the beauty and brilliance of God's universe will help us to appreciate the miracle of life and sing with vigor and vitality, *How Great Thou Art.*

"Through him all things were made; without him nothing was made that has been made" (John 1:3, NIV).

October 2
October is Breast Cancer Awareness Month

Years ago, a forty-year-old young lady scheduled an appointment with me because of swelling and bruising on her breast. She thought the swelling started after bumping into something. Upon observing her breast, I was almost lost for words and had to maintain my composure. It was apparent this did not start from a bump. The skin on the breast was dimpled and reddish orange in color, and I could see a lump protruding out of the breast skin.

My medical training said she had waited too late for cure. Despite my thoughts, I referred her to an oncologist. She followed his recommendations to have surgery and extensive chemotherapy and subsequently became cancer free. Following successful treatment, she would come to my office for her annual physical examination and we'd rejoice together about her miraculous healing. She is a very fortunate lady with an excellent outcome despite waiting so long to be examined. What appeared to be inconceivable in my mind was made possible through God. Hear Jesus as he says to the disciples, "With man this is impossible, but with God all things are possible" *(Matthew 19:26, NIV)*.

Talk with your internist, family practitioner, or gynecologist about getting a mammogram. Most importantly, make the decision to eat healthy and get moving to lower your risk for getting breast cancer and live your best possible life.

"An ounce of prevention is worth a pound of cure."
~ *Benjamin Franklin*

October 3
Sacrificial Giving

"Then a poor widow came and dropped in two small coins. Jesus called his disciples to him and said, 'I tell you the truth, this poor widow has given more than all the others who are making contributions. For they gave a tiny part of their surplus, but she, poor as she is, has given everything she had to live on'" (Mark 12:42-44, NLT).

This is a lesson about surplus giving versus sacrificial giving. In this scripture, Jesus pays high commendation to a generous but poor widow. He observes how those with abundant means give only a tiny portion of their surplus, that which they don't even need to live. While the one with limited means gives all she has.

How often is this still the case in our communities today? There are numerous unnamed women and men who make sacrifices out of proportion to their means. They go without clothes, food, sleep, and money for their families, churches, and community. They won't have a bank full of money to leave after they die because they laid it all out on the court of life.

Sacrificial giving is godly giving. It means giving up that which you need as demonstrated by the poor widow or that which you dearly love demonstrated best by God: "For God so loved the world that he gave his only Son, so that everyone who believes in him will not perish but have eternal life" (John 3:16, NLT).

"One person gives freely, yet gains even more; another withholds unduly, but comes to poverty. A generous person will prosper; whoever refreshes others will be refreshed" (Proverbs 11:24-25, NIV).

October 4
Faith and Disappointment

"Now faith is the substance of things hoped for; the evidence of things not seen"
(Hebrews 11:1, KJV).

Suppose you commit to do everything right. You eat healthy organic foods, exercise thirty to forty-five minutes four to five days a week, get the proper rest, and sleep eight hours a night. You make annual visits to the doctor and regularly receive a clean bill of health. You spend time each day in prayer and meditation, attend church regularly and tithe every Sunday. Your work ethic is impeccable, and you volunteer at a homeless shelter two times a month. Nevertheless, life's unhappy moments occur and test your faith.

A heart attack, job loss, your child diagnosed with cancer or one is arrested for substance abuse or perhaps more than one of these disrupts your perfect life. Without an unwavering faith, these circumstances could lead to situational stress resulting in a host of physical or emotional ailments.

Jesus reminds us, "In this world you will have trouble" *(John 16:33, NIV)*. There will be challenges that may seem impossible to overcome. These discouraging experiences occur in the lives of believers and nonbelievers. The distinction with a difference is your faith in what God can do. Remain prayerful. You are never alone. Remember Jesus on the cross in his darkest hour. He never stopped talking to God. Expect God to make a way. Continue to believe that God is behind the scenes working out the best plan for your life circumstances. As you continue to trust God, the solution will become clear.

"But you must continue to believe this truth and stand firmly in it. Don't drift away from the assurance you received when you heard the Good News. The Good News has been preached all over the world, and I, Paul, have been appointed as God's servant to proclaim it" (Colossians 1:23, NLT).

October 5
Monkey See. Monkey Do.
Monkey Get in Trouble Too.

I am reminded of a story about a man who bought a monkey so he could have some fun. The monkey would mimic all of his owner's actions. At first, it was cute and comical. But then, it became quite annoying. The monkey would follow behind the man repeating every action he took. "How do I stop this madness?" the man asked himself

One day, he decided to let the monkey see him shave. He lathered his face and neck. And then, took a knife and placed the dull side of the knife on his neck, pretending to shave. Then, he left the room, leaving the door ajar to see what the monkey would do. The monkey lathered his face and neck. Then, picked up the knife and placed the sharp blade on his neck and cut his carotid artery. As a result, he bled to death.

Sometimes when we copy the behavior of others, we end up hurting ourselves. The Almighty Sovereign God has a special plan for every human being. God will guide you to discover your mission and purpose in life. Open your heart and mind to God. You have been fearfully and wonderfully made (*Psalm 139:14, KJV*). When you discover your purpose, you will discover joy and peace on earth.

"Don't copy the behavior and customs of this world, but let God transform you into a new person by changing the way you think. Then you will learn to know God's will for you, which is good and pleasing and perfect" (Romans 12:2, NLT).

October 6
Friendship and Love

"And the song, from beginning to end, I found again in the heart of a friend."
~ Henry Wadsworth Longfellow

A year before my husband passed, I backed out of the garage one day, and two birds flew onto the hood of my car. Awestruck, I continued slowly out of the driveway until they flew away. But this was not the end of my bird encounter. Twenty minutes later, when I arrived at work and parked my car, two birds flew onto my hood. I shared the moment with my husband, and we laughed together about the unusual occurrence.

Did this incident have any spiritual significance or was it just coincidental? Was there a message for me? Long after my husband passed, I thought about those birds. Perhaps God was saying that in the near future, Cecil, my best friend would make his earthly transition. But know this, nothing would separate the love you have for each other because love never ends.

Years ago, the song "I believe" was sung masterfully by Frankie Laine. The song reminds us that while we may not have the answers to the why's and how's of life, by faith we do see enough evidence that life goes on.

Every time I hear the birds sing in the early morning or watch one fly through the trees in my back yard, I believe. Although the wind (breath of God) passed over my beloved husband, through God's magnificent universe, I am reminded of him and healed a little more each day by the simplest of things in life.

"Friendship is born at that moment when one person says to another: 'What! You too? I thought I was the only one."
~ C.S. Lewis

October 7

Emotional Health

Depression is extremely common, yet for some reason people choose not to share when they feel depressed. Many patients present to the doctor's office with physical complaints that may actually be hiding depression rather than be a true primary physical disorder. Why do we tend to not think of ourselves as being depressed?

The feeling of depression is a natural state. It becomes a problem when one remains in this state over a long period of time, and it interferes with normal day-to-day activities. While it shouldn't, in our society, depression carries with it a negative connotation. Each part of us must be healthy to keep us in balance. Before I retired, I used to remind patients about the mind, body, and spirit connection and encouraged professional counseling.

If not attended to, depression can make you feel overwhelmed and helpless. No one wants to feel out of control. As a result, the mind masks this feeling through manifestations of physical symptoms, substance abuse, or other self-destructive behaviors.

Here are two questions primary care physicians ask patients to help identify persons at risk for depression:

1. Over the past two weeks how often have you been bothered by loss of interest or pleasure in doing things?
2. Over the past two weeks, how often have you been bothered by feeling down, depressed, or hopeless?

If your answer is more than half of the time for either, I strongly encourage you to talk with your doctor.

"Weeping may go on all night, but joy comes with the morning" (Psalm 30:5, NLT).

October 8
Breakthroughs, Health, Righteousness, and Glory of the Lord!

Chapter 58 of Isaiah is all about the purpose of true fasting—to break the chains of injustice, to share your food with the hungry, to house the homeless, to clothe the naked, and to not turn away from your own flesh and blood. As you can see, fasting is more about justice and righteousness than it is about personal image. These are challenging tasks, but the results would transform the world individually and collectively. "Then shall thy light break forth as the morning, and thine health shall spring forth speedily: and thy righteousness shall go before thee; the glory of the Lord shall be thy reward" (*Isaiah 58:8, KJV*).

In other words:

You will emerge like a bright shining star who speaks healing words of wisdom and peace to those you meet.

Your body is no longer constrained but moves with ease and more easily heals.

Your mind is clear, no longer controlled by imaginations and false knowledge.

Your soul is deeply connected to the Almighty Sovereign God. Wherever you go, God's *righteousness* leads the way. And after you leave, the glory of the Lord will remain with the people you touch.

"Then shall thy light break forth as the morning, and thine health shall spring forth speedily: and thy righteousness shall go before thee; the glory of the Lord shall be thy reward" (Isaiah 58:8, KJV).

October 9
October is Intimate Partner Violence Awareness Month

"Her brother Absalom saw her and asked, 'Is it true that Amnon has been with you? Well, my sister, keep quiet for now, since he's your brother. Don't you worry about it.' So, Tamar lived as a desolate woman in her brother Absalom's house" (2 Samuel 13, NLT).

Yes, stories about rape and sexual assault are in the Bible. In 2 Samuel, King David's daughter, Tamar was raped by her brother. As this story demonstrates, intimate partner violence occurs in families and is oftentimes kept secret. Tamar is told to keep quiet. In the end, it tears her apart, leaving her devastated and depressed. Victims must not remain silent.

Feminist activist, Gloria Steinem reported that since 9/11/2001, more women have been killed by "intimate partners" than all the victims in the September 11 massacre and the American victims in the Iraq and Afghanistan wars combined.

During one's lifetime, more than 1 in 3 women and 1 in 4 men have experienced sexual violence, physical violence, or stalking by an intimate partner. To add to these unnerving facts, the health consequences from such violence may lead to physical ailments, psychological distress, and risk-taking behaviors.

The impact of intimate partner violence or domestic violence is devastating to the physical and emotional lives of those affected. Survivor services must be enhanced, and perpetrators must be held accountable.

"The ultimate weakness of violence is that it is a descending spiral, begetting the very thing it seeks to destroy."
~ *Dr. Martin Luther King, Jr.*

October 10
Frederick Douglass Patterson

"I learned a lesson with regard to race that I never forgot: how people feel about you reflects the way you permit yourself to be treated. If you permit yourself to be treated differently, you are condemned to an unequal relationship."
~ *Frederick Douglass Patterson*

Frederick Douglass Patterson's legacy as an educator is unmatched. He was born on this day in 1901. Dr. Patterson served as President of Tuskegee University for eighteen years, and his many accomplishments included transforming Tuskegee Institute into a full-fledged university, founding the School of Veterinary Medicine, the Commercial Dietetics Program, and the university's engineering and commercial aviation programs.

In addition to his work as an educator, Dr. Patterson founded the United Negro College Fund (UNCF). UNCF supports thirty-seven private historically black colleges and universities throughout the United States and administers 10,000 scholarships every year. Since its inception in 1944, UNCF has raised over $3.6 billion.

Frederick Douglass Patterson is a hero, a hidden figure whose accomplishments are not well-known. His footprints are not only deep in Tuskegee Institute but in all historically black colleges. It is easy to confuse him with the great abolitionist and orator because he was named after him.

But Frederick Douglass Patterson stands tall with greatness and power for his contributions to education, and his footprints are deep in the soil of the United States of America.

"For as he thinketh in his heart so is he" (Proverbs 27:3, KJV).

October 11
She Was Not Afraid To Ask
(Joshua 15:16-17; Judges 1: 12-13)

Achsah (/ˈæksə/; Hebrew) was the only daughter of Caleb (one of the spies, along with Joshua who urged the Israelites to trust God and enter the land of Canaan).

Caleb remains faithful to God down through the years as a gallant warrior in Israel's army. One of the customs was for daughters to marry into a specific ethnic or cultural group of the father's choice. Caleb promises to give his daughter in marriage to whoever obtains a specific military victory. Othniel wins the battle and Achsah becomes his wife. Then, Achsah has Othniel ask Caleb for a piece of land, and Caleb gives Othniel a large portion of land as a dowry for his daughter.

Caleb loved his daughter. There was nothing he wouldn't give her. Perhaps that's why she didn't stop after her first request. When Othniel refused to ask her father for more, Achsah asked him directly for a spring of water. Her father responds by giving her not one but two sources of spring water.

Some might say that Achsah was not content with her father's gifts and wanted more. And, that's possible. But at no time is she described to be disrespectful or mean-spirited. Perhaps she was thinking about her future family.

Could this story be symbolic of God giving blessings beyond what we ask or even think? In this particular Bible story, Achsah received more than she had asked for. What would she have received if she had never asked? Christians must not be shy to petition God nor should they doubt God if the answer is not what's expected. God's answer could be yes, no, or wait. Faith in God means being obedient to God regardless of the answer or outcome.

"Now unto him that is able to do exceeding abundantly above all that we ask or think, according to the power that worketh in us" (Ephesians 3:20, KJV).

October 12
Choice

"It was scrubbing those household toilets with my mother that I saw and breathed income inequality. I decided to make a difference."

These are the words of a twenty-nine-year-old young lady, Alexandria Ocasio-Cortez. She is the youngest person elected to congress. She is bright, authentic, articulate, and courageous, all of which it takes to be a leader.

Her humble beginnings are remarkable and inspiring, but what I like most of all about the above quote is when she says, "I decided to make a difference." God has given us free will to do as we please. We can spend our days here on earth moping, brooding, and grumbling about our situation or we can choose to do something about it. Not only did she want to do something about her situation, but she wanted to make a difference. That makes her a servant-leader.

She is bright—graduating with honors from Boston University. She is authentic—not afraid to tell her story even if it makes some uncomfortable. She is articulate—able to connect with people from every walk of life and she uses today's technology as a powerful communication tool. She is courageous—not afraid to speak truth to power regardless of political affiliation.

"I can do all this through Christ who gives me strength" (paraphrased Philippians 4:13, NIV).

October 13
Acting Like an Eagle

"Bless the Lord, O my soul, and forget not all his benefits: who forgiveth all thine iniquities; who healeth all thy diseases; who redeemeth thy life from destruction; who crowneth thee with lovingkindness and tender mercies; who satisfieth thy mouth with good things; so that thy youth is renewed like the eagle's" (Psalm 103:2-5, KJV).

Psalm 103 begins with praise to God for four benefits: forgiveness, redemption, lovingkindness, and renewed youth like an eagle. How is an eagle's youth restored? An old fable gives insight. As they begin to age, the eagle returns to their dwelling nest for an extended period of time. During this time, they pound their beak on a rock until it falls off, then patiently wait for a new beak to grow. After the new beak forms, the eagle plucks away all the old feathers and new healthy feathers grow. Once this is complete, they are again able to mount up their wings and soar high above the clouds and storms. It must have been very painful for the eagle to pound its beak into a rock, but, it had to be done to complete the rejuvenation or restoration process. What is this fable saying?

Like the eagle, at some point in life, human beings will contemplate how they want the rest of their life to be. There's a lot outside of your control but there's a lot you can change. What does being renewed like an eagle look or feel like to you? Are you satisfied with your physical, mental, and spiritual health habits?

God can satisfy your mouths (your desires) with good things. God gives you the strength to pluck away those unhealthy habits and replace them with fresh, empowering, and transformative behavior. Rejuvenation does not happen overnight. It takes patience, but the promise has already been made.

"But they that wait upon the Lord shall renew their strength; they shall mount up with wings as eagles; they shall run, and not be weary; and they shall walk, and not faint" (Isaiah 40:31, KJV).

October 14
The Nobel Peace Prize

Annually six international prizes are awarded by the Nobel Foundation for outstanding achievements in the fields of physics, chemistry, physiology or medicine, literature, economics and for the promotion of world peace.

On this day in 1964, Dr. Martin Luther King, Jr. was awarded the Nobel Peace Prize for the promotion of world peace. At the time of the award, Dr. King was thirty-five years of age and the youngest winner ever of the prize. Dr. King pledged "every penny" of the prize money, which amounted to about $54,000 to the civil rights movement.

He was in the hospital for a check-up when he learned about the award. Here are some of his first comments taken from a New York Times article: "I do not consider this merely an honor to me personally, but a tribute to the disciplined, wise restraint and majestic courage of gallant Negro and white persons of goodwill who have followed a nonviolent course in seeking to establish a reign of justice and a rule of love across this nation of ours."

Dr. King said, he felt gratification in knowing "the nations of the world," in bestowing the prize on him, "recognize the civil rights movement in this country as so significant a moral force as to merit such recognition."

"Injustice anywhere is a threat to justice everywhere. We are caught up in an inescapable network of mutuality, tied in a single garment of destiny. Whatever affects one directly, affects all indirectly."
~ *Dr. Martin Luther King, Jr.*

October 15
Faith is Real

"Now faith is the substance of things hoped for, the evidence of things not seen" *(Hebrews 11:1, KJV).*

A counselor tells a student she doesn't have the ability needed to reach her dream profession and that she should aim for something that requires less skill. A job supervisor refuses to nominate a highly qualified person for a promotion, and instead, the less qualified person gets the job. He says this person has unique talents. You are told your idea won't work, and then your boss earns praise for your idea after making a few subtle changes. Life experiences like these are designed to lower your self-worth. But don't let them discourage you. Believe in yourself. Your life is to be lived according to God's expectation of you, not anyone else.

While reading the scripture, "Faith is the evidence of things not seen," I had a moment of insight about self-worth and value. Christians agree that faith in God is our proof of God. I believe that faith in God is also proof of my human value.

God had you in mind before you were formed in the womb. Every organ in your body was formed by God. You are not a chance happening. You were miraculously conceived when one sperm (one of 150 million) from your father successfully fertilized one egg from your mother. At the moment of fertilization, your genetic make-up was known. If any other sperm had made the connection with your mother's egg, you would not exist. You are the evidence of things not seen.

The Almighty Sovereign God believes wholly in you. You must believe in yourself. You are a special part of the evidence that God exists. There will always be people who will treat you with ridicule and contempt. Pray for them. There will be those who try to frighten you. Fear God instead. Stay true to God in mind and heart. "No weapon forged against you will prevail, and you will refute every tongue that accuses you" (*Isaiah 54:17, NIV*). In other words, pay no attention to people who use disempowering words. Press forward toward your dreams with holy confidence.

Whether you were raised by your biological, foster-care, or adoptive family, you are in the family of God with a specific mission on this earth that only you can fill. If you don't do it, it will be left undone. You are proof that God exists.

"For you created my inmost being; you knit me together in my mother's womb. I praise you because I am fearfully and wonderfully made. Your works are wonderful, I know that full well" (Psalm 139:13-14, NIV).

October 16
The Road to Recovery from Grief

Death of a loved one is difficult to comprehend and contend with, whether it is the death of an adult or child. I think it's most paralyzing when a young child dies. As I write this reflection, a raging hurricane tore through the panhandle. One of its victims was an eleven-year-old girl killed instantly by a tree that fell through the roof. I was six-hundred miles away, but my heart broke for her family. Human beings cannot understand why infants and children suffer and die, or why death comes like a thief in the night and snatches a bride from her husband. Not to mention cancer that sometimes lingers around almost teasing families anxiously hoping for physical healing that does not happen.

Who wants to travel the road of grief after the loss of a loved one? Not many. Death is uncomfortable for most people. Oftentimes, grieving people hear unhelpful messaging, "Be strong. It's time to move on." So, people cover up their true feelings and emotions about their loss. As a result, the grieving process is hindered.

Indeed, the grief road is rough, but it will slowly smooth out. Your broken heart will mend and when it does, you will begin to see and feel new meaning in your loved one's life. If you experienced the death of your child, you may start to feel their spirit soar through another child's laughter. If it was your spouse who died, you will discover beautiful ways to keep their memory alive. You may hear echoes of their wisdom through others or see someone who has the dignity and presence of your loved one that warms and helps heal your heart.

"You have turned my mourning into joyful dancing. You have taken away my clothes of mourning and clothed me with joy" (Psalm 30:11, NLT).

October 17
To Be or Not To Be Yourself

"I had to learn very early not to limit myself due to others' limited imaginations."
"I have learned these days never to limit anyone else due to my limited imagination."
~Mae C. Jemison

Born on this day, in the State of Alabama. Mae C. Jemison is a physician, chemical engineer, scientist, and astronaut. Flying aboard the Endeavor in 1992, Dr. Jemison is the first African American female astronaut to travel to space.

Dr. Jemison stands out not only for her intellect, but her spirit of service, courage, curiosity, and healthy self-knowledge. While attaining her degree in chemical engineering, she also fulfilled the requirements for a B.A. degree in African and African American studies. After medical training, she joined the Peace Corps to serve others. And no one can deny, it takes courage and curiosity to fly into outer space.

Who are you? You are not Dr. Mae C. Jemison, but you are a child of God and you also were given the gift of life for a very special reason. It is up to you to discover your reason for being. Never give up. Don't listen to the naysayers - including yourself if you are speaking words of defeat. Self-defeat is not productive. Whether you are one or 101, as long as you are alive, you can be something. You burst forth on this planet with energy. Use every last ounce of your God given energy.

"Greatness can be captured in one word: lifestyle. Life is God's gift to you, style is what you make of it."
~Mae Jemison

October 18
Determining Your Lot in Life:
All that Glitters is Not Gold

"The whole countryside is open to you. Take your choice of any section of the land you want, and we will separate. If you want the land to the left, then I'll take the land on the right. If you prefer the land on the right, then I'll go to the left" (Genesis 13:9, NLT).

Abraham made the above offer to his nephew Lot. Lot had been with Abraham since his own father died, but an argument between their herdsmen led to them going their separate ways. Abraham offered Lot the gift of choice, and Lot surveyed the land choosing the best and richest land near the Jordan river. But his choice for riches led to danger, mockery, and shame.

God has given us the gift of choice. The choices you make are yours. You make choices about finances, health, marriage, divorce, and jobs. It's always your decision. If things don't work out, there is a human tendency to blame others. The only person responsible for your choices is you. It is human nature to justify one's self by casting blame on other's. It satisfies our conscience. The husband says he can't lose weight because of his wife's good cooking. The parishioner would tithe if she had more money.

The blame game started with Adam and Eve. Both disobeyed God and chose to eat from the tree of the knowledge of good and evil. When confronted by God, Eve blamed the serpent for tricking her. Adam blamed God. Every person must assume responsibility for their choices. It may not always be easy, but it is possible with God's help. The wisest choice is to stay close to God every day. "In everything you do, put God first, and he will direct you and crown your efforts with success" (*Proverbs 3:6, TLB*).

"This day I call the heavens and the earth as witnesses against you that I have set before you life and death, blessings and curses. Now choose life, so that you and your children may live" (Deuteronomy 30:19, NLV).

October 19
Health is Wealth

My husband lived twenty-eight years after a heart attack. Our years before this life-changing event were stressful. He was in his eleventh year as a college president and my private medical practice was at its peak. Our eating habits were poor, and we did not exercise. One year in a cardiac rehab program and a vegetarian diet started to make a difference. Most importantly, my husband stopped smoking cigarettes.

One year later, he had open heart surgery. Surgery was a success, and he was able to gradually resume a safe cardiac rehab program. Although the need for cardiac bypass surgery was a surprise, the year before surgery was like a preparation period. Had he not made lifestyle changes, the outcome after surgery could have been more challenging. God's word says, all things work together for good.

Cecil's faith in God and self-confidence encouraged him to sign up for the 15K Jacksonville River Run. This run is 9.7 miles long, but the distance did not discourage him. He went to work on his body, mind, and spirit. Two years later, at age fifty-two, he completed the River Run in one hour and forty-four minutes. It takes a lot of courage to attempt this feat. Even more so after a heart attack and open-heart surgery. I was cheering him on at the finish line.

"Hold yourself responsible for a higher standard than anybody else expects of you. Never excuse yourself. Never pity yourself. Be a hard master to yourself-and be lenient to everybody else."
~ *Henry Ward Beecher*

October 20
What Are You Asking For?

"Sometimes you ask God for something and you don't know what you're asking."
~Mahalia Jackson

Two of Jesus's disciples, James and John, ask Jesus if they could sit in places of honor next to him when his kingdom reigned. The other disciples became indignant and annoyed at their unfair request. In their thinking, Jesus would become king here on earth, set Jerusalem free, and reign supreme on Mount Zion. They all believed they deserved special recognition when this happened.

James, John, and the other disciples didn't know what they were asking. As soon as it became evident that Jesus would not reign on earth, their demeanor changed. All the disciples who wanted to be next to Jesus had deserted him before he was even crucified. While Jesus prayed in Gethsemane, Peter, James, and John fell asleep. Judas betrayed him. Peter denied he even knew Jesus.

The disciples are no different from human beings today. How often do you ask Jesus for something grandiose—something that's not in accordance with the will of God? How often do you ask for something good for the wrong reasons? Things like: I want to be a pastor, an evangelist, a writer, singer, or write gospel music, so I can make plenty of money, be admired for my voice, or earn world recognition.

Jesus' answer to his disciples is the same answer today. If you're asking to feed the hungry, clothe the naked, provide shelter for the homeless, and to help set the oppressed free, then you'll always be next to me. Pray to always be a servant in God's kingdom.

"But among you it will be different. Whoever wants to be a leader among you must be your servant, and whoever wants to be first among you must be the slave of everyone else"(Mark 10:43-44, NLT).

October 21
Prevention Works

Without any prompting from her physician, a fifty-five-year-old woman requested a colonoscopy. She had been checked once a year with non-invasive stool testing, an acceptable way to screen. But she wanted to have a colonoscopy. She had no symptoms of abdominal pain nor had she seen blood or black colored stools. Yet, when the colonoscopy was performed, the specialist discovered colon cancer. This unfortunate discovery turned into a fortunate consequence because the cancerous tumor was successfully removed with no subsequent need for chemotherapy, and the lady has been cancer free for well over eight years. Prevention works.

A fifty-two-year-old man completed a fecal stool test to screen for colon cancer. This test checks for traces of hidden blood that cannot be seen with the naked eye. His stool tested positive for blood. Positive findings require a follow-up colonoscopy, which he agreed to have. The colonoscopy revealed a colon cancer that was found early enough to be surgically removed with no need for chemotherapy. Prevention works.

If you are forty-five years or older and have not been screened for colon cancer, please contact your primary care physician about getting this test done today.

"He who cures a disease may be the most skillful, but he that prevents it is the safest physician."
~ *Thomas Fuller*

October 22
Healthy Decision-Making

One day while driving, I saw a pink car with the words, "Love you Mom" skillfully and boldly displayed on the trunk. As I passed the car, I noticed a beautifully painted breast cancer ribbon on the passenger front door. I pondered on this wonderful way to honor their mother. Unfortunately, there was one glitch. The driver in the pink car was smoking a cigarette. At that point, my attention moved away from the tribute he was paying to his mother to the harm he was doing to his body.

Tobacco is still the leading cause of preventable death in the United States. Smoking causes chronic lung disease, lung cancer, and many other types of cancer as well.

It is Breast Cancer Awareness month and attention is given every year to this important issue because breast cancer screening saves lives. But cigarette smoking still has to be addressed. There has been a significant decrease in the number of persons who smoke cigarettes. However, forty-two million Americans still smoke cigarettes. If you know someone who smokes, encourage them to make the healthy decision to quit.

During the time I practiced medicine, I asked patients about cigarette smoking at every office visit. I celebrated those who had quit and told them, "This is the best health decision you will ever make." My advice to those who smoked was similar, "The best health decision you will ever make is the decision to quit smoking. Tobacco cessation is not easy, but it is possible."

"Then an old sage remarked, it's a marvel to me that people give far more attention to repairing results than to stopping the cause when they'd much better aim at prevention."
~Joseph Malin

October 23
God's Creative Love

From beginning to end, throughout the Bible, the overarching theme is a message of love. It was love that formed this breathtaking universe and its wonders: the sky ... the stars ... planets ... moon ... sun ... oceans ... mountains ... valleys ... and deserts. It was love that made it possible for animals, plants, and humankind to be created and pro-created down through the ages. Unfortunately, catastrophes such as tsunamis, earthquakes, hurricanes, volcano eruptions, flooding, and tornadoes make our love connection with the Almighty Sovereign God feel weaker. But God's love is everlasting.

When our health fails or we have lost a loved one to illness, divorce, mental illness, or incarceration, it can seem like the love that keeps the world ticking is not making our life clocks run well.

In spite of these challenges, God's love is still as abundant and unconditional as it has and will always be. Nothing is beyond the boundary of God's love, not our families, churches, communities, nations, or universe. No one and no situation, no matter how disruptive or challenging, is beyond the boundary of God's love.

"The Lord appeared to us in the past, saying: "I have loved you with an everlasting love; I have drawn you with unfailing kindness" (Jeremiah 31:3, NIV).

October 24
What Does It Mean to Love the Lord
With Your Whole Heart?

If you think about it, to love the Lord with your whole heart is quite similar to the way you love a special person in your life. When that special person in your life presents you with a gift, you find a way to show appreciation for what he/she has done for you. When we are in the presence of our love, we are excited. We are sensitive to what makes them happy and do things that make them happy. We spend time with them; we love talking with them and love listening to them.

The heart is the center of who you are. All of our emotions are linked to our heart: love, hate, joy, sorrow, anger, fear. When you love God with all your heart, God will take every emotion you experience and bless, nurture, and shape them into God's will for your life and for those whose lives you touch.

"You must love the LORD your God with all your heart, all your soul, and all your mind" (Matthew 22:37, NLT).

October 25
What Does It Mean to Love the Lord With All Your Soul?

You are alive because God breathed into your soul. Your soul is your innermost being and your connection to the Holy Spirit. It is the soul that helps you discover God's purpose for your life. But it is your faith in the Almighty Sovereign God that gives your soul spark and drive.

Recall when the angel came to Mary to announce that she would be the mother of Jesus, the savior of the world. She responded with faith, "Be it unto me, according to thy word" (*Luke 1:38, KJV*). She followed with a powerful soliloquy that began, "My soul doth magnify the Lord, and my spirit hath rejoiced in God my savior" (*Luke 1:46-47, KJV*).

It is through our soul that we worship and praise God. It's our soul that gets happy. Mahatma Gandhi said it this way: "When I admire the wonders of a sunset or the beauty of the moon, my soul expands in the worship of the creator." To love the Lord with all your soul is to stay attuned to the Living God. When you love the Lord with your soul, your relationship with God and with human beings is deep, meaningful, and rich.

"You must love the LORD your God with all your heart, all your soul, and all your mind" (*Matthew 22:37, NLT*)

October 26
What Does It Mean to Love the Lord With All Your Mind?

Philippians 2:5 says, "Let this mind be in you, which was also in Christ Jesus." When you love the Lord with your mind, you'll have to think a lot more spiritual thoughts. Making room for thoughts about God is challenging in this highly technological world. To love the Lord with your mind requires your will to be involved. It takes a conscious effort. Both your will and your conscious involve your mind. The Psalmist begins his prayers with "I will."

"I will never pray to anyone but you" (*Psalm 5:2, NLT*). "I will thank you, LORD, with all my heart; I will tell of all the marvelous things you have done" (*Psalm 8:1, NLT*). "I will bless the Lord at all times; his praise shall continually be in my mouth" (*Psalm 34:1, KJV*). Each time you speak these words and begin with I will, you are willing it to be so and it will happen. The mind is powerful.

When you love the Lord with all your mind, you give the power of the mind over to the Lord. As a result, your thoughts are more positive, peaceful, and joyful. You are able to think honest, just, pure, lovely, good report, virtuous, and praise thoughts that Paul speaks about in Philippians 4:8-9. This is not easy. The mind is like a message board filled with comments, notes, jottings, news, and reminders on every imaginable subject. I find the practice of meditation to be helpful. I refer you back to the February 7 reflection for how I meditate. Remember, "You will keep in perfect peace those whose minds are steadfast, because they trust in you" (*Isaiah 26:3, NIV*).

"You must love the LORD your God with all your heart, all your soul, and all your mind." (Matthew 22:37, NLT).

October 27
Harvest Time

"When the harvest time approached, he sent his servants to collect his fruit" (Matthew 21:35, NIV).

Harvest time is the time for gathering the rewards of one's work. Jesus used this parable about a landowner and the tenants who worked his land to teach a spiritual lesson about ownership.

The landowner planted a vineyard, dug a winepress for crushing grapes, built a wall around the vineyard and a watchtower. He rented the vineyard to some tenants and moved away for an extended period of time, and the tenants worked hard to grow crops.

With harvest time approaching, the landowner sent servants to collect his share of the crop. However, the tenants didn't want to give up any of the harvest and resorted to multiple violent tactics including murdering the landowner's son. They refused to let anyone come and collect the fruits of their hard labor. Ultimately, they forgot who owned the land.

Like these tenants years ago, human beings forget who really owns the land...who gives us the jobs, the houses, the money to accumulate wealth. We own nothing. We are merely tenants who are permitted to work in God's vineyard.

God created you and is a divine watchtower over your life. While you sleep, the angels stand guard.

The Almighty Sovereign God desires to collect a share of the crop each person earns. Ten percent of our earnings, ten percent of our time, and ten percent of our talent. When you give back to God, your crop gets sweeter and bigger. There is more rejoicing and meaningfulness in life, less anxiety, and less greed.

"Honour the Lord with thine substance, and with the first fruits of all your increase" (Proverbs 3:9, KJV).

October 28
Thoughts on Meditation

"You Should Meditate Every Day" is the title of an editorial in the New York Times that is quite interesting. I practice meditation on a regular basis and was glad to see a focus on mind health. The writer's primary concern was that technology (internet and social media) had overpowered his mind making him feel disconnected, distracted, resentful, and cynical. He noticed real change after he started meditating daily. Now, he feels that he is no longer controlled by technology. As expected, he acknowledged meditation to be an effective Buddhist practice known for centuries that he is now using and encourages others to join in.

The editorial comments were mostly from people who agreed with the benefits of meditation: "Combats stress and anxiety; settles my mind; simple but not easy" were examples of the usual comments. One naysayer found it unhelpful and a complete waste of time. I didn't read any comments from people who were willing to try meditation.

While meditation is usually associated with Buddhism, it is also a Christian practice that comes with a promise. "Keep this Book of the Law always on your lips; meditate on it day and night, so that you may be careful to do everything written in it. Then you will be prosperous and successful" (Joshua 1:8, *NIV*). "I meditate on your precepts and consider your ways" (Psalm 119:15, *NIV*).

Meditation is healthy and calming. While in Buddhism, one selects a mantra to keep the mind from wandering, the Bible encourages reflecting on scripture. Spend time memorizing passages of scripture. Most people know the Lord's prayer and the twenty-third Psalm by heart, but our minds have room for much more. Indeed, scriptures are soothing and even healing.

"My son, pay attention to what I say; turn your ear to my words. Do not let them out of your sight, keep them within your heart for they are life to those who find them and health to one's whole body" (Proverbs 4:20-22, NIV).

October 29
Words of Gratitude

The mind tends to focus on the missing elements in life. Unfortunately, this can lead to despair, jealousy, selfishness, apathy, and nonbelief. This is why a daily gratitude journal helps reframe your life picture. Sometimes in my journaling, I take a meaningful word and think of words that align with each letter in that word. Today's word is grateful. When I think about being grateful, I am more mindful that:

- Generosity scatters to others and increases to itself.
- Refreshing thoughts are like Vitamin C for the brain—brightening and cleansing.
- Appreciation is an attitude of gratitude.
- Thanksgiving goes back and forth and forth and back.
- Empathy is a source of grace to both the giver and recipient.
- Freedom from sin is a blessing and possible only through Jesus Christ.
- Understanding means to stand under another person and see from their perspective.
- Love never fails.

"But giving thanks is a sacrifice that truly honors me. If you keep to my path, I will reveal to you the salvation of God" (Psalm 50:23, NLT).

October 30
Forgiveness Is Important in Salvation

The heart of God's love is forgiveness. It is impossible to appreciate the love of God without experiencing forgiveness.

My story about forgiveness is one that will always stay with me. I asked God to bring to my mind things that were hindering my spiritual growth. As I listened, I jotted down all that came to mind. Then, I prayed the prayer of salvation and shredded the piece of paper. I can still picture in my mind and feel in my heart when God's world became alive in me, through people, music, plants, animals, and the total environment. I fell in love with God.

When you accept Jesus as your Lord and Savior, forgiveness of sins is immediate. You enter into an intimate relationship with Jesus that is accompanied by joy, liberation, and peace. You are born again.

Next, you must become rooted and grounded in God's word so that when cares, troubles, and challenges arise, you will not be tempted to lose hope and fall away.

Prayer of Salvation: O God, I am a sinner. I am sorry for my sins. I am willing to turn from my sins. I receive Jesus Christ as my Savior. I confess him as Lord. From this moment on, I want to follow you and serve you in the fellowship of your church. In Jesus name, AMEN.

October 31
The Bread of Life

Undeniably, eating is one of the most satisfying pastimes in life. Besides the three meals eaten on most days, food is a big part of Thanksgiving, Christmas, weddings, funerals, anniversaries, schools, banquets, parties, church activities and many other events. And there are shopping malls, where we may find almost as many restaurants and fast food places as there are places to shop.

Even in the days when Jesus walked the earth, food played a central role. Some people followed Jesus because of the food he passed out. If we are honest with ourselves, sometimes we follow Jesus for the food (blessings) he gives. In the Gospel of John 6:25-27 (*NLT*), Jesus said, "I tell you the truth, you want to be with me because I fed you, not because you saw the miraculous sign."

Jesus used this opportunity to teach, and his message was something like this: Food is important to our physical bodies, but there is another type of food necessary for spiritual life. In essence, he was saying, don't spend all your time laboring for perishable things like food but spend much more time laboring for food that brings everlasting life.

If one's physical body gets weak after one or two days without food, what happens to your spiritual body if you fail to take in God's word for days, weeks, or even months? Our souls need nourishment. Our soul is most important because it is where the spirit dwells. Our soul keeps us alive. It is the soul that makes us laugh, cry, love, and feel the burdens of other human beings. It is our soul that longs desperately to find peace with our Creator. We need to feed our souls.

"...Man shall not live by bread alone, but by every word that proceeds out of the mouth of God." (Matthew 4:4, KJV)

November 1
What Do I Have To Give?
(A Reflection Especially for Women)

What do I have to give? Perhaps Mary asked this question to herself when the angel Gabriel informed her that she was chosen to be the mother of Jesus. It was unclear to Mary, but her abiding faith accepted the angel's proclamation.

So in the fullness of time, the seed of God was planted in a poor, dark-skinned, unwed girl who lived in the ghetto of Nazareth. God's decisions are beyond human understanding. The Bible does declare, "For my thoughts are not your thoughts, neither are my ways your ways, declares the Lord" (*Isaiah 55:8 NIV*).

Not unlike Mary, you may never have seen yourself as the fragrant rose or delicate orchid that completes God's work of love, but you are. From the beginning of time, God saw you as the answer to what was missing in creation. From the living rib of man, God breathed life into a woman. With God's breath came all the feminine beauty and emotional connection the world ever needed. Nothing was added after the woman. You added the finishing touch to God's creation.

"When fear has risen within her, she will raise her hands even higher, taking deep and careful breaths as the daylight reminds her: She is guided. She is seen. And by grace she will make it through all of these things."
~*Morgan Harper Nichols*

November 2
Food in Fallow Ground

"Much food is in the fallow ground of the poor, and for lack of justice there is waste" (Proverbs 13:23, NKJV).

Fallow land is uncultivated, unpolished, and unrefined. Yet, with plowing and fertilization, it becomes rich and cultivated, producing a harvest of healthy crops.

In the United States, the Census Bureau data defines poverty as an annual income of $25,750 or less for an average family of four. Think about this fact: Four people trying to live on $25,750 a year. Forty-three million people live at this level right now. Poverty leads to physical and mental illness, homelessness, illiteracy, and violence. Poverty is similar to fallow land and well worth an investment.

Investing in poor people is like investing in undeveloped land. If given a chance, that budding group would lead to a cultivated harvest of research scientists, superior teachers, physicians, entrepreneurs, and computer scientists who will lead the nation and world in creative solutions to the myriad problems that the world faces. Indeed, much food is in the fallow ground of the poor.

"He that oppress the poor to increase his riches, and he that gives to the rich, shall surely come to want" (Proverbs 22:16, KJV).

November 3
Harriet Tubman's Prayer

Harriet Tubman shares a story about prayer in her memoir. She had blocked a doorway to prevent an overseer from seizing a fugitive slave. The overseer picked up a heavy weight to hit the fugitive but missed and hit Harriet instead knocking her unconscious.

After an extended period of time, she awakened from the coma not able to perform up to par. This was not a good sign for a slave, especially one who had been defiant. It meant she could be more easily sold off into the deep south. She started to pray. At first, Tubman prayed that her master be changed, heart softened, and converted.

When she learned there were plans for her to be shipped away, her prayer changed: "Oh Lord, if you aren't ever going to change that man's heart, kill him Lord and take him out of the way." Not long after, he died, and she expressed heartfelt sorrow to the point of wanting to "bring that soul back." She was in her teens and living under the cruel institution of slavery when she prayed this prayer.

Oftentimes, prayers only make sense to the one praying, and that's how it should be. Prayer is a time to be thankful, but it's also a time to cry and express our heartfelt emotions to God. This is what Ms. Tubman was doing. Prayer is a conversation. This means we need to also spend time listening to God for answers. We may not like the answer, but it will be according to God's will. In the Lord's prayer, it says, "Thy will be done." A common way of expressing it goes like this, "God said it, I believe it, and that settles it for me."

"This is the confidence we have in approaching God: that if we ask anything according to his will, he hears us" (1 John 5:14, NIV).

November 4
Childbirth: A Labor of Love

Childbirth and motherhood are gifts from God. While the nine months before the baby is born is miraculous, it pales in comparison to the birthing process. During pregnancy, the baby is nurtured in a warm, safe, and protected environment. Around forty weeks, the baby slowly moves down the birth canal. While the baby is tucked away in the warm placenta, the mother undergoes grueling painstaking work in order to push the baby out of the birth canal.

The birth of a baby is no small feat. Although technological advances make delivery fairly smooth, there is still the hard labor the mother undergoes, as well as the potential for complications and even death of the mother or baby. In my opinion, there is no greater miracle than the birth of a baby. This is best expressed by the unspeakable joy shared by parents and grandparents.

Thank you, God for the miracle of birth and for giving mothers the courage to risk their lives to bring new life into the world. A baby is divine evidence life will go on.

"You made all the delicate inner parts of my body and knit me together in my mother's womb" (Psalm 139:13, NLT).

November 5
Being an Advocate For Children

The "Greatest Love of All," is a song about our children. When Whitney Houston sang this song, she made you feel secure about the future of our children. The children she sang about would grow to become courageous and moral leaders. The starting point begins with the time spent with parents. Parents are children's best advocates, providing security, leadership, and guidance.

A young father with three children shares how much he loved spending time with his two sons. At the time of our conversation, his daughter was one month old so much of her time was still with his wife. While other parents bring their children to events and usually remain on the sidelines with their attention directed to their cell phones, this was no sideline father. When they visit parks, fairs, or festivals, he goes on rides with his sons. He plays fun games with them at family entertainment centers.

The father shared he grew up with much older parents, and his father was ill most of his childhood, limiting special time with him. This father wanted to make sure his children didn't miss quality time with him.

In our highly sophisticated society, there is an abundance of activities for children to be involved in: soccer, band, football, ballet, cheerleading, basketball, baseball, piano lessons, and taekwondo just to name a few. These are all good. But what shapes their emotional and psychological growth most of all is quality time with their parents. Indeed, children are our future.

"See that you do not despise one of these little ones. For I tell you that their angels in heaven always see the face of my Father in heaven" (Matthew 18:10, NIV).

November 6
Choice: You Make It. You Own It.

Life starring Eddie Murphy as Ray and Martin Lawrence as Claude is brilliant. The movie is filled with many life lessons, one of which is the freedom to choose. It portrays how environment and community shape the actions and experiences of two ordinary African American men. Set in the Depression, the action takes place during a time when the community is suffering some of the worst ravages of a collapsing economy. The economy had caused five times as much unemployment in the African American community. People chose a variety of hustles to survive.

One of the hustles was bootlegging. Ray and Claude drive to Mississippi to pick up a truckload of illegal whiskey. To have some fun, they visit a bar where Ray chooses to gamble the bootleg money away. Claude chooses to allow a woman to seduce him and lose the rest of the money.

As life choices go, they end up in the wrong place at the wrong time. A man is murdered, and they are falsely accused, arrested, and sentenced to *Life* in prison. Both are justifiably angry about being falsely imprisoned. However, Claude spent years blaming Ray, "You're responsible for the whole situation. You're the reason I'm here. I blame you for everything. I regret the day I met you." This mindset imprisoned him not only physically but mentally.

God has given every human being free will. We have the power to make choices. Free will might lead to poor decision-making when life circumstances are discouraging. Taking ownership of one's choices is the first step to overcoming life's burdens. When I own my choices, I can start doing something about them.

"I believe that we are solely responsible for our choices, and we have to accept the consequences of every deed, word, and thought throughout our lifetime."
~ Elizabeth Kubler-Ross, MD

November 7
Best Friends (1964)

College has a tendency to make you bold and brazen. After high school, my best friends and I went our separate ways. Carolyn attended Fisk University, Pat left for Spelman, and I went to Howard University. But we all headed home at Christmas time to share stories, have fun, and be a little adventurous.

I can't remember whose idea it was, but the three of us decided to go to a movie theater downtown. We'd heard the theaters had integrated and were now open to African Americans. This had happened during the six months we were away in college. The year was 1964, in Jacksonville, Florida. Only one year had passed since the historic March on Washington, and we ventured out on our own, not telling our parents.

The ticket counter was external to the theater. It housed one lady who sat inside a glass booth. When we asked for three tickets, she told us that only two of us could come into the theater at a time. We were dumbfounded and asked for an explanation. She informed us that the NAACP had agreed to this stipulation. We decided to go to the other main movie theater about five minutes away and were given the same explanation.

From our viewpoint, the agreement was ridiculous, but we didn't know the whole story. Plus, when we left for college six months earlier, Jacksonville was still a totally segregated city. The path to integration would be slow and deliberate. The wisest decision would have been to discuss this with our parents before making our move. They would have discouraged this undertaking for our safety. But adventurous young best friends felt safe and invincible. Afterall, we had completed a semester of college and were happy to be together again. Prayer and religion were not included in this venture. The blessing is that God was with us every step of the way. And God said, "Not quite yet."

"You chart the path ahead of me and tell me where to stop and rest. Every moment you know where I am. You know what I am going to say even before I say it, LORD. You both precede and follow me" (Psalm 139:3-5, TLB).

November 8
Courage

"Ain't I a Woman"
~ *Sojourner Truth*

Sojourner Truth was born into slavery around 1797 and walked into freedom in 1826. Although she never learned to read or write, she was courageous and spoke truth to power on the abolition of slavery and women's rights. She was driven and guided by her faith in the Almighty Sovereign God.

Ms. Truth had the courage to challenge the myth of the inferiority of women in 1852, when she gave a speech at the Women's Rights Convention in Akron, Ohio. One man, present at the convention insisted that women would lose their special privileges such as being "helped into carriages and lifted over ditches." To which, Sojourner Truth replied:

"Nobody ever helped me into carriages, or over mud puddles, or give me any best place! And ain't I a woman? Look at me, look at my arm. I have plowed and planted and gathered into barns—and no man could head me—and ain't I a woman? I have born'd five children and seen 'em most all sold off into slavery, and when I cried out with a mother's grief, none but Jesus heard...and ain't I a woman."

Thank you, God, for women like Sojourner Truth who had the faith to believe in an Almighty Sovereign God, the courage to speak the truth, and the fortitude to fight for justice and freedom for all people.

"If the first woman God ever made was strong enough to turn the world upside down all alone, these women together ought to be able to turn it back and get it right side up again! And now they is asking to do it, the men better let them."
~ *Sojourner Truth*

November 9
Death is a Part of Life

The movie, *Imitation of Life* was released about sixty years ago. It is one of those movies that stays with you forever. For me, one sub-theme about death is just as thought provoking as the major themes of self-hatred and pretense.

The protagonist has a remarkable understanding about death. She faces a major illness with courage and seems to understand that death is a part of life. She shares joyfully the kind of funeral she desires and explains eloquently how it must celebrate her grand entry into eternity. She saves money for her funeral and when it is time, the funeral is replete with beautiful music, a marching band, and a horse-drawn hearse. Now, that's a true Living Will.

Birth and death are major life events. Just as we prepare for the birth of a child, we ought to prepare for death. Pre-arrangements for death (burial plans, wills, trust, living wills) help ease financial burdens as loved ones grieve the loss of their loved one.

"Even though I walk through the darkest valley, I will fear no evil, for you are with me; your rod and your staff, they comfort me" (Psalm 23:4, NIV).

November 10
Environment

"The Earth is the Lord's, and everything in it, the world, and all who live in it."
(Psalm 24:1, NIV).

God's universe is fully integrated with life sustaining systems: sun, moon, water, air, wind, soil linked together miraculously to support human life and itself. Natural resources like oil, natural gas, water, coal, phosphorous, and rare earth elements are necessary for the healthy existence of the total universe.

While specific natural resources are more abundant in one country than another, I don't believe God meant them to be restricted for that country's primary use and manipulation. And they certainly should not be used as bargaining chips when there are humanitarian needs for specific resources in certain parts of the world.

God is always our guide for how to live and share. We all breathe the same air. There is the same sun, moon, and sky regardless of what country you live in. Can you imagine a God who would only let the sunshine in the Eastern Hemisphere? Or withhold the moon from certain countries based on specific criteria? The point is that God loves all of us equally. It is God's desire that we love and respect each other regardless of our country of origin.

Dr. Martin Luther King, Jr. asserted, "We are caught up in an inescapable network of mutuality, tied to a single garment of destiny. Whatever affects one directly, affects all indirectly."

"Our most basic common link is that we all inhabit this planet. We all breathe the same air. We all cherish our children's future. And we are all mortal."
~John F. Kennedy

November 11
Faith: Looking for the Messiah

"When the men came to Jesus, they said, 'John the Baptist sent us to you to ask, 'Are you the one who is to come, or should we expect someone else'" (Luke 7:20 NIV)?

Posed to Jesus, this question of doubt by John the Baptist did not align with how John lived. It was John who declared with boldness to turn your minds back to God. It was John who preached to prepare a pathway for the Lord's coming. John had the honor of baptizing Jesus.

John was imprisoned for speaking the truth. From prison, he questioned Jesus. "Are you the one who is to come, or should we expect someone else" (*Luke 7:20, NIV*)? In essence, have I wasted my life seeking the wrong person? If you are the Messiah, why am I incarcerated? Surely, you have the power to get me out.

Jesus sent a message back to John: "Tell him what you have seen and heard—the blind see, the lame walk, the lepers are cured, the deaf hear, the dead are raised to life, and the Good News is being preached to the poor. And tell him, God blesses those who are not offended by me" (*Luke 7:22, NLT*). Then, Jesus delivered an eloquent oration about the life of John the Baptist. But at the end of the oration, he said, "I tell you, of all who have ever lived, none is greater than John. Yet, even the most insignificant person in the Kingdom of God is greater than he" (*Luke 7:28, NLT*).

What is Jesus saying? When you can't see the hand of God at work, your faith is the proof that God's hand is working. John had moments of disappointment. But his reward was huge and predetermined before he was born. All Christians have moments of despair. Our eternal victory is also predetermined. Not unlike John the Baptist, we must remain faithful and believe that the hand of God is at work even in the midst of discouragement.

"Blessed is the man who does not fall away on account of me" (Luke 7:23, NLT).

November 12
Family: Remembering Mama

Warm memories of my mother fill my heart when I hear Shirley Caesar sing, "I remember Mama." Mama, as we called her, was a praying woman, highly intelligent, strong, and royal in appearance. She spoke and carried herself like she had studied and trained at a high-class boarding school. Yet, she was raised in a poor country village called Four Mile Creek about five miles outside of Bainbridge, Georgia.

Our mother shared her life story with her children numerous times. She walked five miles (to and from) school. She used an outdoor toilet, drank water from a well pump, and washed clothes in a big black iron pot. Although her family was poor, all their nutritional needs were met by farming and sharing in the community.

Mama made sure her children were aware of their history. On many weekends, she would pack the car and drive four hours to visit her mother. There, we had to use the outhouse.

Mama achieved much during her ninety-two years of life and never expressed bitterness about any hardships she endured. She talked with passion about the endearing love, the belonging nature, and the safe and happy home where she was raised. As I reflect, this is what contributed to her intellect, strength, and great love for humanity. She loved the quote, "Where there is great love, there are great miracles." Indeed, she is my miracle. I remember Mama in a happy way. Thank you, God, for mama.

"She is clothed with strength and dignity, and she laughs without fear of the future" (Proverbs 31:25, NLT.)

November 13
The Full Extent of Jesus' Love:
The Foot Washing Savior (John 13:1-16)

Have you ever been invited to dinner and upon entering the home the host or hostess invites you to remove your shoes? And not for fear that your shoes might soil their perfect flooring, they invite you to soak your feet in a basin filled with warm filtered water and healing herbs. Shortly thereafter, they take a fresh warm towel and gently pat your feet dry as a whole-hearted way of expressing welcome to you.

This activity is similar to the foot washing experience during the time when Jesus walked the earth. It was a hospitable custom performed by the host, house servant, or the guest as they enter a home after walking on a dusty or unclean road.

The foot washing experience is the way Jesus chose to reveal the love he had for his disciples. They could not fathom how Jesus would carry out such a humbling act. When Jesus uses this ritual, it becomes transformational.

In this act, Jesus is the host and the servant. Foot washing is a metaphor for God's eternal love. Through this action, Jesus is welcoming the disciples into his divine home and what a welcome it is! When Jesus holds the disciple's feet in his hands, it represents an embodiment of divine love and intimacy he has for the whole person. It says, I will forever hold you in my hands. It is a sign that there is no separation between the disciples and Jesus so long as they accept his unconditional love. It embodies the lesson - going forward they were to do the same for themselves and for others.

On Maundy Thursday in our church, not only is holy communion celebrated, but our pastor enacts the foot washing ritual which Jesus did the night before he was crucified. During this time, water is poured into a basin, and the pastor sprinkles water on the foot of willing congregants and then dries the foot with a towel. It is a meaningful and humbling experience and helps me to appreciate this special night before the crucifixion.

My prayer is that you be ever reminded that God's love holds you in divine hands. Like the disciples, there is no separation between you and God so long as you accept divine unconditional love.

"For I am convinced that neither death nor life, neither angels nor demons, neither the present nor the future, nor any powers, neither height nor depth, nor anything else in all creation, will be able to separate us from the love of God that is in Christ Jesus our Lord" (Romans 8:38-39, NIV).

November 14
Forgiveness: Seventy Times Seven

If you do a word search in this book of reflections, you'll discover forgiveness is present multiple times. Most of us know why. Forgiveness is not an easy virtue to attain. Even when we want to forgive, it's difficult.

In our society, there's always the potential of being offended. Before we leave home, while driving, or using another mode of transportation, at work, shopping, and then back home, at some point, someone has probably offended us.

The Lord's Prayer says, "forgive us our debts as we forgive our debtors" (*Mathew 6:12, KJV*). St. Francis of Assisi says, "Where there is injury, pardon." In the Bible, Peter asks Jesus how often should he forgive his brother (or sister), and Jesus answered seventy times seven. So, what's the answer?

Give up on being right. Don't go to bed angry. Let go and let God. Don't live in the past. Pray for the one who has offended you. These are all good steps, but sometimes nothing seems to make a difference. When you struggle with forgiving others, consider searching your heart and memory for the answer to this question: What has God forgiven you for?

Sit quietly for a few minutes. Get a pen and start writing a list of things God has forgiven you for. Add to the list things that could have happened to you based on chances you took or choices you made but didn't happen. Start writing. Say a prayer of thanksgiving for God's unmerited grace and forgiveness during foolish times in your life. Rip up the sheet of paper. Now, choose to let the spirit of unforgiveness go. Forgiveness is the pathway to love. When we forgive, love abounds in our lives, souls, and minds.

"While I know myself as a creation of God, I am also obligated to realize and remember that everyone else and everything else are also God's creation. This is particularly difficult for me when my mind falls upon the cruel person, the batterer, and the bigot. I would like to think that the mean-spirited were created by another force and under the aegis and direction of something other than my God. But since I believe that God created all things, I am not only constrained to know that the oppressor is a child of God, but also obliged to try to treat him or her as a child of God."
~Maya Angelou

November 15
The Altar Call

"Earth has no sorrow that heaven cannot heal."
~ Thomas Moore

A most engaging part of Christian worship is when the minister invites the congregants to come to the altar for prayer. It is a time for people to bring their cares and concerns to God. One of the old hymns of the church calls the altar, the mercy seat, the place where you can lay your burdens down. Even though the congregants spend time praying at home, it is an act of faith to walk down the aisle and kneel at the altar - for it is the place that symbolizes the presence of the Almighty Sovereign God.

Is it old fashioned? Some might think so. Does it take up too much time? Some might think so. Is it done just for show? Some might think so. Prayers are not answered. Some might say so. These are the words from the naysayers. However, Christian believers have seen miracles happen, prayers answered, or gained clarity and understanding about life situations.

When my husband gave the altar call followed by the altar prayer, he would end with a charge to the congregation, reminding us to leave our burdens there at the altar and to not take them back to their seats. The altar call is an act of faith. The next step is trust that God will answer our prayers. Don't be afraid to heed the call to come to the altar for prayer.

"The name of the Lord is a fortified tower; the righteous run to it and are safe" (Proverbs 18:10, NIV).

November 16
Giving is the Heart of Christianity

...For it is in giving that we receive. It is in pardoning that we are pardoned. It is in dying that we are born to eternal life.
~St. Francis of Assisi

There are many people that help save lives by regularly donating blood and plasma. These are safe procedures, but it still takes courage. Then, there are those who make huge contributions to another's life. For example, when they donate one of their kidneys or a portion of their lung or liver to one in need. Although these surgeries are more complex, unless something goes wrong, the donors and recipients recover and afterwards lead productive lives.

In my opinion, the evidence of Christianity is giving motivated by love and sacrifice. Christians, as well as non-Christians, perform selfless acts all the time. There have been times when individuals have given their lives protecting or shielding another. These courageous acts usually occur in crisis moments. In 2019, we read about several people who used their body to ward off massacres at schools and churches. These are noble acts of selfless giving.

Suppose someone you loved had a major illness, but it had been determined that he/she would fully recover if all of their blood was removed and replaced by another person's blood. However, the person who gives up their blood would die. What would your response be? I believe I know my response. This is a hard price to pay, but such a price has been paid.

Human beings have a major sickness called sin. Sin leads to spiritual death. The Almighty Sovereign God made it possible for us to fully recover through Jesus Christ. Jesus' blood was emptied out on the cross. How it happened that his blood would cover so many is a divine mystery. Songwriter, Lewis E. Jones said it this way, "There is power— power wonder working power in the blood of the Lamb."

The Almighty Sovereign God through Jesus Christ gives absolute assurance that if we believe, then we have eternal life. Death is only a part of life. It is not the end.

"For God so loved the world that He gave His only begotten son that whoever believes in him would not perish but have eternal life" (John 3:16, KJV).

November 17
The Amazing Power of Grace

Forty-three years ago, the power of God's grace became alive to me. I had moved back to Jacksonville, Florida, to work in a medical clinic at the university hospital. My relationship with Jesus Christ had been restored for two years, and I was loving my journey.

Shortly after arriving, I learned that a very special high school teacher's only daughter was dying from cancer. Mary (as I shall call her) was thirty-three years of age, a few years older than me. I wasn't even sure if she remembered me. Her mother, my former teacher, was brilliant, wise, kind, and loving.

I went to visit my teacher's daughter, and I was a bit uneasy upon arriving in her hospital room, but she welcomed me. Mary was lying in bed and appeared quite weak, her voice barely above a whisper. She was very thin but pretty as always. During the brief time there, I assisted her with a cup of water and turned her in bed. Mostly, I sat with her. As Mary lie at her weakest moment, her presence exhibited elegance, poise, and grace.

After the visit was over and I was back in the lobby of the hospital, my eyes were drawn to a decorative display of stone. Engraved in the stone were the words: My grace is sufficient for you. My power is made perfect in weakness.

That was a defining moment for me. At that point, I realized what I saw in Mary was the Almighty Sovereign God demonstrating perfect strength in weakness. Mary died a few weeks later, but I'll always remember the strength of God manifested in a frail human being.

"My grace is sufficient for you. My power is made perfect in weakness" (2 Corinthians 12:9, NIV).

November 18
A View From Another Side

There is an insightful quote that reads: "I would agree with you, but then we'd both be wrong." I have to admit this quote describes my attitude more often than I'd like to concede. And this is probably true for most people. On any given subject, human beings hold one view and are unlikely to be swayed to other perspectives. For example, Christians believe Jesus is the way to life. Muslims believe Allah leads the way. Some people believe healthcare is a universal right while others believe healthcare is a privilege. The political climate in our country is in a state of flux. In each scenario, most people feel their way is right. How do you come together with such divisiveness?

The philosopher, Friedrich Nietzsche said it this way: "You have your way. I have my way. As for the right way, the correct way, and the only way, it does not exist." Making a declaration that my way is right and other ways are wrong moves away from healing and wholeness at every dimension of life.

Consider this, we are connected to every human being; this connection makes us ONE. Yes, the person who irritates you the most is a part of you. When you harm someone, you are harming yourself as well. Jesus put it this way, "Love your neighbor as yourself" (*Mark 12:31, NIV*).

Once we can agree on our human connection, we will become more open to other person's truth, acknowledging their viewpoint with respect. We will be more willing to understand other people's behavior and practice forgiveness. We will start to understand the impact of culture on individual and community behavior.

We cannot live only for ourselves. "A thousand fibers connect us with our fellow men [and women]; and among those fibers, as sympathetic threads, our actions run as causes, and they come back to us as effects."
~ Henry Melvil

November 19
The Loneliness of Grief

In my opinion, death is the most challenging life event we face. Loss of a loved one regardless of age is painful, shocking, and disruptive. Death most often leads to feelings of angst, apprehension, uncertainty, and sorrow. There is never a right time for someone we love to die. Indeed, it is hard to prepare for death even when death is expected. What's more, after death comes the grieving and mourning process, which is even more difficult. Climbing the mountain of grief is a herculean task.

When my husband died, I felt the penetrating effect of grief. During the early months of mourning, I started reading a variety of books on death and dying in search of answers and solace. I reacquainted myself with Elisabeth Kübler-Ross, MD, a psychiatrist whose pioneer work in hospice care changed the way death and dying is viewed globally. One of her recommendations is to not only write letters to your beloved but also to write what you think their response would be. I did this sometimes and found it to be a rewarding activity.

One of the hardest issues for me was loneliness. In fact, I did not recognize these feelings until one day through my tears, I blurted out to myself how lonely I felt. Writing this book of reflections has been healing. Other people's life stories, parables in the Bible, more prayer, journaling, and volunteer work keeps me in the present and inspired. Still, it is part of my journey and cannot be excluded.

Recovering from the death of your life-partner is no small feat, but I am finally beginning to feel comfortable again in my own skin.

"You have turned my mourning into joyful dancing.
You have taken away my clothes of mourning and clothed me with joy,
that I might sing praises to you and not be silent.
O Lord my God, I will give you thanks forever" (Psalm 30:11-12, NLT)!

November 20
The Coffee Table

A lot of things that seem important lose their significance in the big picture of life. Take David and Meri, a happily married couple. David has a behavior that nettles Meri. He likes to take his shoes off and place them beneath their stylish coffee table. Instead of enjoying time together, Meri's temperament changes each time this happens. Time and time again, Meri shares her feelings with David. He stops for a while, but as habits go, his shoes end up back under the coffee table.

Then something happens. David has a massive heart attack and almost dies. This gave Meri time to reflect on the multiple times she complained about David leaving his shoes under the coffee table. As the thought enters her mind that he might not survive, this act seems so little. David is blessed to recover. When he arrives home from the hospital and sits to rest, something blocks his path as he tries to stretch his legs out under the coffee table. Meri has placed all his shoes there. They both laugh heartily and embrace. And as they caress, David and Meri feel the warmth of each other's body. And somehow, both know that in addition to the healing of David's physical heart, a miraculous healing was taking place inside both David and Meri.

Consider this exercise: Make two columns on a piece of paper. In one, write down what you love about your mate and in the other, write down what annoys you. Now, write down things your mate love about you and what you do that annoys your mate. Be honest. Based on your list, who's the most patient?

Regardless of the genuine love spouses or partners share, at times they are impatient with each other. If it's not the shoes under the coffee table, it's the smelly clothes next to the laundry bin, the lid off the toothpaste, socks on the floor, the loud TV—the list is endless. Are these annoyances worth the stress on your emotions and your relationship?

"When couples love God first, they love each other better."
~ Brela Delahoussaye

November 21
An Inspiring Hero

"Once you learn to read, you will be forever free. Knowledge makes a man unfit to be a slave."
~ *Frederick Douglass*

Frederick Douglass was born into slavery in 1818. During slavery there were slave codes that banned African Americans from learning to read or write. Even during slavery, there were a few ways around injustice. Douglass was taught to read by his slaveholder's wife. The full story is found in *The Life and Times of Frederick Douglass*.

Douglass was a smart man, and he was determined to learn to read. His oppressor also knew that reading would open the door to a wealth of knowledge and eventual freedom. Douglass gains his freedom and becomes a great orator and abolitionist.

Not being able to read is a much more crippling disability than many a physical ailment. Thirty-two million adults in the United States cannot read. In my opinion, sharing narratives on how many in the enslaved population learned to read against all odds may inspire others to learn to read, thereby reducing the twenty-first century illiteracy rate.

I read a story about a man who learned to read at age fifty-four. When he was in sixth grade, his school gave up on trying to educate him. A learning disability combined with multiple family problems made learning difficult. One day, he heard his sick mother express her disappointment in the school for abandoning her son. Her advocacy on his behalf empowered her son. After she passed, his passion to learn to read intensified. He discovered an adult literacy program that was able to help him. There are adult literacy programs across the nation. If you know someone who needs this assistance, refer them to https://www.nld.org or call 1-877-389-6874.

"You don't have to burn books to destroy a culture. Just get people to stop reading them."
~ *Ray Bradbury*

November 22
A Hidden Figure

"Shoot for the moon. Even if you miss, you'll land among the stars."
~*Norman Vincent Peale*

Recently, there was an article in the New York Times about Raye Montague. Her important life story was hidden for years. Montague was gifted with high intellect, discipline, determination, courage, and confidence. When she told her story, she'd start with the above quote.

Her childhood dream was to become an engineer, but there were challenges and obstacles that she had to overcome. Montague grew up in Arkansas during the era of Jim Crow and was denied entry into the engineering program at the University of Arkansas at Fayetteville. Because of this, she studied business at the African American college in Arkansas.

Montague never gave up her dream to become an engineer. Except for some computer programming at night school, she had no formal training as an engineer. She learned her skill set on the job, working as a clerk typist for several years before becoming a computer systems operator and computer systems analyst at the Naval Ship Engineering Center in Washington, DC.

She was promoted to program director of the Naval Sea Systems Command integrated design, manufacturing, and maintenance program, and she also served as the division head of the Navy's computer-aided design and computer-aided manufacturing program.

Her most outstanding achievement was to lay out, step by step, how a naval ship might be designed using a computer. No one else had been able to do this. Montague accomplished this mission. After this, she began advising other government agencies, private sector companies, and the automobile industry.

At the height of her career, she briefed the Joint Chiefs of Staff every month and taught at the United States Naval Academy in Annapolis, Maryland, though her work was not acknowledged publicly until 2012.

Ray Montague was a woman who trusted herself. She did not let discriminatory racial and gender practices stop her from becoming a first-class engineer. Montague said, "God sends you what you need." Not only did God send her what she needed, God sent her to Washington, DC and placed her in the Department of the Navy. She went on to say, "People put obstacles in your way. You find a way to achieve despite the system not because of the system."

"You can do anything you want to do provided you are educated. You can be anything you want to be. There is no such thing as women's work or men's work. You might have to work harder. In my case, I had to run circles around people, but, eventually, I went from the bottom to the top, essentially, with the Navy."
~ Raye Montague

November 23
An Unspoken Bible

(Author unknown/Story paraphrased)
"So, take some time from your busy day to help some brother find his way, and refuse to look down on any man unless you look down to help him to be the very best he can."
~Nan Campbell Fletcher

One Sunday morning, a megachurch reached its capacity of 3,000 persons. The choir and the congregation were singing praises to God. The prayers were powerful, and members couldn't wait to hear the sermon. As the pastor was about to mount the pulpit, a man, woman, and their two children entered the church. They looked for seats but there were none. Their clothes and shoes were in disrepair. All eyes were on them.

The family started to walk slowly down the aisle in search of seats. People looked uncomfortable, but no one said anything. The family moved closer and closer to the pulpit, and when they realized there were no seats, they sat down on the carpet.

The tension in the air was thick. Then another family started walking down the aisle. They were members of the church but not well known. But there was something special about this family. Their humility and modesty in dress were noticeable.

The pastor was taken aback and held back from preaching. The family reached the other family sitting on the carpet and sat down on the carpet to worship with them, so they wouldn't be alone. People started moving towards the pulpit from all over the church. They all sat down together and filled the space surrounding the pulpit.

Everyone choked up with emotion. When the pastor gained control, he said, "What I'm about to preach, you will never remember. What you have just seen, you will never forget. Be careful how you live. You may be the only Bible some people will ever read."

"When I am with those who are weak, I share their weakness, for I want to bring the weak to Christ. Yes, I try to find common ground with everyone, doing everything I can to save some. I do everything to spread the Good News and share in its blessings" (1 Corinthians 9:22-23, NLT).

November 24
Identity and Humanity

Then Jesus demanded, "What is your name?" And he replied, "My name is Legion, because there are many of us inside this man" (Mark 5:9, NLT).

In this passage of scripture, Jesus meets a man described as being controlled by demons. He lives in a cemetery and does repeated acts of harm to himself. In today's society, this man would be labeled homeless and mentally ill.

In the United States today, a large portion of the homeless population are mentally ill with no medical or mental health care. They don't live in cemeteries or wander around naked, they sleep on sidewalks, in abandoned buildings, in the woods, under bridges and tunnels and eat out of garbage cans.

As for the man in the cemetery, Jesus showed him empathy and respect. He asked his name. When you want to know a person's name, you demonstrate feelings for them. You humanize the person. Jesus was not afraid to talk with Legion. The conversation allowed the demons to bargain on how they would die. In the story, Jesus causes the demons to be expelled from the man. What happens next? The man is observed to be clothed and in his right mind, desiring to be of service to humankind.

Striking up conversations with persons who are mentally ill and homeless can be more meaningful than passing out supplies and food. It might lead to the person getting treatment for their mental illness.

"Successful people build each other up. They motivate, inspire, and push each other. Unsuccessful people just hate, blame, and complain."
~Anonymous

A Woman Filled With Empathy

"The arc of the moral universe is long, but it bends toward justice."
~ Dr. Martin Luther King, Jr.

One-hundred sixteen years ago, a prison reform activist was born on this day. Frances Joseph-Gaudet, an African American, began her visionary mission when racism was rampant in the United States. Not only did she make visits to prisons to pray with those incarcerated, but researched the circumstances surrounding their imprisonment, found many to be innocent, and advocated for their release.

She asked the question, "If you had good reason to believe a prisoner guiltless and you could get him out of his distress, would you not do so?" Her research compelled her to make pleas to judges on behalf of innocent men and women in prison. She was successful in getting some released.

In 1902, she raised enough funds to open, Colored Normal and Industrial School, an orphanage and boarding school for poor and homeless children. The campus encompassed one hundred five acres and numerous buildings.

In 1992, the Innocence Project began for the purpose of using scientific data (DNA) to exonerate those who have been wrongly convicted as well as working to reform the criminal justice system. Similar to years ago, when Mrs. Joseph-Gaudet bravely tackled prison reform, a lot of innocent people are in prison today. Never think that your work against injustice is in vain.

Were half the power, that fills the world with terror,
Were half the wealth, bestowed on camps and courts,
Given to redeem the human mind from error,
There were no need of arsenals or forts.
~ Henry Wadsworth Longfellow

November 26
A Prayer for the Thanksgiving Season

Almighty Sovereign God, Creator of all humankind, I humbly request to enter into your divine presence. I am thankful for the free gift of eternal life. Thank you for families and friends; thank you for churches, communities, and all nations of the world.

We are blessed to live in a time when technology and science have discovered medications that can cure cancer, manage diabetes and high blood pressure, prevent heart attacks, manage HIV/AIDS, and keep people alive whose kidneys have failed. Yet, oh Lord, there remains a large disparity between blessings from you and how they get filtered down to close the gaps in healthcare delivery; gaps that exist throughout the world including the United States of America, the richest country in the world.

Help us to remember that every good and perfect gift comes from you. Inspire everyone, especially those in power, to ensure that the poor who need medical help will have easy and free access to what you have provided. Have mercy upon all of us and help us to remember who is in charge of everything and what role we have in helping bring your Kingdom closer to earth as it is in heaven.

We are blessed to live in a time when there is enough money for every human being to have decent housing, wholesome nutrition, healthcare, and good education. While some people have these blessings, there are too many people who do not.

While we enjoy thanksgiving fellowship and a hearty meal, keep the concerns of the poor and have-nots close to our hearts, not just today, but every day until as often quoted by Dr. Martin Luther King, Jr. "justice rolls down like water and righteousness as an overflowing stream."

Now, Lord, please bless the food we are about to receive, and may it nourish our physical bodies in such a way that it stirs our souls to higher levels of loving and giving. AMEN

November 27
Faith is Real and Fast

Ten months ago, my Goddaughter accepted an executive position at a prestigious university. The salary and benefits were outstanding. The job seemed like a dream come true.

Marie and her three young children packed and moved from Washington, DC to Boston. While the children were starting to adjust to their new school, Marie was beginning to question her dream job. There was deception, malicious talk, and disparaging writings occurring among highly educated people. She was in a toxic work environment, and her dream job turned into a nightmare.

After praying and seeking God's direction, Marie felt that regardless of the prestige and salary, staying on this job was not in her best interest. She began to seek out new positions, started packing for the move back to Washington, and soon thereafter resigned. Marie interviewed for one position in Washington that seemed promising and comparable to the job she was leaving, but when she left Boston nothing was definite.

Marie's faith was being tested. She knew it wouldn't be easy, but her faith was strong. Uprooting her children concerned her the most but staying in that work environment would soon affect her health and home life. She stepped out on faith and didn't look back. Shortly after arriving in Washington, even before she had finished unpacking, she was offered the new position.

Dr. Martin Luther King, Jr. said, "Faith is taking the first step, even when you don't see the whole staircase." If Marie had not stepped out on faith, she would still be trying to work things out in a dysfunctional work setting. Marie kicked doubt out of the way.

"When one door closes, another opens; but we often look so long and so regretfully upon the closed door that we do not see the one which has opened for us."
~ *Alexander Graham Bell*

November 28
The Number One Life Concern

A poll was taken to find out the life issue that concerns most people. Healthcare was number one. Even when we make the wrong health choices, we still want to be healthy.

Do you know anyone who wants to be unhealthy or sick? It may seem so considering the lifestyle choices many Americans make: physical inactivity, unhealthy eating, cigarette smoking, and alcohol over-consumption. These unhealthy choices may result in heart disease, cancer, chronic lung disease, the leading causes of death in America.

Health is more valuable than gold, silver, or all the money in the world. We cannot pay for good health. No one has enough money to buy health. Although some may try.

There are no guarantees on having good health. But it is time for us to not only reflect on our health choices but to take actions that improve the health of our bodies, minds, and spirits.

"I am come that they might have life, and that they might have it more abundantly" (John 10:10, KJV).

November 29

The Power of Imagination

"The man who has no imagination has no wings."
~Aristotle

When you involve others in your dream, it comes alive. Consider Eddie Murphy's character, Ray in the movie *Life*. Ray is falsely accused of murder and sentenced to life in prison. Long before he was incarcerated, Ray's dream was to own a club named, "Ray's Boom-Boom Room." Although he was poor, he did not allow his situation to keep him from dreaming.

The power of Ray's imagination is dramatized in a scene where he invites the other inmates to his dreamed-up club. They are able to picture the reality of it in their own minds. He talks directly to each one and shares the role they play at his club. The smiles on their faces is evidence of what they imagine and how happy they were to be included. The movie director brings the viewers into the action as we too see the club with each of the prisoners being involved.

You could say that prisoners live in a cave of darkness. At least for a brief time, Ray's imagination helped them escape the pains of institutionalized oppression.

"As a man [or woman] thinketh in his heart, so is he" (paraphrased Proverbs 23:7, KJV).

November 30

The Joy in Sharing

"Then Nehemiah the governor, Ezra the priest and teacher of the Law, and the Levites who were instructing the people said to them all, "This day is holy to the Lord your God. Do not mourn or weep. For all the people had been weeping as they listened to the words of the Law" (Nehemiah 8:10, NIV).

The people of God had been listening to the Law of God for six hours straight. Men, women, and children listened attentively. While their understanding was limited, they mourned and cried because it was God's word they were hearing. When you absorb God's word into your innermost being, it transforms your thinking and your behavior. After such an extended period of time, it was time for action.

Nehemiah urged the people to stop mourning and crying and encouraged them to celebrate by eating rich foods and drinking sweet drinks. Most importantly, he told them to share with people who have nothing and to stop looking downcast. He told them the best antidote for grieving is to be joyful in the Lord. Because joy is a source of strength against divine anger. "The joy of the Lord is your strength," he says to the people.

Every day is a day of Thanksgiving. The season of Thanksgiving illuminates God's goodness and makes all other days of the year more meaningful. Nehemiah is saying, go out and demonstrate your commitment to God by being generous. Donate to a local food bank. Volunteer at a food bank or soup kitchen. Deliver Thanksgiving meals. Generosity nourishes your soul with joy and makes you strong in the Lord.

"Nehemiah said, 'Go and enjoy choice food and sweet drinks, and send some to those who have nothing prepared. This day is holy to our Lord. Do not grieve, for the joy of the Lord is your strength'" (Nehemiah 8:11, NIV).

December 1
World AIDS Day

"It's not the years in your life that count. It's the life in your years."
~*Abraham Lincoln*

Each year, December 1 is World AIDS Day. It is a day set aside to increase awareness of the disease and to show support for those living with the illness. It's also a day to reflect over the past, present, and future of the AIDS epidemic.

AIDS is caused by the HIV virus. The virus weakens the body's immune system making it difficult to fight infections. If left untreated, AIDS is deadly. Over 500,000 people have died from AIDS in the United States.

Thirty-nine years ago, AIDS was a mysterious disease that brought mayhem, panic, fear, shame, confusion, and death. Although it was first reported in five previously healthy gay men in Los Angeles, it quickly became an epidemic affecting people of every age, race, and gender.

People with AIDS were shunned like those with leprosy during biblical days. Lepers were considered defiled and wherever they went, they were forced to shout out, *"Unclean, unclean."* Individuals with AIDS didn't cry out unclean, others simply spurned them as if they were. Years ago, my first patient with AIDS had a prolonged hospital stay because family and community shelters refused to take him in.

Education has helped to allay some of the misguided beliefs. Excellent treatment makes it possible for persons with AIDS to live out their normal life expectancy. There has been a lot of progress, but still no cure or vaccine exists to prevent the disease. People need to be vigilant about being tested and getting treated.

"Everyone thought I was going to die like a year later, they didn't know. So I helped educate sports, and then the world, that a man living with HIV can play basketball. He's not going to give it to anybody by playing basketball."
~*Magic Johnson*

December 2
Life Work

"Your profession is not what brings home your weekly paycheck, your profession is what you're put here on earth to do, with such passion and such intensity that it becomes spiritual in calling."
~Vincent van Gogh

What work could you do regardless of whether you were paid or not? You take this work on like it is a mission. This work brings meaning to your life; you feel totally committed to it. It is work that motivates you to go above and beyond your salary. It's work that changes the lives of those you work with. Life work might be considered one's calling. Some people are born teachers. These teachers have the special gift of communication and understanding. While they are born with this gift, they perfect it with constant practice.

Some men and women are called to the ministry. Jeremiah was called by God. "The word of the Lord came to me," saying, "Before I formed you in the womb I knew you, before you were born I set you apart; I appointed you as a prophet to the nations" (*Jeremiah 1:4-5, NIV*). Sometimes you may feel fear and doubt. But God will reassure and guide you.

My mother would say I expressed the desire to become a doctor around the age of two or three. To be sure, I left for college with intention of becoming a physician. At one time, I had given up my childhood dream. After a few detours, my dream was fulfilled. God kept pushing me forward and made it happen.

Perhaps you are like me now and have retired. God's calling is still on your life. A life-work is a life of service. It may be different after retirement, but you'll still discover ways to serve humankind.

"God has a vision for our lives that is greater than any vision we can have for ourselves or that others can have for us."
~William Watley, PhD

December 3
Godly Love

The story of the prodigal son (*Luke 15:11-32, NLT*) is an excellent example of the extent of God's love. It is a story about a father and his two sons and how they deal with broken relationships.

One son asks his father for an early inheritance before the father dies. The father grants his request. Then, the son alienates himself from the family, spends all his money, and ends up on the streets, homeless and helpless. The other son stays with his father to earn his merit by hard work. The father loves both sons and is heartbroken over the one who has left.

Eventually, the alienated son realizes his mistakes and comes back home. He returns with an attitude of confession and repentance. The father is elated and welcomes him with open arms. Their relationship is restored with joy and celebration.

The brother who remained at home to work hard and support his dad is overcome with anger and refuses to join in the celebration. He felt no compassion for a brother who left the family and wasted all his money. He couldn't understand his father's loving response. He wanted him to compare his worth to his undeserving brother, but like God, the father looked at his young son's heart. He was overjoyed to have his son back home. Now, he had both sons again.

Are you more like the brother who remains at home, hardhearted, unforgiving, and self-righteous? Or, like the father who shows unconditional love, unmerited grace, forgiveness, and mercy?

"Love suffers long and is kind; love does not envy; love does not parade itself, is not puffed up; does not behave rudely, does not seek its own, is not provoked, thinks no evil; does not rejoice in iniquity, but rejoices in the truth; bears all things, believes all things, hopes all things, endures all things" (1 Corinthians 13:4-8, NKJV).

December 4
Tis the Season

It's twenty-one days before Christmas and many people have already started preparing for celebrations, parties, and family get-togethers. Even now, Christmas trees are in homes, offices, and every department store. Some neighborhoods look like winter wonderlands. Festive music, Christmas movies, and of course the Nutcracker ballet prepares hearts and minds for the holiday season.

As you continue to get ready for the season, please be reminded of the population of people who dread holidays. Some have to struggle and pray extra hard just to get through them. This is a difficult time for those who have experienced the death of a wife, husband, parent, or child. It is also a difficult time for children with incarcerated parents.

There are those with loved ones who are hospitalized with major illnesses. And, lastly those who are isolated because of incarceration or homelessness. Consider the gift of time. It is a very important portion of your life. Every moment is precious and when you give some of your valuable time away to someone or a family in need during the Christmas season, it makes the season much more treasured.

"Use each precious moment with all the precious seconds in it to love each other for Christ's sake, for the next precious moment may very well be too late. So, take some time from your busy day to help some sister or brother find their way and refuse to look down to help him or her to be the very best they can."
~*Nan Campbell Fletcher*

December 5
Mental Health

Her husband Elkanah would say to her, "Hannah, why are you weeping? Why don't you eat? Why are you so downhearted? Don't I mean more to you than ten sons" (1 Samuel 1:8, NIV)?

Hannah struggled with infertility for years. Although her husband reminds her of his endearing love, for Hannah, it wasn't enough. She wanted the blessing of motherhood. As a result, she became severely depressed. Even during biblical times, depression was real. In addition to Hannah, David was filled with despair and Jeremiah cried all the time. Both Elijah and Jonah were so depressed they felt life was not worth living any more.

In today's society, depression is a major medical problem. Symptoms of depression include sadness, fatigue, loss of self-worth, poor concentration, difficulty sleeping, loss of interest in most activities, loss of appetite, weight loss, and even thoughts of suicide.

There are two types of depression. One type is caused by a stressful or traumatic event. Hannah's depression was related to stress of infertility. The other type of depression results from your genes. This means that you are at greater risk to develop major depression if your parents, siblings, or children suffer from depression. Either type can be treated.

Sometimes professional counseling is needed. Don't be ashamed to take care of your mental health. Remember, God heals our bodies, frees our mind, and nourishes our soul. Our emotional well-being is just as important as our physical well-being.

"A pearl is a beautiful thing that is produced by an injured life. It is the tear [that results] from the injury of the oyster. The treasure of our being in this world is also produced by an injured life. If we had not been wounded, if we had not been injured, then we will not produce the pearl."
~Stephan Hoeller

December 6
Kindness

"Therefore, as God's chosen people, holy and dearly loved, clothe yourselves with compassion, kindness, humility, gentleness and patience" (Colossians 3:12, NIV).

I'd like to share a story about a man of below average intellect but a genius in being kind. I'll call him Fred. People called Fred stupid. Most people either laughed at him or felt sorry for him. Regardless of how he was treated, Fred remained kind, non-judgmental, and compassionate. These virtues were effortless for him. He never had to think about being kind to those who were unkind to him. It was as if he was unaware of a spirit of meanness.

Fred performed selfless good deeds without a second thought. His integrity was impeccable. Fred was strong and athletic and would use these talents to help others. Although the woman he loved deserted him multiple times, he was loving and kind each time she returned to him. Fred's life was filled with joy and prosperity. Both overflowed to the people's lives he touched.

Some might say Fred's behavior was related to his low intellect. If so, then Jesus must have had a low IQ. For this is how Jesus lived. These ideals are found in the Sermon on the Mount, also called the Beatitudes (*Matthew 5*). Although the Beatitudes seem impossible to follow perfectly, Jesus would not make goals that are impossible to achieve. As Paul says, your commitment to God will keep you pressing forward toward not just earthly achievements but, most importantly, toward your eternal goals.

"I don't mean to say that I have already achieved these things or that I have already reached perfection. But I press on to possess that perfection for which Christ Jesus first possessed me. No, dear brothers and sisters, I have not achieved it, but I focus on this one thing: Forgetting the past and looking forward to what lies ahead. I press on to reach the end of the race and receive the heavenly prize which God, through Christ Jesus, is calling us" (Philippians 3:12-14, NLT).

December 7
Mother Dear

The blood sweat and tears of great grandparents, grandparents, parents, aunts, uncles, and cousins who lived during the fifties and sixties must always be cherished and remembered. My maternal grandmother was Queen B. Williams. We called her Mother Dear. She was one of those community change agents.

Mother Dear was a voter registration campaign director in the state of Florida. She registered the highest number (7,212) of persons in the state. For her work, she was cited in *The Crisis*, the official publication of the National Association for the Advancement of Colored People (NAACP).

She was a leader in the Order of the Eastern Star where she campaigned for educational scholarships and organized oratorical contest for prospective college students. My sister and I, and many other young people, were recipients of scholarships from these contests.

Although we know national leaders who worked for social justice and reform, there are many like my grandmother who were in the background doing less glamorous work. Because of their faith in God, along with their commitment to social justice and reform, young people today have opportunities that were only dreams when they lived.

"We've come this far by faith, leaning on the Lord."
~ *Albert A. Goodson*

December 8

Telling Your Story

"Go home to your family and tell them how much the Lord has done for you, and how he has had mercy on you" (Mark 5:19, NIV).

Jesus gave the demon-possessed man specific instructions after he had healed him. He wanted to follow Jesus. In fact, he begged Jesus to let him come. But Jesus said no and told the man to go home and tell his story. Why did Jesus tell him no?

Perhaps his story was too powerful for the people in his community not to see his total transformation. They only knew about his wild animal-like behavior. His family and community needed to see how he had changed. The change could have a major impact on many lives. Sure enough, it says that, "the man went away and began to tell in the Decapolis how much Jesus had done for him. And all the people were amazed" (Mark 5:20, NIV). Decapolis refers to ten cities. This means his story spread over ten cities and impacted Jews and Gentiles alike.

The desire to follow Jesus is humbling. The will to be obedient to Jesus is humbling and rewarding.

Regardless of where you are in your Christian journey, you have a story to tell. Your story will continue throughout your walk with Jesus. The new chapters in your life will not only help you but will help every life you touch. With Jesus, your life story is uplifting, inspiring, and illuminating. There are many persons who need to hear your story.

"I love to tell the story, 'Twill be my theme in glory, To tell the old, old story of Jesus and his love.'"
~ Katherine Hankey

December 9
Rejection is Not Forever

Oprah Winfrey is a trailblazer of the highest degree. She grew up in extreme poverty to become a billionaire and philanthropist. As a young child, her living arrangements were unpredictable, almost as if she was rejected. She took turns living with her grandmother, mother, and father. Her talent, intellect, determination, and God's grace helped her succeed. Many doors were opened to her because of her skills.

By the age of eighteen, she became Nashville's first African American female co-anchor of an evening news program. A few years later, she was hired to anchor an underperforming morning talk show. Under her leadership, it became quite successful and was renamed the Oprah Winfrey Show. The show held high ratings for twenty-five years. In January 2011, she purchased a television network and named it OWN (the Oprah Winfrey Network.)

Ms. Winfrey's life is a true success story, but what is most meaningful about Ms. Winfrey's life is how she nourishes her soul. In spite of all of her achievements, she strives to move to a higher level of thinking, understanding, and being. Because of this, she connects with people at the level of their soul, that part of us that where love, hope, peace, and joy abound.

"For nothing shall be impossible with God" (Luke 1: 37, KJV).

December 10
Human Rights Day

I read an article in The New York Times that reported a twenty-seven-year-old female, forty weeks pregnant went into labor inside a police station holding cell. Before taking her to the hospital, the officers handcuffed her wrists and shackled her ankles. The story goes on to say that for nearly an hour, she experienced excruciating labor pains while in police restraints. The police officers disregarded the physicians request to remove the restraints even though it is illegal to restrain a pregnant woman in the state of New York. They eventually removed some of the restraints but left her right hand cuffed to the hospital bed.

Labor pains are often described to be the worst pains one will ever feel. Her pain was accompanied by the physical pain and mental anguish of being shackled during childbirth. By ignoring the advice of the physicians, in addition to placing her life in danger, the police were mocking and scoffing her. They were insensitive to her pain and vulnerability. Fortunately, the baby and mother survived.

When I read this report, I thought about Jesus Christ. Jesus was abandoned, shackled, and nailed to a cross until he died. I can't imagine how painful this was but his cries from the cross give some indication of his suffering. While he agonized, those around him (like the policemen) were insensitive to his pain as they mocked and scoffed him.

The young woman's arrest was related to a child custody case. Was this deserved punishment for a societal sin? What is God saying? Shackling a pregnant woman is tantamount to shackling the baby's life to come—not just this baby's life but all babies. Babies are our future and pregnant women and babies must be given special care.

While we recognize Human Rights Day annually, we must keep in mind that every day is Human Rights Day.

"Human kindness has never weakened the stamina or softened the figure of a free people. A nation does not have to be cruel to be tough."
~ Franklin D. Roosevelt

December 11
Service: Troop 2416 Wants To Help!

One Sunday afternoon, members of a Girl Scout troop stood at the entrance of a large grocery store in my community. They were collecting food and other personal supplies for a local food pantry.

The Girl Scouts were surrounded by multiple carts filled with a variety of grocery items. Just before entering the store, they would hand customers a small piece of paper. In addition to the heading, Troop 2416 wants to help, the name of a local food pantry, mission statement, and names of items in greatest need were on the small sheet of paper.

The mission was creative: to allow families and individuals to select the food and personal items that would be most useful. Using this model maintained the dignity of each person and reduced waste from unwanted food items.

These young girls were performing an important service on a Sunday afternoon. The look on their faces showed how much they enjoyed the activity, and they made it easy for others to join them in donating to those in need. The number of filled grocery carts spoke volumes about the success they had in serving others.

Troop 2416 reminds me of the Bible story where 5,000 people were fed from one little boy volunteering five barley loaves and two small fish. The disciples asked the question, "But how far will the loaves and fish go among so many?" The Girl Scout troop demonstrated what it means to follow Jesus and what can be accomplished when something is placed in God's hand.

"When they had finished eating, Jesus said to Simon Peter, "Simon son of John, do you love me more than these?" "Yes, Lord," he said, "you know that I love you." Jesus said, "Feed my lambs" (John 21:15, NIV).

December 12
Motherly Wisdom

In her book, *"Wouldn't Take Nothing For My Journey Now,"* Dr. Maya Angelou shares how at sixteen, she felt devastated after being fired from a job. Through tears, she told her mother what happened. Angelou says her mother's face became "radiant with indulgent smiles." After her mother hugged her, she said, "Fired? Fired?" She laughed. "What the hell is that? Nothing. Tomorrow you will go looking for another job. That's all."

As her mother continued to use her handkerchief to dab Maya's tears, she added, "Remember you were looking for a job when you found the one you just lost. And think about it, if you ever get fired again, the boss won't be getting a cherry. You've been through it once and survived."

Indeed, it is no wonder that Maya Angelou rose up through the ashes of life's hard challenges. Her mother instilled in her wisdom that no amount of money could buy. What's more, Dr. Angelou ingested her wisdom and shared it with the world.

"Happy is the man who finds wisdom, and the man who gains understanding; for her proceeds are better than the profits of silver, and her gain than fine gold. She is more precious than rubies, and all the things you may desire cannot compare with her" (Proverbs 16:16, NKJV).

December 13
Finding Meaning in Loss

When my husband died, I experienced miracles of support. One miracle was developing a close friendship with one of Cecil's friends. In fact, I consider Angela both a daughter and a friend. She pointed me to the book, *Man's Search for Meaning* by Victor Frankl. Dr. Frankl was a psychiatrist imprisoned during the holocaust in Germany.

In the book, one of his patients sought guidance from Dr. Frankl after the death of his wife. The patient thought it would be impossible to find meaning in life without his wife. Dr. Frankl asked him to "flip the script." What would his response be if he had died and his wife had lived?

This scenario was just the thing that helped the patient begin the healing process. He could not bear the thought of his wife being alone without him. Life would have been difficult for her, and he would not want her to have to face life alone.

Indeed, this story still helps me to this day. I would not have wanted my darling husband with poor health and limited vision to be alone without me. God helps us to find meaning even in the death of a loved-one.

"For my thoughts are not your thoughts, neither are your ways my ways," declares the LORD. "As the heavens are higher than the earth, so are my ways higher than your ways and my thoughts than your thoughts" (Isaiah 55: 8,9, NIV).

December 14
Stress Versus Peace

I'm convinced the Lord doesn't want us to be filled with stress. This is emphasized repeatedly in God's word: "Let not your heart be troubled" (*John 14:1, KJV*). "Do not be anxious about anything, but in every situation, by prayer and petition, with thanksgiving, present your request to God" (*Philippians 4:6, NIV*). "Let the peace of Christ rule in your heart since as members of one body you were called to peace. And be thankful" (*Col. 3: 15, NIV*).

Stress is hard on the body if it persists. Under stress, the body releases large amounts of chemicals into the blood. These chemicals make the heart rate, blood pressure, and breathing go up. As a result, the body has more oxygen in the blood. The oxygen fills the muscles with energy needed to respond to the stress. Once the stress or threat eases off, heart rate, blood pressure, and breathing return to normal.

In today's society, stress lingers. This means blood pressure, heart rate, and breathing can remain high, which can cause all kinds of medical problems. Heart attack, high blood pressure, diabetes, and cancer are a few diseases that can be caused by stress.

We need a storehouse of healthy habits to counteract our stress filled lives. Bible study, meditation, exercise, sleep, healthy eating, and fun/family times are relaxing activities that help. Also, consider reducing screen time (phone, iPad, TV). In children, reduced screen time improves sleep, lowers body mass index, improves social behavior, reduces aggression and improves school performance. In adults, there is increased mental clarity and productivity. "Thou will keep him in perfect peace, whose mind is stayed on thee: because he trust in thee" (*Isaiah 26:3, KJV*).

"Within you, there is a stillness and a sanctuary to which you can retreat at any time and be yourself."
~ Hermann Hesse

December 15
Mismatched Shoes

One day during the Christmas holiday season, I saw a middle-aged man walking down the street wearing mismatched shoes. It looked like the shoes didn't quite fit because he appeared to walk lop-sided. His clothes were tattered, but it was his shoes that captured my attention.

In my opinion, wearing mismatched shoes is about as close to walking barefoot as you can get. It is illegal to walk into any public place without shoes, so while unfashionable, he was protected from the environment and wouldn't break the law if he had to enter a public place.

Still, wearing mismatched shoes takes away from one's humanity in its own unjust unique way. I didn't know if he was hungry or homeless, but one thing for sure, his shoes bothered me most.

I have a friend who has an online business that sells a variety of inexpensive apparel. I purchased six pairs of men's shoes and took them to a Goodwill store. My plan is to continue making this donation on a monthly basis. While the man I saw on the street may not benefit directly from my activity, someone else will. A fire can spread from a tiny spark.

Then the LORD said to Cain, "Where is your brother Abel?" "I don't know,"
he replied. "Am I my brother's keeper" (Genesis 4:9, NIV)?

December 16
Transformation of a Caterpillar

"Humans can reproduce only human life, but the Holy Spirit gives birth to spiritual life. So don't be surprised when I say, You must be born again" (John 3:7, NLT).

I am amazed how a caterpillar changes into a butterfly. If you look closely on the leaves of trees, you will find some very tiny eggs. A tiny egg grows and after a few days a caterpillar is hatched. Once hatched, the process for changing into a butterfly starts. A huge amount of energy and nutrients are needed for this process, so the caterpillar eats a lot. It is reported on average that a caterpillar will eat 2,700 times its own body weight before it is ready for the transformation to take place. As the caterpillar increases in size, it sheds its skin multiple times. Once fully grown, it spins itself into its transitional state known as a chrysalis. This is a hard shell or covering. Inside the chrysalis, the body of the caterpillar starts to break down and be reorganized. During this period, all of the structures of a butterfly are formed. It takes about ten to fifteen days before a beautiful adult butterfly emerges. This transformational process is called metamorphosis.

The Christian journey is quite similar to the life cycle of a butterfly. When we are born again, our spiritual life starts. We are called babes in Christ. Like the caterpillar, we are hungry. Our hunger is for the word of God: "You must crave spiritual milk so that you can grow into the fullness of your salvation. Cry out for this nourishment..." (*1 Peter 2:2-3, NLT*). Our nourishment is God's word, preaching, prayer, and fellowship.

Like the caterpillar, we must shed harmful things in our lives and form a chrysalis. The butterfly's journey to new life takes about two weeks. Our journey is much longer. Christianity is a journey that will last the rest of our lives. It begins when we accept Jesus Christ as Lord. We grow and mature. But we are always becoming. When we cross over to the other side, we will be all that God created us to be.

"Therefore, if any man be in Christ, he is a new creature: old things are passed away; behold, all things are become new" (2 Corinthians 5:17, KJV).

December 17
The Hospital Waiting Room

Have you ever spent time in a hospital waiting room? It's an unsettling place to be, especially during the Christmas season. This is the time when homes are filled with the energy of excited children, joyful music, happy millennials, and lots of tasty foods. Oftentimes when loved ones are in intensive care units, waiting rooms can become an unwanted second home, a lonely second home where uncertainty permeates the environment.

During the holidays, many of us are more mindful of the hungry and homeless population. There are opportunities to give through churches, grocery stores, and Salvation Army baskets; even fast food restaurants participate in giving. But hospital waiting rooms are far from people's minds.

As you reflect on your blessings during this Christmas season, remember those sitting in lonely hospital waiting rooms. Say a healing prayer for them and their loved ones. The energy from your prayers will make a difference. In *The 50 Prayers of Pope Francis*, Shane DeCreshio said, "Prayer is powerful. It can heal, prayer can give, and it can change lives."

Almighty Sovereign God, thank you for the gift of Joy to the world. May your healing love be felt by those sitting in hospital waiting rooms not knowing the future but with hopeful hearts prayerfully wait for the best outcome for their loved ones. AMEN

December 18
Dew Drops of Mercy

One Sunday morning as we sang the hymn, "Jesus, the Light of the World," the lyrics "dew drops of mercy" touched my heart. Have you ever awakened to see the dew drops that cover the grass? Dew drops completely cover the grass, and in a similar manner, God's mercy covers us completely.

The author of this great hymn, Charles Wesley must have added the word 'dew' to remind singers of the value of everything on God's earth.

Scriptures in the Bible that reference 'dew' are associated with bounty and divine blessings. Hear Isaac as he says to Jacob, "May God give you heaven's dew and earth's richness—an abundance of grain and new wine" (*Genesis 27:28, NIV*).

Hear God's promise, "I will be like dew to Israel. He will blossom like a lily, Like a cedar of Lebanon he will send down his roots" (*Hosea 14:5, NIV*).

Lastly, a Jewish prayer begins, "May dew fall upon the blessed land. Fill us with heaven's finest blessings. May light come out of the darkness to draw Israel to you as a root finds water from dew."

Next time you observe the dew on the grass or on beautiful roses, think about God's complete love and blessings that always cover and protect you.

"Walk in the light, beautiful light, come where the dew drops of mercy shine bright, shine all around us by day and night, Jesus, the light of the world."
~Charles Wesley

December 19
Birth: Adoption is Divine

Children who have been adopted or who are in foster care may sometimes feel unsure of themselves or have a lower self-image. When you read some of the Bible stories about adopted persons, you discover them to be no different in God's eye. One familiar example is Moses.

Moses was born during a time when Pharaoh, the Egyptian king, ordered all male Hebrew babies to be drowned in the Nile River. Rather than face death from the king's decree, the mother of Moses placed him in a small papyrus basket and let it drift down the river. This was intended for his death, but destiny said, *not yet*. The king's daughter discovers the baby and hires one of the Hebrew women (his actual mother unbeknownst to her) to nurse him. After a period of time, the mother gives her baby up, and he is adopted into the house of Pharaoh.

Many years pass, and Moses murders an Egyptian for beating a Hebrew and runs away for forty years. During this time of exile from his homeland, Moses encounters God on the backside of the desert. It was here that God chooses Moses to lead the liberation of the people of God who had been enslaved for 430 years.

An adopted person changed the course of history. The good news is that every human being was chosen by God. All of us are here on this earth for a very special reason. Moses discovered God's will for his life. I believe most Christians want to know God's will for their life too. I encourage you to continue to strengthen your personal relationship with Jesus Christ. Try to live according to God's word. Do a self-evaluation. What are your special gifts or talents? Do they need to be honed? Remain prayerful and attuned to God. Rest assured, God will direct your heart and path.

"You don't choose your family. They are God's gift to you, as you are to them."
~ *Desmond Tutu*

December 20
And How are the Children?

There is a tribe in Africa known as the Masai tribe. The Masai tribe has a special way of greeting one another. Rather than ask, 'how are you' or say, 'nice to see you' they ask, "And how are the children?" The response to the greeting is, "All the children are well."

The greeting and the response are indicative of the value the tribe places on their children. The greeting means they are highly conscious of their children's powerlessness. Their welfare is most important.

The question and answer says the children are safe, protected, and properly cared for.

Well cared for children are the responsibility of the entire nation. Ensuring that all children have access to quality education, healthy nutrition, safe housing, and healthcare. When this is done, we can rest assured that the nation's future will be bright for generations to come. "And How are the Children?"

"If anyone causes one of these little ones—those who believe in me—to stumble, it would be better for them to have a large millstone hung around their neck and to be drowned in the depths of the sea" (Matthew 18:6, NLT).

December 21
Self-Care: Healthy Decision-making

Self-care is critical to healthy living. The foundation of self-care is adequate rest, followed by healthy eating and exercise. Consider rest. The most important factor in achieving optimal health is free. Adults need eight hours of sleep and children less than twelve years of age need ten to eleven hours of sleep each night. During sleep, the body rejuvenates. Rest and sleep strengthen our immune system, and memory. It also aids in brain development for children.

Choosing to eat healthy is self-care. What does your body feel like after you eat? Are you energetic or sluggish? Food that supplies the most energy are fruits and vegetables and lots of water.

Physical activity and exercise are self-care activities. Exercise gives us stamina, the strength to endure and keep going for a long time. Physical activity produces hormones in the brain that boost our mood and increase our tolerance to pain.

Because we have so much on our life-plate, we make choices. Please choose not to let self-care drop to the bottom of the to-do list. On an airplane, the stewardess instructs us, if oxygen is necessary to place your mask on first before assisting anyone else. Then, you can help others. Self-care is the wisest choice you can make.

To paraphrase a poem by Elizabeth Barrett Browning, "How do I love me, let me count the ways?"

December 22
Divine Confidence

Here's a true story about inspiration and faith in God. A dear friend was diagnosed with breast cancer at the age of forty-eight. Cheryl practiced prevention. She had a yearly mammogram and did monthly self-breast exams. In fact, two years before her diagnosis, she underwent a biopsy to evaluate something not looking right on her mammogram. The biopsy was negative. The next year her full mammogram was normal.

Another year passed. Cheryl felt a lump in her breast while doing a self-check. At this time, God gave her a message, "You're going to have a storm. But fear not, everything is going to be alright." She told her doctor about the message she received from God, and they moved forward.

A biopsy was performed with the results confirming breast cancer. Cheryl chose to have both breasts removed because of a family history of cancer. Subsequently, she received six months of chemotherapy. A year after this treatment, Cheryl underwent breast reconstruction surgery.

She has been cancer free for eight years and practices a healthy lifestyle that includes prayer, meditation, service, communion with other saints, regular exercise, growing her own herbs and eating plenty of organic vegetables.

The Almighty Sovereign God planted seeds of confidence into Cheryl's being and the rest is divine history.

"What a friend we have in Jesus, all our sins and griefs to bear! What a privilege to carry everything to God in prayer. O what peace we often forfeit, O what needless pain we bear, all because we do not carry everything to God in prayer."
~ Charles Converse

December 23
Making Preparation for the Lord (Part 1)

"Listen! I hear the voice of someone shouting. 'Make a highway for the Lord through the wilderness. Make a straight, smooth road through the desert for our God'" (Isaiah 40:3, NLT).

A lot of things had to take place to prepare for the birth of Jesus. The birth of John the Baptist had been prophesied seven-hundred years earlier. To fulfill this prophecy, the angel Gabriel came to Zechariah, the Jewish priest, to inform him that he and Elizabeth were about to be blessed with a great son. He explained that he would be the forerunner of the Messiah. The angel even told him that his son's name would be John.

Zechariah was not listening with his spiritual ears and had forgotten what Isaiah prophesied. All he could think about was how on earth could he and his elderly wife have a baby. He wanted Gabriel to provide proof. Doubt had overcome his faith in God.

The angel Gabriel admonished Zechariah and made it impossible for him to speak until the baby was born. The entire time Elizabeth carried the baby, Zechariah only used sign language and writing tablets. When the baby was born, the people wanted to name the baby after the father, but Zechariah wrote down for all to see, "His name is John." Instantly, Zechariah started speaking again.

I suppose the angel didn't want Zechariah speaking words of doubt. Nothing must get in the way of the most important events in history. How often has God reassured you that everything will work out? Does doubt cloud your faith? Do you start talking negative? Acknowledge your feelings of doubt, and then wait patiently for God to act. Rest in the Lord. What God has in store for you will happen. It might be better to remain quiet rather than speak words of doubt.

"John replied in the words of Isaiah the prophet, 'I am the voice of one calling in the wilderness, Make straight the way for the Lord'" (John 1:23, NIV).

December 24
Making Preparation for the Lord (Part 2)

.   God chose a virgin named Mary to be the mother of our Lord and Savior Jesus Christ. An angel appeared to Mary to announce her divine gift. Mary's initial response was innocent, "But how can this happen? I am a virgin" (*Luke 1:34, NLT*). She did not ask for proof or how she would know for sure. Once she was told that the power of God would overshadow her, Mary responded, "I am the Lord's servant and I am willing to accept whatever God wants. May everything you have said come true" (*Luke 1:38, NLT*).

Mary's joy burst into a song of praise and prophecy known as the Magnificat. Her song demonstrates the depth of her faith and relationship with God. I suspect Mary had spent a lot of her time with God. Her words were an ever-flowing stream of who God is. Mary sang about God's endless mercy, concern for the poor, social justice, strong arm of protection, and great faithfulness.

The good news is that you too are God's chosen vessel with a specific purpose to fulfill on this planet. How will you know your purpose? Like Mary, you have to trust God, take time to read the Bible, spend time in prayer and meditation. God will speak to you through the preached word and gospel music. Also, listen to your parents or a person God has placed in your life who serves in a parental role. God's will for your life comes through parents, godparents, and godly people directed to you.

"Being confident of this very thing, that he which hath begun a good work in you will perform it until the day of Jesus Christ" (Philippians 1:6, KJV).

December 25
A Christmas Gift Like No Other

"For to us a child is born, to us a son is given, and the government will be on his shoulders. And he will be called Wonderful Counselor, Mighty God, Everlasting Father, Prince of Peace" (Isaiah 9:6-7, NIV).

In Bethlehem, Joseph and Mary, a band of homeless shepherds, and three wise men unexpectedly meet to experience God's blessings. Joseph and Mary are in town to register for a census. Mary is in the last days of her pregnancy. Soon after they arrive, she gives birth to baby Jesus.

At the time of his birth, an angel of the Lord appears before the band of shepherds to announce Jesus' birth. The shepherds run to the village and find the first family. They are overcome with joy and so are all the people they share the news with. Three wise men see a shining star that leads them to Jesus' exact location. They worship Jesus and present him with expensive gifts.

The Christmas story describes who God is and how God moves in our lives. There was no big media event for all the world to see. Neither was there a town crier, sixty-two gun salute, or a stream of social media messages that Christ the Lord is born. It was personal and peaceful. A helpless infant born to poor parents was the way God gently eased into human history to bring love, joy, and peace to all. Homeless shepherds were the only ones to receive the announcement. Through God's way, no one is outside the boundary of God's love. God's movement in our lives is the same today as it was in the past.

God's gift to us is not a package we'll find under a Christmas tree. The Christmas season comes and goes. God's gift has been packaged in such a way that it will last throughout eternity. My prayer is that your daily walk with the Lord will be filled with the gifts of godly joy and peace.

"Hail the heaven-born Prince of Peace! Hail the Sun of Righteousness! Light and life to all He brings, Risen with healing in His wings, Mild He lays His glory by, Born that man no more may die, Born to raise the sons of earth, Born to give them second birth. Hark! the herald angels sing, Glory to the newborn King."
~ *Charles Wesley*

December 26
Love of Family and Storytelling

My husband, Cecil, was an avid storyteller, and I loved to hear stories about his father's life. Cecil's father had been dead thirteen years when we met, but I was introduced to Charlie Cone through Cecil. He shared stories about him over and over again and they were always a joy to hear. I could feel the reverence, love, and pride Cecil had for his father. When we made visits to his mother's home, the conversation around the dining table centered around his father.

One story I recall was the time his father used wood to explain the power of brotherhood among three brothers. He showed them three separate pieces of wood. Then, he tied them together to demonstrate how hard it would be to separate them. He encouraged his three sons to stay together like the pieces of wood strapped as one. "Let nothing separate you from the love and care of the family." Indeed, throughout the thirty-five years Cecil and I were together, there was an endearing love and bond the brothers had for each other and for their mother.

Keep the memory of your loved ones alive by sharing stories about their life. Storytelling is healing and is an excellent way to ease the grief from a loved one's death. Remember, the Bible started out through the oral tradition which is the same as storytelling.

"Sharing tales of those we've lost is how we keep from really losing them."
~Mitch Albom

Faith: It's Good to be Alive

Roy Campanella's autobiography, *It's Good To Be Alive*, is a book I'll always remember. I read it at the age of twelve. It still moves and inspires me to this day.

Mr. Campanella is one of the greatest catchers in the history of baseball. Before a tragic car accident, he played with the Brooklyn Dodgers for ten years. The Dodgers were just about to move to California when the accident happened. The accident left him paralyzed from the shoulders down.

At the age of thirty-seven and in the prime of his life, his baseball career was over.

At first, he was angry and depressed with no will to live. Adjustment to the rehab program was slow, but there were several things that helped him find meaning in life again. During his stay, his relationship with his son improved. Then, he marveled how people of all ages were struggling with physical handicaps but still resolved to live beyond their hardship. Gradually, he adjusted to the program and remained in the center for months, learning strategies for self-care.

One day on his way home from the rehab center, another car accident happened causing a car fire. The therapist was able to drag him out of the car. As he lay on the grass, he shared that he feared he would die. This accident made him realize how much he wanted to live. I believe the second accident inspired the title of his book, "*It's good to be alive.*" From then on, Mr. Campanella adjusted to his physical disability. Even before the accident, and afterward, he was loved and respected by other baseball players and fans. The team owners continued his salary after he was paralyzed. Once he left rehab, the Dodgers hired him to work as an assistant supervisor of scouting and a special coach and mentor to young catchers.

Life events can abruptly change the course of our life at any age. It is normal to feel disbelief, anger, doubt, and despair. But with God's help, family, and supportive friends, you will find guidance and strength through the situation.

"There hath no temptation taken you, but such as is common to man: but God is faithful, who will not suffer you to be tempted above that ye are able; but will with the temptation also make a way to escape, that ye may be able to bear it" (1 Corinthians 10:13, KJV).

December 28
Family Conflict in the Midst of Grief

Sometimes grief from the loss of a loved one is placed on hold because of family conflicts. Family members stop speaking, take each other to court, or become personally offended if they are left out of a will. Personal property is often a major source of conflict. Things get worse when there is no will or trust. I saw a movie once where two sisters were fighting for a father's multimillion-dollar estate while he lay critically ill in the hospital. Why fight about another's property?

In the Gospel of Luke 12:13-21, Jesus is in the midst of a crowd when a man asks him to make his brother divide the inheritance with him. Although it is not written in the text, the brother must have refused to give him a portion of the estate. The brother seeking money was probably debt laden and was looking for a way out.

Jesus refuses to be an arbitrator. His answer suggest that the man's request is prompted by covetousness. Jesus responds, "Watch out! Be on your guard against all kinds of greed; a man's life does not consist in the abundance of his possessions" (*Luke 12:15, NIV*).

When the primary reason for living is to accumulate as much wealth as possible, then the most important reason for life is missed. You end up miserable and constantly looking for legal and sometimes illegal ways to accumulate even more wealth.

"But seek ye first the kingdom of God, and His righteousness; and all these things shall be added unto you" (Matthew 6:33, KJV).

December 29
Remembering My Father

"To a Father Growing Old Nothing Is Dearer Than a Daughter."
~Euripides

If my father was alive, this would be his 115th year of life. He was forty-three years old when I was born and a marvelous provider and protector of his family. In our family, my dad was the one who grocery shopped. My sister reminded me that he did a lot of the cooking too. Every Friday, he'd come home with grocery bags filled with lots of healthy foods such as carrots, potatoes, chicken, and fish.

He learned and excelled at the game of tennis, winning many local tennis tournaments. There were multiple trophies in our home, the evidence of his skill at playing tennis. In Althea Gibson's memoir, she writes about playing tennis with some excellent African American tennis players while visiting in Jacksonville, Florida. One of them was my father.

His formal education was limited to the sixth grade, but he was a wise man and a visionary. I remember him taking business courses at a night school. Regardless of his job, he performed it with pride and dignity. He worked as an elevator operator and later as a US postal handler. After retiring in the mid 50's, he started his own successful landscaping business.

A few years after completing medical school, my father shared his concerns that a medical degree might make it difficult for me to find a husband. It was heartwarming to hear that my father's primary concern was for his daughter to be protected. He had a crippling stroke about six months before our wedding and was unable to attend. I didn't have to tell him the news. All I had to say was, "Guess what, Daddy?" His response was barely above a whisper, "You got married." Exactly three months after our wedding, he passed away. He was able to leave his earthly tabernacle, and his daughter would now be protected by her husband.

"A father's tears and fears are unseen, his love is unexpressed, but his care and protection remain as a pillar of strength throughout our lives."
~Ama H. Vanniarachchy

December 30

Mountains

"Stop staring at mountains. Climb them instead, yes, it's a harder process but it will lead you to a better view.
~Author Unknown

Kate Winslet and Idris Elba star in the movie *The Mountain Between Us*. The movie takes place on a snow-covered mountain following the crash of a chartered plane. The pilot dies leaving two strangers and a dog to face the mountainous terrain. They have limited water and food and no cell phone service. They face slippery slopes, a mountain lion, perilous snowstorms, and bitter cold. After multiple risk-filled events, they are rescued. How did they overcome their mountain of difficulties?

Trust was a major factor. They had to trust themselves and each other. As they acknowledged their fears and stopped blaming each other for their predicament, they were better able to face the mountains of uncertainty. During perilous situations, they used their innate survival skills to help each other. Every life-threatening encounter seemed to not only increase their trust in the other but instilled in them the belief that they would survive.

In a similar way, we face a variety of mountains with no magical solutions. There is no getting around mountains of debt, illness, death, divorce, hate, or anger. And just like Alexis and Ben, we will have to face and tackle our mountains.

Where do you place your trust? Saving for a rainy day is wise. A skillful doctor is a blessing. So is a well-trained lawyer or a faithful minister. However, they are finite. To climb those mountains in our lives, we need to place our trust in God. Is your faith weak? All you need is just a little. Jesus says, "...if you had faith even as small as a mustard seed, you could say to this mountain, 'Move from here to there,' and it would move. Nothing would be impossible" (*Matthew 17:20, NLT*).

"Trust in the Lord with all your heart; do not depend on your own understanding. Seek his will in all you do, and he will show you which path to take" (*Proverbs 3:5-6, NLT*).

December 31
End of Year Prayer

Dear Lord,

Over the past year, there are persons who have been burdened beyond their strength and taxed beyond their ability to cope. Some individuals have felt betrayed. Others are trying to overcome the death of a loved one. Some have stumbled before strong temptations and paid prices that only you understand the depths of the cost.

Others have taken a risk in going to college, starting a new job, forming a new relationship or ending and old one. Some of us have faced extended illnesses or had to care for a loved one with a major sickness.

Yet, in spite of all of these various situations, we believe in the reality of your presence. That you love us. That you saved us. We sincerely believe that everything you do is worthy of our trust.

We believe that you are the one who brings meaning out of chaos. That you are absolute and powerful. You are yet present, participating and aware of the details of all creation. And that you will intervene on our behalf.

Thank you, Almighty Sovereign God, for bringing us through this year. As we start a new year, a new decade, help us to run the race of life with patience and courage. And to keep looking unto you, Jesus Christ, the author and finisher of our faith. AMEN

"The faithful love of the Lord never ends! His mercies never cease. Great is his faithfulness; His mercies begin afresh each morning" (Lamentations 3:22-23, NLT).

Sources

January 12

Martha Whitmore Hickman, *Healing After Loss Daily Meditations for Working Through Grief* (William Morrow 2002) November 9th meditation.

January 15

https://share.america.gov/life-legacy-martin-luther-king-jr/ (Accessed January 25, 2019)

January 17

Michelle Obama, *Becoming* (Crown New York, 2018), 59, 83, 91

January 25

Cherita, *A Poem of Love (not published 1993)*

January 27

https://www.washingtonpost.com/archive/lifestyle/style/1990/12/16/leontyne-price-in-her-own-voice/e2d726bf-fed3-4e41-bd64-ca45fe7a253e/ (Accessed 10/1/2018)

February 4

Rosa Parks with Jim Haskins, (Rosa Parks, My Story) Puffin Books 1992, 115-116

February 6

Earl Conrad, *Harriet Tubman, A Biography* (Paul S. Eriksson, Inc. New York 1943) 36

February 11

A. Lee Henderson, *Religious Experiences and Journal of Mrs. Jarena Lee, "A Preachin' Woman"* (AMEC Sunday School Union/Legacy Publishing Nashville, Tennessee 1991) 22

February 17

Maya Angelou, *I Know Why the Caged Bird Sings* (Random House New York 2015) 21,81

March 20

http://www.satucket.com/lectionary/Jonathan_Daniels.htm
Accessed March 19, 2019

March 22

https://www.biography.com/activist/mary-mcleod-bethune Accessed
June 5, 2019

March 23

Michelle Obama, *Becoming* (Crown New York 2018) 375.

March 31

Martha Whitmore Hickman, *Healing After Loss Daily Meditations for
Working Through Grief* (William Morrow an imprint of HarperCollins
Publishers 2002).

April 3

https://www.cdc.gov/features/sexualviolence/index.html Accessed
December 2, 2018.

April 9

www.americamagazine.org April 12, 2019

April 13

https://www.biography.com/activist/helen-keller Accessed April 13,
2019

April 15

https://www.history.com/this-day-in-history/titanic-sinks Accessed
April 14, 2019

April 19

http://blog.africaimports.com/wordpress/2009/05/an-african-folk-
tale-about-wisdom Accessed April 15 2019.

April 27

https://www.moody.edu/about/our-bold-legacy/d-l-moody/ accessed July 24, 2019

Mark Ellingsen, *Reclaiming our Roots Volume 2 Martin Luther to Martin Luther King* (Trinity Press International Harrisburg, Pennsylvania 1999) 220

May 1

C.D.C. Reeve, Translated by G.M.A. Grube, *Plato Republic* (Hackett Publishing Company, Inc. Indianapolis/Cambridge 1992) 35, 36

May 4

Cecil Wayne Cone, *Why do the Righteous Suffer?* In Preaching on Suffering and a God of Love, Henry J. Young editor (Fortress Press Philadelphia 1978) 51-52.

May 9

Wyatt North, *Mother Teresa A Life Inspired*, © Wyatt North Publishing, LLC 2014).

May 25

https://www.webmd.com/special-reports/grief-stages/20190711/how-grief-affects-your-body-and-mind

May 26

Elephant and the blind men. Jain World website.

https://jainworld.com/education/jain-education-material/jain-stories/elephant-and-the-blind-men/

accessed 1/19/2019

May 31

Misty Copeland, *Life in Motion: An Unlikely Ballerina* (Simon and Schuster New York London Toronto Sydney New Delhi 2014).

June 3

Rosa Parks with Jim Haskins, *Rosa Parks My Story* (Puffin Books Penguin Group 1992) 48-51.

June 6

James H. Cone, Martin & Malcolm & America (Orbis Books Maryknoll, New York, 1991), 124-125.

https://www.biography.com/activist/mary-mcleod-bethune accessed June 5, 2019.

June 10

https://www.poetryfoundation.org/poems/52494/the-heart-of-a-woman accessed June 10, 2019.

June 14

Kenneth W. Osbeck, *101 Hymn Stories* (Kregel Publications Grand Rapids, MI 1982) 28-31.

June 17

https://www.youtube.com/watch?v=XdSLp4MmDRM accessed June 17, 2019.

June 27

https://www.truthfulwords.org/biography/crosbytw2.html

Accessed June 20, 2019

July 3

The New Interpreter's Bible Volume XI Luke and John, page 298.

July 4

Kenneth W. Osbeck, *101 Hymn Stories* Kregel Publications Grand Rapids, MI 1982) 44.

July 5

Studs Terkel, *An Interview by James Baldwin, James Baldwin: The Last Interview: and other Conversations* (Melville House Publishing 2014).

July 15

https://www.biography.com/scholar/maggie-lena-walker accessed July 14, 2019.

July 18

https://www.britannica.com/biography/Saint-Katharine-Drexel accessed July 18, 2019.

July 28

Bernard Binlin Dadié, *The Black Cloth* (The University of Massachusetts Press 1987) 12-16.

July 29

Edited by John W. Blassingame *Source: Slave Testimony: Two Centuries of Letters, Speeches, Interviews, and Autobiographies*, (Louisiana State University Press Baton Rouge 1977) 268-274.

August 2

Fyodor Dostoyevsky, *The Brothers Karamazov* 1(Penguin Books, Baltimore Maryland 1958) 56.

August 5

Cone, Juanita Fletcher. "Faith for Tomorrow." In the Communicator-African Methodist Episcopal Church Sunday School Union, 44-45. Edited by A.L. Henderson. Nashville, Tennessee 1994

August 14

Gwendolin Sims Warren, *Ev'ry Time I Feel the Spirit* (Henry Holt and Company, New York, 1997), 32-33.

August 17

https://www.ncdcr.gov/blog/2015/12/31/selma-burke-renowned-fdr-portrait-on-the-dime (April 1, 2019

www.encyclopedia.com

August 25

The Schomberg Center for Research in Black Culture, *365 Days of Black History 2007 Engagement Calendar* (Pomegranate Communications, Inc. 2006).

August 28

Journal: Good medicine. Published by the Physicians Committee for Responsible Medicine| Spring 2019| Volume. XXVIII, No.2.

September 4

W. Terry Whalin, *Sojourner Truth American Abolitionist,* (Barbour & Company), 133-134.

September 15

www.history.com Birmingham Church Bombing, January 27, 2010, accessed September 15, 2018.

September 16

Gwendolyn Sims Warren, *Ev'ry time I feel the spirit* (Henry Holt and Company, New York 1997), 68-70

September 17

Fyodor Dostoyevsky, *The Brothers Karamazov* 1(Penguin Books, Baltimore, Maryland 1958) 340.

September 20

www.elitedaily.com accessed 4/29/2019

September 22

Gwendolyn Sims Warren, *Ev'ry Time I Feel the Spirit (Henry Holt and Company, New York 1997),* 23-24.

September 23

https://www.franciscanmedia.org/saint-martin-de-porres/ accessed July 20, 2019.

September 24

https://lisasingh.com/southeast-travel/martin-luther-kings-defining-moment-a-kitchen-in-montgomery-alabama-past-midnight/ accessed January 25, 2019

September 26

Gwendolyn Sims Warren, *Ev'ry time I feel the spirit* (Henry Holt and Company. New York 1997), 178-179.

September 30

https://laurenkfoster.wordpress.com/category/black-history-month/ accessed February 16, 2019

https://en.wikipedia.org/wiki/William_Augustus_Hinton accessed February 16, 2019

October 5

Frances Joseph-Gaudet, *He Leadeth Me*, (Louisiana Printing Company Limited New Orleans, 1913), 50, 51.

October 9

https://www.politifact.com/punditfact/statements/2014/oct/07/gloria-steinem/steinem-more-women-killed-partners-911-deaths-atta/ Accessed November 15, 2016.

http://www.cdc.gov/violenceprevention/pdf/NISVS-Fact-Sheet-2014.pdf accessed December 15, 2017.

October 10

https://www.tuskegee.edu/discover-tu/tu-presidents/frederick-d-patterson accessed October 9 2018.

October 14

https://www.nytimes.com/1964/10/15/archives/martin-luther-king-wins-the-nobel-prize-for-peace.html accessed October 14, 2018.

October 28

https://www.nytimes.com/2019/01/09/opinion/meditation-internet.html accessed October 28, 2018

November 2

https://aspe.hhs.gov/poverty-guidelines accessed December 1, 2018.

November 3

Earl Conrad, *Harriet Tubman*, (Paul S. Eriksson, Inc. New York, 1943), 18.

November 8

Cecil Wayne Cone, *The Constitution and the People of African Descent* (Howard Law Journal, 1987).

November 19

Elizabeth Kubler Ross MD & David Kessler, *On Grief and Grieving*, Scribner New York London Toronto Sydney New Delhi, 2005), 212, accessed May 15, 2016.

November 21

Frederick Douglass, *The Life and Times of Frederick Douglass* (Facsimile Edition Citadel Press Secaucus N.J. 1983), 67-70.

https://medium.com/@OneYoungWorld /32-million-american-adults-cant-read-why-literacy-is-the-key-to-growth-818996739523 accessed November 21, 2018.

November 22

Katherine Q. Seelye, *Raye Montague, Navy's 'Hidden Figure' Ship Designer*, Dies at 83.

https://www.nytimes.com/2018/10/18/obituaries/raye-montague-a-navy-hidden-figure-ship-designer-dies-at-83.html accessed November 22, 2018.

November 25

Frances Joseph-Gaudet, He Leadeth Me (Louisiana Printing Company, Limited New Orleans 1913), 21.

www.innocenceproject.org accessed November 22, 2019 The project works to exonerate the innocent through DNA testing and reform the criminal justice system to prevent further injustice.

December 9

Kathleen Elkins, From poverty to a $ 3 billion fortune—the incredible rags-to-riches story of Oprah Winfrey https://www.businessinsider.com/rags-to-riches-story-of-oprah-winfrey-2015-5 accessed December 7, 2018.

December 10

Ashley Southhall and Benjamin Weiser, Police Forced Bronx Woman to Give Birth While Handcuffed, Lawsuit Says https://www.nytimes.com/2018/12/06/nyregion/pregnant-inmate-shackled-lawsuit.html

accessed December 8, 2018.

December 12

Maya Angelou, *Wouldn't Take Nothing For My Journey Now* (Random House New York), 79-80.

December 13

Victor Frankl, *Man's Search for Meaning* (Beacon Press Boston Massachusetts Beacon Press 1959, 1984, 1992, 2006) accessed through online publication.

December 16

http://lifecycle.onenessbecomesus.com/larvae.html accessed December 15, 2018.

December 27

It's Good to be Alive (1974) The Story of Roy Campanella. https://www.youtube.com/watch?v=fHk4_AHMyZw

About the Author

Juanita Fletcher Cone is dedicated to promoting optimal health through public education. Before retiring in December 2017, she practiced internal medicine for 37 years. She is board certified by the American Board of Internal Medicine.

Cone completed her BS and MD degrees from Howard University in Washington, D.C. She completed internal medicine training at Bridgeport Hospital in Bridgeport Connecticut. Then, she moved back to her hometown where she practiced internal medicine in Jacksonville, Florida for 23 years.

Cone was ordained an itinerant elder in the African Methodist Episcopal Church. In 2000, she moved to Atlanta where she completed a specialty in preventive medicine at Morehouse School of Medicine. During this time, she completed two years of study at the Interdenominational Theological Center in Atlanta.

The last 14 years of her medical practice were spent with The Southeast Permanente Medical Group here in Atlanta. During a portion of this time, Cone served as Physical Program Director for Health Promotion and Disease Prevention.

In 2018, she authored her first book, *Footprints: Faith, Wellness & Forging Ahead Through Life's Challenges*. In addition to writing, she spends her time volunteering as an advocate for children in foster care, working with young adults at a homeless shelter, and maintaining a personal wellness program to nourish her own body, mind, and soul.

Living Water for the Thirsty Soul: 365 Stories of Hope, Health, & Healing is a collection of daily reflections that you can use in your own quiet time. You won't get bored. She shares her insight and guidance on personal and family stories, Bible wisdom, stories of present and past historical figures, and life virtues. *Living Water for the Thirsty Soul* is Dr. Cone's second book.

Made in the USA
Columbia, SC
27 April 2020

93566396R00250